Romantic Days
and Nights®
IN LOS ANGELES

Help Us Keep This Guide up to Date

Every effort has been made by the author and editors to make this guide as accurate and useful as possible. However, many things can change after a guide is published—establishments close, phone numbers change, hiking trails are rerouted, facilities come under new management, etc.

We would love to hear from you concerning your experiences with this guide and how you feel it could be made better and be kept up to date. Although we may not be able to respond to all comments and suggestions, we'll take them to heart, and we'll make certain to share them with the author. Please send your comments and suggestions to the following address:

The Globe Pequot Press
Reader Response/Editorial Department
P.O. Box 480
Guilford, CT 06437

Or you may e-mail us at:
editorial@globe-pequot.com
Thanks for your input,
and happy travels!

ROMANTIC DAYS AND NIGHTS® SERIES

Romantic Days and Nights®

IN LOS ANGELES

*Romantic Diversions
in and around the City*

SECOND EDITION

by Stephen Dolainski

The
Globe
Pequot
Press

GUILFORD, CONNECTICUT

Romantic Days and Nights is a registered trademark of The Globe Pequot Press.
Cover illustration by MaryAnn Dube
Text design and Illustrations by M.A.Dube
Spot Art by www.arttoday.com
Map by Mary Ballachino

Library of Congress Cataloging-in-Publication Data

Dolainski, Stephen.
  Romantic days and nights in Los Angeles: romantic diversions in and around the city / by Stephen Dolainski. — 2nd ed.
        p.   cm. — (Romantic days and nights series)
  Includes index.
  ISBN 0-7627-0540-X
  1. Los Angeles (Calif.)—Guidebooks.   I. Title.   II. Series.
        F869.L83D65   1999
        917.94'940453—dc21   99-35753
                                                                  CIP

Manufactured in the United States of America
Second Edition/First Printing

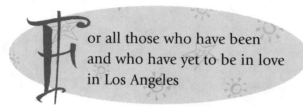

For all those who have been
and who have yet to be in love
in Los Angeles

LOS ANGELES ENVIRONS

118

210

2

25

405

5

23

170

27

134

Pasade

101

14

Hollywood Blvd.

Beverly Glen Blvd.

Sunset Blvd.

Beverly Blvd.

5

23

N9

27

Mulholland Hwy.

Sunset Blvd.

4

20

3

2

Wilshire Blvd.

17

Santa Monica Blvd.

16

15

N9

1

4

5

Los Angeles

Malibu

8

7

Santa Monica

Olympic Blvd.

To Oxnard
See insert

29

Santa Monica Fwy.

21

La Cienega Blvd.

42

10

105

405

91

Pacific Ocean

1

110

605

40

13

Long Beach

Santa Catalina Island

6

Avalon

N

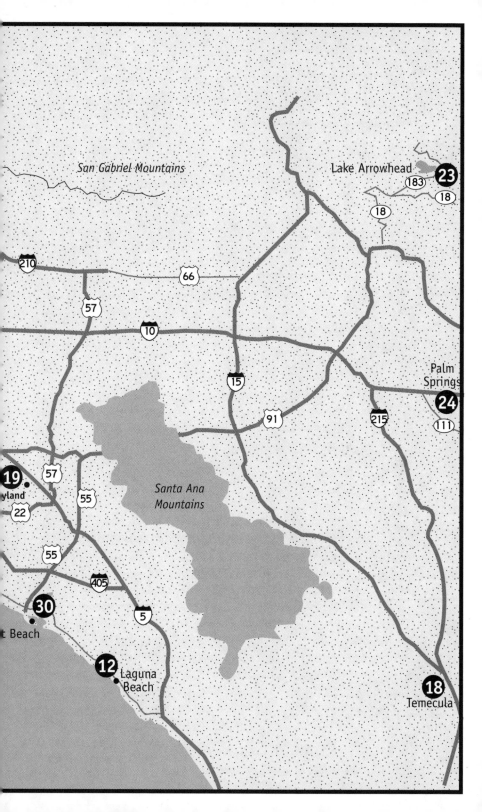

Contents

Acknowledgments

I̲T'S EASY TO AGREE to undertake a project like this guidebook. It's impossible to accomplish the task without considerable help and support from friends and colleagues like Al Hassan, Judy Stearns, Liza Yetenekian Smith, Peter Hoffman, Lillian Lepore and Shari Frazier, Ellen Payne, Mark Lamana, Tina Rubin, Sandra Rochowansky, Bob Carter, Ken Batchelor, Merrill Lee Williams, Linda Adams, Janis Flippen, Robert Deuel, Cindi Pietrzyk, Shelley Wolf, and Laura Strom.

Thank you all.

Introduction

EW AMERICAN CITIES ARE IN the media spotlight like Los Angeles. So much is seen, read, and heard about the City of Angels, that everybody thinks he knows the city and has something to say about it. Usually, it's not good—too big, too sprawling, too smoggy, too crowded, too violent. Well, those of us who love living in Los Angeles—and who have been in love in Los Angeles—think the city gets a bad rap. Question a Los Angeles–basher, I say, and chances are you'll uncover someone who hasn't seen the city through the eyes of love.

Los Angeles is a rich territory, romantically speaking. Depending on what you consider to be romantic—a moonlit walk on the beach, a horseback ride in the mountains at sunset, stargazing in the desert, an evening at the theater, dim-sum brunch in Chinatown, a hot air balloon ride, a candlelight dinner for two, a massage and a Roman bath, or a stroll through a world-class art museum—Los Angeles is brimming with possibilities. I've tried to encompass as much of this city's rich romantic territory as possible in these thirty itineraries by venturing out of Los Angeles proper occasionally to suggest intimate escapes in Santa Barbara, Palm Springs, and Orange County.

Although it might seem more fun and romantic to spontaneously take off for a spur-of-the-moment getaway, you'll probably be disappointed to find there's no room at the inn when you arrive. Planning is the key to a successful getaway, especially if the trip is to commemorate an anniversary, birthday, or other occasion. Always ask about romance packages or other special rates. Depending on the time of year, some hotel room rates differ by $100 or more. Call a local florist to arrange for flowers to be in your room on arrival. Generally, hotel check-in time is 3:00 or 4:00 P.M., and checkout time is between 11:00 A.M. and noon. Ask about the policy on early check-in and late checkout times. Most hotels will accommodate you if possible. It's almost always possible to check in early. You may not be able to get into the room, but you can leave your luggage with the hotel or the bell captain, then take off for lunch and afternoon activities. When you return to the hotel, your luggage should be waiting for you in your room. When it's time to leave, if you can't hold on to the room for a late checkout, then reverse the procedure. Leave your luggage with the hotel, finish your sightseeing or shopping, and pick up your bags later in the afternoon. Innkeepers, concierges, and restaurateurs are all delighted to help with the special arrangements that go into a romantic experience like a candlelit dinner for two, a violinist or guitarist serenading the two of you, or a marriage proposal in a hot air balloon. In fact, almost every innkeeper, concierge, and restaurateur I spoke with while researching this book told me at least one "romantic" anecdote.

Part of planning an intimate escape for the two of you includes anticipating what it's going to cost. Room rates for hotels, inns, and B&Bs are always listed within the text. The price ranges listed for dining out are approximate. Expensive means $50 or more per person for dinner, $25 or more for lunch. Moderate is $25 for dinner, $15 for lunch. Inexpensive is $15 for dinner, $10 for lunch. The cost of drinks, wine, tax, and tip are excluded in these estimates. Other significant costs, such as hot air balloon rides, massages, and guided tours, are also listed to help you plan accordingly.

Finally, it really doesn't matter where you go for your romantic escape or how much you spend. With someone special at your side, even a simple peanut butter and jelly sandwich on a beach in Malibu can turn out to be an unforgettably romantic experience.

The prices and rates listed in this guidebook were confirmed at press time. We recommend, however, that you call establishments before traveling to obtain current information.

The Best of the Los Angeles Area

BEST ROMANTIC DINING

Amelia's (Newport Beach)
Bernard's (Downtown Los Angeles)
Diaghilev (West Hollywood)
El Encanto Terrace (Santa Barbara)
Geoffrey's (Malibu)
Il Cielo (Beverly Hills)
Raymond Restaurant (Pasadena)
Ristorante Villa Portofino (Catalina)
Rose Garden Tea Room (Huntington Library)
Ti Amo Ristorante (Laguna Beach)

BEST ROMANTIC SMALL HOTELS

Beverly Hills Inn (Beverly Hills)
Carriage House (Laguna Beach)
Château du Lac (Lake Arrowhead)
El Encanto Hotel and Garden Villas (Santa Barbara)
Hotel Villa Portofino (Catalina)
Inn at Playa del Rey (Los Angeles)
Malibu Beach Inn (Malibu)
Ojai Valley Inn (Ojai)
Villa Rosa (Santa Barbara)
The Willows Historic Palm Springs Inn (Palm Springs)

BEST ROMANTIC OUTDOOR ADVENTURES

Biking in Upper Newport Bay Ecological Reserve (Newport Beach)
Desert night hike (Desert Safari, Palm Springs)
Hiking the Gabrielino Trail (Los Angeles)
Horseback riding in Santa Monica Mountains
(Adventures on Horseback, Malibu)
Hot air balloon ride (A Grape Escape Balloon Adventure, Temecula)
Island Packers Channel Islands excursion (Ventura)
Mountain jeep tour (Pink Moment Jeep Tours, Ojai)
Ocean kayaking (Malibu Ocean Sports kayaking, Malibu)
Weekend sailing lessons (Santa Barbara Sailing Center, Santa Barbara)

BEST GARDENS FOR LOVERS

Central Garden (Getty Center, Bel-Air)
El Molino Viejo (Pasadena)
Hotel Bel-Air (Bel-Air)
Huntington Library, Art Collections,
and Botanical Gardens (San Marino)
Japanese Garden (rooftop) at New Otani Hotel
(Little Tokyo, Los Angeles)
Japanese Garden at Ritz-Carlton Huntington Hotel (Pasadena)
Virginia Robinson Garden (Beverly Hills)

BEST SPOTS FOR ART AND CULTURE LOVERS

Avenues of Art and Design (West Hollywood)
The Getty Center (Bel-Air)
Huntington Library, Art Collections,
and Botanical Gardens (San Marino)
Japanese American National Museum (Little Tokyo, Los Angeles)
Los Angeles County Museum of Art (Museum Row, Los Angeles)
Museum of Latin American Art (Long Beach)
Music Center of Los Angeles (Los Angeles)
Norton Simon Museum (Pasadena)
Pasadena Playhouse (Pasadena)
Southwest Museum at LACMA West (Museum Row, Los Angeles)

BEST PLACES TO WATCH THE SUNSET

Dockweiler State Beach, Playa del Rey (Los Angeles)
El Encanto Terrace restaurant (Santa Barbara)
The Getty Center (Bel-Air)
Heisler Park (Laguna Beach)
Malibu Beach Inn (Malibu)
Palisades Park (Santa Monica)
Splashes restaurant (Laguna Beach)

BEST PLACES TO HOLD HANDS

Balboa Island (Newport Beach)
Central Garden (Getty Center, Bel-Air)
El Molino Viejo (Pasadena)
Electra Craft harbor cruise (Oxnard)
Huntington Library, Art Collections, and Botanical Gardens (San Marino)
Japanese Garden (rooftop) at New Otani Hotel
(Little Tokyo, Los Angeles)
Japanese Garden at Ritz-Carlton Huntington Hotel (Pasadena)
Lawn glider at El Encanto Hotel and Garden Villas (Santa Barbara)
Proposal Bench at Loyola Marymount University
(Playa del Rey, Los Angeles)
Surfrider Beach (Malibu)
Walking tour of West Hollywood (West Hollywood)

Romancing the City

Heart of the City

BUNKER HILL, DOWNTOWN LOS ANGELES

ROM THE FREEWAY, DOWNTOWN LOS ANGELES looks like another city center of tall buildings, bearing corporate logos and neon letters spelling out names of banks and oil companies. But at the close of business on Friday, the daily commotion of the business week calms down and the central city is ready to reveal its many subtly pleasing aspects. The weekend is the time to discover that downtown Los Angeles also has a romantic side. In fact, an acquaintance of mine, who has worked downtown for years, once surprised her husband on their anniversary with a weekend stay downtown. They took in the theater one evening and the art museum the next afternoon. In between there was time to stroll around Bunker Hill and shop for jewelry. The weekend turned out to be one of the most romantic of her marriage.

PRACTICAL NOTES: This itinerary involves a good deal of walking, albeit only within a short distance of your hotel. But people seem to be very concerned about crime and safety in Los Angeles, so a comment about safety seems to be in order: Of course, Los Angeles is a big city, and it has its share of crime. But statistically, at least, downtown Los Angeles has a lower crime rate than Seattle, not to mention New York, Miami, and Chicago. So, while the usual precautions one takes in a big city should not be abandoned (don't wear expensive jewelry or flashy watches, for instance), extreme concern about personal safety in the downtown district seems to be unwarranted.

The **Regal Biltmore Hotel** has a variety of weekend packages that may include dinner at the hotel's signature restaurant, Bernard's (about $300 per couple); upgraded amenities on the tenth-floor Regal Club

Floor with extras like continental breakfast, afternoon tea, use of the health club, and validated parking (about $200 per night); or a suite (from about $179 per night).

DAY ONE: *Afternoon*

When the two of you check in at the **Regal Biltmore Hotel** (506 South Grand Avenue; 213-624-1011, 800-245-8673; Web site: www.thebiltmore.com; $235-$2,000), you'll be surrounded by magnificent hand-painted ceilings, faux travertine columns, gilt, and charming decorative details like the "Biltmore angels." The Biltmore, one of the Historic Hotels of America, has been a grand hotel from the day it opened in 1923. Its architectural style may not be immediately recognizable—it's a synthesis of elements of Spanish Rococo Revival and Italian Renaissance palatial—but its historical and cultural status in Los Angeles is unquestionable. The motion picture Oscar statuette was conceived and sketched on a hotel napkin here in 1927 at the founding banquet of the Academy of Motion Picture Arts and Sciences. Over the years everyone has slept here—presidents, movie stars, royalty. A 1997 renovation brought a lighter touch in color scheme, carpeting, and floral fabrics to guest rooms and hallways. (If you're really interested in the history and architecture of the hotel, plan your visit for the second Saturday of the month, when the Los Angeles Conservancy conducts tours of the historic property starting at 10:00 A.M.)

Romance AT A GLANCE

✷ *After checking into the* **Regal Biltmore Hotel** *(506 South Grand Avenue; 213-624-1011), explore the city's downtown* **Jewelry District** *and* **Fashion District.**

✷ *After dinner at the elegant* **Bernard's,** *the hotel's fine dining room, enjoy a theater, dance, or music performance at the* **Music Center** *(213-972-7211). Later have a nightcap in the revolving lounge atop the* **Westin Bonaventure Hotel & Suites** *(404 South Figueroa Street; 213-624-1000).*

✷ *Visit the landmark* **Central Library** *(630 West Fifth Street; 213-228-7000) and stroll through the* **Bunker Hill** *section of downtown, where public sculpture abounds. Along the way stop in at the* **Museum of Contemporary Art (MOCA)** *(250 South Grand Avenue; 213-621-2766) and then have lunch alfresco in the courtyard of the museum at* **Patinette at MOCA** *(213-626-1178).*

The Biltmore's 3:00 P.M. check-in leaves you and your partner time to explore two intriguing districts downtown, the Jewelry District and the Fashion District. Leave the hotel by the exit through Rendezvous Court to Olive Street and Pershing Square. Walk over 1 more block to Hill Street and turn right. The **Jewelry District** is centered on Hill Street and

Broadway between Sixth and Seventh Streets. At street level a sprawl of stalls and small stores trade in all manner of gold and jewelry. Display windows and counters glitter with a treasure of gold chains, bracelets, rings, precious and semiprecious stones, watches, and other jewelry. The air is a rich polyglot of languages—Armenian, Hebrew, Russian, Spanish, Japanese, and heavily accented English. The scene is reminiscent of a *souk*, or bazaar, in Cairo or Damascus or Istanbul, with eager vendors trying to draw your attention.

As tempting as it might be to shop for jewelry as a memento of your weekend, if you're serious about purchasing a fine piece of jewelry, then you'll probably want to visit one of the more upscale establishments. Because this district is also the wholesale market, many of the important vendors are not open to the public. One that is, however, offers a well-established reputation as well as services especially geared toward visitors. Vartan Fouad Ashour of **Vartan and Kesheshian Fine Jewelry Company** in the California Jewelry Mart (607 South Hill Street, Suite 500; 213-622-5743) is a specialist in diamonds. He's been in business for twenty years, designing and manufacturing his own merchandise. His tiny shop on the fifth floor is open on Saturdays and is a glittering showcase of engagement and wedding rings, anniversary rings, earrings, necklaces, and watches. On my recent visit a couple in their forties who were about to be married cooed and hugged as Ashour and his wife helped them with the final details of their diamond wedding rings.

At Seventh Street walk south about 4 blocks to Los Angeles Street and the Fashion District. (You can also take advantage of the DASH shuttle buses that run along this stretch of Seventh Street. The fare is only a quarter; call 213-808-2273 for schedules.) The **Fashion District** is the wholesale and manufacturing center for the garment industry in Los Angeles. But its colorful, street fair atmosphere makes it a favorite destination for weekend urban explorers. In the blocks around Los Angeles Street west of Seventh, there's a dizzying collection of retailers, wholesalers, and manufacturers, selling clothing, textiles, accessories, shoes, ribbon, and fabrics. But you don't even have to buy anything to have a good time here. Sidewalk hawkers try coaxing you to enter shops to buy everything from pink suits to yard goods. Few street scenes in Los Angeles are as entertaining. Several retail shops are clustered along Santee Alley (between Santee Street and Maple Avenue, from Olympic Boulevard to Twelfth Street) and in the **Cooper Building** (860 South Los Angeles Street; 213-622-1139; 213-627-3754). Several times during the year, the **California Mart** (110 East Ninth Street; 213-630-3600), the huge wholesale market, opens to the public for "Super Sale Saturdays."

Backtracking along Hill Street to Pershing Square, you'll see the Biltmore across the square. Cross over to Olive Street and go into the hotel through the original arched, columned entrance. You'll be stepping into the splendid **Rendezvous Court,** a grand distinguished space that harks back to another era, when ladies wore gloves and veiled hats and gentlemen stood when a lady entered or left the room. The trickling fountain and the classical music should be immediately soothing if the two of you are worn out from sight-seeing and shopping. The hotel used to serve afternoon high tea in the Rendezvous Court, but, alas, has discontinued regular tea service except for groups and at holidays (Valentine's Day and Christmas; $23 per person, includes tea, champagne, tea cakes and tarts, and finger sandwiches).

DAY ONE: *Evening*

DINNER

Bernard's (expensive) at the Biltmore has been regarded for many years as the place to go in downtown Los Angeles if you want hushed elegance, traditional pampering, romance, and an ambitious kitchen. Executive chef Roger Pigozzi's Continental-California menu features plenty of seafood, such as grilled Chilean sea bass with risotto and eggplant, or a trio of grilled swordfish, salmon, and tuna with artichokes, caramelized onions, and sun-dried tomatoes. There's game, such as sautéed venison loin medallions with chanterelle mushrooms and juniper berry sauce, and, of course, meats: steaks, chops, and rack of lamb. The service is still pampering, and altogether, the experience is a special occasion.

Your plans for the evening should include the theater—you'd be missing a highlight of this itinerary if they don't. The **Music Center of Los Angeles** (135 North Grand Avenue; 213-972-7211) is the city's principal performing arts complex and the major cultural attraction in downtown Los Angeles. The Music Center sits atop seven acres of Bunker Hill and comprises three separate venues: the 3,000-seat **Dorothy Chandler Pavilion** (213-972-7211), which hosts the opera, Philharmonic, and other musical performances; the **Ahmanson Theater** (213-972-7211 or

213–628–2772), where big musicals and dance shows check into town; and the small, 700-seat **Mark Taper Forum** (213–972–7211 or 213–628–2772), one of the top regional theaters in the country.

A hotel car can take you to the Music Center, where you can stroll hand in hand around the central plaza, listening to the sidewalk musicians and singers. The 1960s buildings of the complex are nothing much to look at, although the Dorothy Chandler does glow regally at night when its chandeliers are lighted. The fountain, however, is always fun to watch as it shoots jets of water into the air, often trapping hapless theatergoers in a spray of water as they try to dash through the momentarily still fountain.

If the night is still young for you when the curtain comes down, then head over to the **Westin Bonaventure Hotel & Suites** (404 South Figueroa Street; 213–624–1000) for a nightcap in the revolving rooftop lounge called the BonaVista. It takes about an hour for the lounge to make a complete revolution, giving you a 360-degree view of the city. The **Gallery Bar** at the Biltmore is quite elegant and also an excellent spot for a nightcap. Although it doesn't offer panoramic views of the city, it does have gorgeous art deco murals on opposite ends of the cozy adjacent niche, the Cognac Room.

DAY TWO: *Morning*

BREAKFAST

A weekend getaway always presents a tempting indulgence: a long, lazy morning with the newspaper and breakfast in bed (the in-room coffeemaker in your one bedroom suite gives you a head start on room service). For you get-up-and-get-going types, the Biltmore's casual eatery, **Smeraldi's,** is also open for breakfast daily from 6:30 to 10:00 A.M. Still another option is the **Original Pantry Cafe** (877 South Figueroa Street, at Ninth Street; 213–972–9279; inexpensive). A Los Angeles institution since 1924, it never closes and serves what many people think are the best hash browns in the city.

After breakfast, you can begin an easy stroll that within a few blocks takes in several of the architectural landmarks of the Bunker Hill section of downtown Los Angeles. The place to begin is the Beaux Arts–style building right across the street from the Biltmore's main entrance, the **Los Angeles Public Library's Central Library** (630 West Fifth Street; 213-228-7000, 213-228-7400). One of the most loved historical landmarks in the city, the library was damaged by an arson fire in 1986. Some 400,000 books were damaged or destroyed, and the library was closed for seven years. The original main building was restored and, together with a new building with an eight-story atrium, was reopened in 1993, bigger and better than ever. It's worth a peek inside to see the second-floor rotunda, with its carefully restored stenciled ceiling, colorful murals, and massive chandelier, as well as the new atrium in the new wing, with its dramatically sculpted pole lights and colorfully contemporary, whimsical chandeliers.

Across the street from the library is the tallest building in Los Angeles and on the West Coast, the 1,017-foot, 73-story **Library Tower,** formerly known as First Interstate Tower (633 West Fifth Street). For some reason the developers did not include an observation deck in the building, so unless you've got business in the tower, about as far as you can go is the lobby, where there's an interesting three-part mural of three painted angels. The mural is called *Unity* and is supposed to represent figures painted in the chapel called Porciuncula visited by St. Francis of Assisi (the original Spanish name given to the Los Angeles River was Rio de los Angeles de Porciuncula). Whatever the derivation, the mural of three white angels (one brunette, two blondes) provoked some critical comment when it was unveiled in 1993 in a city noted for its widely diverse ethnic populations.

A few paces north of the tower are the **Bunker Hill Steps.** This monumental stairway, built in 1990, wraps around the base of the tower linking Fifth Street with Hope Street above. The Bunker Hill Steps are sometimes referred to as Los Angeles's version of Rome's Spanish Steps, although the similarity is hard to discern. Nevertheless, the sweeping stairstep has its own unique attraction. At the base is a small pool filled with water that has flowed down from the top through a stairstepping fountain of fonts and little pools. Landings break up the stairs and are inviting places to sit, quietly perched for a few minutes above Fifth Street. At the top of the steps, an exquisite nude sculpture called *Source Figure* (Robert Graham, 1992) stands atop a cylindrical base that seems to mimic the trunk of the palm trees nearby. Her hands are open, as if to offer the water to the city below. (There's also an escalator if you find all those stairs intimidating.)

At the end of the block (Hope and Fourth Streets), the **Stuart M. Ketchum YMCA** presents a bit of a surprise: A landscaped plaza punctuated with several sculptures wraps itself around the building, providing very nice views of the northeast portion of the city and, if it's clear, the San Gabriel Mountains beyond. Across the street in the **Mellon Bank Center** plaza stands Alexander Liberman's *Ulysses* (1988), a massive but well-scaled, white-painted steel sculpture of tubes and curved shapes.

Walking east together through the plaza will bring you to Grand Avenue. Turn left for a 3-block walk (the longer crosstown blocks) to the **Museum of Contemporary Art (MOCA)** at California Plaza (250 South Grand Avenue; 213-626-6222, 213-621-2766). Along the way, at the crest of the small hill on Grand Avenue, you'll come across a little circular fountain that pops and bubbles and hiccups in the forecourt of **Water Court.** In the large plaza behind it, a clever design of fountains and pools and amphitheater-style seating areas has created one of the city's most interesting urban spaces. Concerts are held here on summer evenings. On a platform above Water Court, a restored version of the historic **Angels Flight,** the world's shortest funicular railroad, transports passengers down a steep grade to the street below or lifts them up. The ride covers a distance of only 335 feet, lasts hardly a minute, and costs 25 cents each way.

Gilded Romance

All that gilt and etched crystal chandeliers inspires romance at the Biltmore Hotel. Back in the 1940s, legendary baseball player Jackie Robinson met his future wife, Rachel, at a luncheon at the hotel. Within a year they were married. Fifty years later the actress Delta Burke wanted a grand, Southern feel for her marriage to the actor Gerald Rainey. The couple chose the Biltmore for the wedding and also had their first anniversary party in the hotel's Crystal Room.

There's something immediately distinctive about the architectural design of MOCA. Renowned Japanese architect Arata Isozaki combined pyramid, cube, and cylinder shapes covered in sandstone, granite, aluminum, and glass to create a stunning structure that suggests something not altogether Western or Japanese. Visitors enter the galleries through a sunken courtyard. The museum's permanent collection holds only art created since 1940. All the major artists from those years—John Baldessari, Willem de Kooning, Sam

Francis, Jasper Johns, Ellsworth Kelly, Roy Lichtenstein, Louise Nevelson, Cindy Sherman, Mark Rothko, Andy Warhol—are represented here. Changing exhibitions present works from the permanent collection, as well as contemporary art that may combine dance, theater, performance, film, video, and music. There's nothing hushed or sedate about a visit to MOCA; it's exuberant and full of life, and the two of you will leave feeling stimulated, even if puzzled or unsure of what you've viewed. MOCA is open Tuesday through Sunday, from 11:00 A.M. to 5:00 P.M. (Thursdays until 8:00 P.M.). Adult admission is around $6.00, with free admission every Thursday from 5:00 to 8:00 P.M.

DAY TWO: *Afternoon*

LUNCH

Patinette at MOCA (213-626-1178; inexpensive) in the courtyard adjacent to the museum's entrance is the place to discuss the form and color of those Ellsworth Kelly canvases you just saw. Try one of the salads, like the mozzarella and tomato salad, which is kissed with Kalamata olives and a drizzle of extra virgin olive oil; the green bean salad with artichokes, cherry tomatoes, Black Forest ham, and a piquant red bell pepper vinaigrette; or one of the sandwiches (the carved, smoked turkey on dark wheat bread is quite substantial) from an imaginative menu of appetizers, soups, sandwiches, and desserts. Sit outside at a table that's shaded by an umbrella.

Walking back along Grand Avenue, stop at the southeast corner at Fifth Street, where there's the sleek **Gas Company Tower.** Go inside for a peek at the lobby "water garden" and to see if you can make sense of Frank Stella's mural *Dusk*, painted on the wall of the adjacent Pacific Bell building. (There's also a little viewing gallery into the Gas Company lobby on Grand Avenue for a different angle.)

As the time draws near to conclude your weekend in downtown Los Angeles, perhaps, like my acquaintance, you'll feel a little bit closer to your partner and to the heart of this one-of-a-kind city as well.

FOR MORE ROMANCE

Extend or alter your visit to downtown Los Angeles with an excursion to Chinatown, Little Tokyo, or Olvera Street (see Itinerary 15, "No Passport Required") or Museum Row (Itinerary 16, "Courting the Muse").

Steppin' ☆ Out with My Baby

WEST HOLLYWOOD

est Hollywood has always been the place in Los Angeles to step out and have a good time. Decades ago supper clubs on the Sunset Strip—Mocambo, Trocadero, and Ciro's—were legendary celebrity haunts where the comings and goings of movie stars were faithfully reported by newspaper gossip columnists. Though the scene in West Hollywood today is funkier at clubs like the Whisky, the Roxy, the Comedy Store, and the Viper Room, it's still possible to capture a bit of the old sophistication. This itinerary focuses on some of those romantic possibilities for you to experience: a Saturday evening group art gallery opening, elegant dining, jazz at an intimate club, and a rousing gospel brunch at the House of Blues on Sunday morning.

PRACTICAL NOTES: Although it's entirely surrounded by Los Angeles, West Hollywood is an independent community. To get more information about West Hollywood and special events like the Saturday night art gallery group openings, contact the **West Hollywood Convention and Visitors Bureau** (Pacific Design Center, 8687 Melrose Avenue, Suite M25; 310–289–2525 or 800–368–6020). Sunday gospel brunch at the House of Blues is very popular, so reserve ahead of time, the sooner the better; call (323) 848–5100. The brochure *A Walking Tour of West Hollywood Apartment Life* costs $2.00 and is available through the Los Angeles Conservancy Walking Tours (523 West Sixth Street, Suite 1216, Los Angeles, CA 90014; 213–623–2489).

DAY ONE: *Afternoon*

You don't have to wait until the sun goes down to step out and check the pulse of West Hollywood. On any blue-skied, sunny day, especially on Saturdays, the place to see and be seen in West Hollywood is **Sunset Plaza**. Sunset Plaza is the section of Sunset Boulevard at Sunset Plaza Drive, just two blocks west of La Cienega Boulevard. You can't miss it—the street widens and the median strip is planted with flowers. Some of the white-frame and brick buildings look vaguely Colonial, a somewhat quaint background for the slender, up-to-the-moment young men and women who strut in and out of the expensive, showy shops. Taking in the scene from a table at a sidewalk cafe, there's no mistaking the sanguine self-awareness of the Southern California good life in this sunny corner of the world where the sidewalks aren't stained and the flowers don't wilt in the heat.

Romance

AT A GLANCE

✳ Take in the West Hollywood scene with lunch at the sidewalk cafe **Clafoutis** (8630 Sunset Boulevard; 310–659–5233; moderate) at **Sunset Plaza,** a trendy stretch of Sunset Boulevard. Then check into the **Wyndam Bel Age Hotel** (1020 North San Vicente Boulevard at Sunset; 310–854–1111 or 800–996–3426), where rich wood, Italian marble, and original art create a sedately elegant environment.

✳ Explore some of city's art galleries clustered on or near Melrose Avenue in a walkable section of the city called the **Avenues of Art and Design.** Periodically, on Saturday evening, several galleries host a group opening. While you view the art, graze on fruit and cheese and sip wine. (Call the West Hollywood Convention and Visitors Bureau, 310–289–2525 or 800–368–6020, for information.)

✳ Dinner is a lushly orchestrated affair of Franco-Russian cuisine at **Diaghilev** (Wyndham Bel Age Hotel; expensive) or a charmingly romantic occasion at **Le Petit Bistro** (631 North La Cienega Boulevard; 310–289–9797; moderate).

✳ Get the day off to a rousing start with a **Sunday gospel brunch** at the House of Blues (8430 Sunset Boulevard; 323–848–5100), then take a quiet hand-in-hand walk through a residential neighborhood to see several historic and architecturally unusual apartment buildings (Los Angeles Conservancy; 213–623–2489).

LUNCH

Sunset Plaza has a near-profusion of sidewalk cafes, which makes it just about the best spot in town for people watching. On the north side of the street, the patio at **Cafe Med** (8615 Sunset Boulevard; 310–652–0445; moderate) is bright and airy, and the menu mixes fresh pasta and salads with pizza from a wood-burning oven. Across the street **Chin**

Chin (8618 Sunset Boulevard; 310-652-1818; moderate) draws legions of devotees who love the chicken salad, pot stickers, and sweet-and-sour orange chicken. We always seem to gravitate to the middle of the block and **Clafoutis** (8630 Sunset Boulevard; 310-659-5233; moderate), with its bistro-ish menu and great people-watching vantage point (tables inside the restaurant in the back have great views of the West Side of Los Angeles). Leave it to West Hollywood to be on the cutting edge, even when it comes to ordering a steak sandwich at Clafoutis. Waiters, rather than writing your order down, send your order to kitchen electronically by punching numbers into the keypad of what looks like a TV remote control. The savory herb-chicken sandwich, by the way, is 380; the steak sandwich, well-done, 381-4. If an ice-blended mocha drink sounds like it would hit the spot, then head over to the north side of Sunset Plaza to **Coffee Bean & Tea Leaf** (8591 Sunset Boulevard; 310-659-1890).

For such a small city—only 1.9 square miles—West Hollywood has quite a lineup of hotels. At one end of the spectrum, there's the ultracool and sexy **Mondrian** (8440 Sunset Boulevard; 323-650-8999 or 800-525-8029), Ian Schrager's hostelry, which is headquarters for hip thirtysomething tastemakers from the worlds of fashion, advertising, and entertainment; then there's the fabled shabby-chic of the **Chateau Marmont** (8221 Sunset Boulevard; 323-656-1010 or 800-242-8328), the long-time haunt of actors and writers, which will always be remembered as the place where John Belushi was found dead; and there are the digs at the **Sunset Marquis** (1200 North Alta Loma Road; 310-657-1333 or 800-858-9758), which are popular with the music industry crowd.

Somewhere in between is the more sedate **Wyndham Bel Age Hotel** (1020 North San Vicente Boulevard at Sunset; 310-854-1111 or 800-996-3426; weekend package with breakfast, from $212). Rich woods, Italian marble, crystal chandeliers, and original art everywhere you turn strike just the right blend of sophistication, elegance, and West Hollywood informality at the Wyndham Bel Age. Suites are stylishly decorated with fine furniture and floral bed covers, and each has its kitchenette and private balcony. The executive suite comes with a bathtub big enough for two (but bring your own bath salts), as well as a CD player. Most romantic (despite the name) is the corporate suite, in which the bedroom is a step up from the sitting area. A white wrought-iron railing marks the divide, and gauzy white draperies pull closed to separate the two areas. Directly across the room is the private balcony. If the weather's warm and the balcony doors are open, you can just lie in bed and let the breeze caress you.

Up on the roof, a pool terrace has nearly 360-degree vistas of Los Angeles—from the Hollywood Hills and downtown Los Angeles to Century City, Santa Monica, and the Pacific Ocean. Quite a backdrop for the frequent weddings held up there.

Sweet Nothings

If, instead of nightclubs and high-energy action, you're looking for a quieter way to savor the afterglow of a fine evening, then go up to the rooftop pool terrace at the Bel Age Hotel. You'll feel as if you're above the whole city. Gaze out over the endless sweep of flickering lights and whisper something sweet and wonderful to each other.

As Saturday afternoon wanes into early evening, a uniquely West Hollywood event gets under way every six to eight weeks—a group opening at a dozen or more of the city's art galleries. Most of West Hollywood's galleries are concentrated on or near Melrose Avenue, just east and west of San Vicente Boulevard in a walkable section of West Hollywood that's called the **Avenues of Art and Design.** There's abundant and reasonable parking at the **Pacific Design Center** (8687 Melrose Avenue at San Vicente Boulevard; 310–657–0800 or for parking call 310–659–7252) from which you can walk. Receptions at the galleries generally begin around 5:00 P.M. and continue until 9:00 P.M. Between nibbles of fruit and cheese and sips of wine, it's a great way for you to see everything from nineteenth-century American art to new Latin American paintings to work by Warhol, Ruscha, Pollock, and Frankenthaler. Often it's a chance to meet artists. If you go, be prepared for anything—one gallery might be serious and sedate; another might be jumpin' to the energy of a young, hipster crowd. It's all part of the fun.

DAY ONE: *Evening*

DINNER

As it is with hotels, West Hollywood is disproportionately blessed with excellent restaurants. Some, like **Morton's** (8764 Melrose Avenue; 310–276–5205; expensive) and **Le Dome** (8720 Sunset Boulevard; 310–

659–6919; expensive), are as well known for their celebrity clientele as their food. Celebrity value, however, does not necessarily equal romantic. One restaurant that turns up on everybody's short list of "romantic" spots is Diaghilev in the Bel Age.

Diaghilev (dinner, Tuesday through Saturday; 310–854–1111; expensive) harks back to another era, Paris or St. Petersburg before the revolution. (Sergey Pavlovich Diaghilev was a Russian impresario and the director of the famous Ballet Russe.) Mirrors and etched glass reflect soft candlelight, setting one of the most romantic moods in any restaurant in town. A red rose decorates every table, and extravagant floral arrangements elsewhere add drama. The tuxedoed headwaiter and Cossack-shirted waiters provide superb service in this hushed, discreet room. The fare is Russian with French overtones: for starters, try *pelmieny,* or plump Siberian ravioli of veal and duck. There's caviar, of course, if you're feeling very extravagant (beluga goes for $95, served with the usual accompaniments). For entrees the filet of sturgeon is light and velvety, served with a lemony sauce and caviar. For chicken Kiev, a tender breaded breast of farm chicken is stuffed with morels and black truffles. And when was the last time your entree was presented to you under a silver *cloche*? But it's that complete attention to detail and presentation that makes Diaghilev so special.

The only problem with Diaghilev is that it's *so* expensive. If spending a ton of money on dinner diffuses your romantic flame, then look to the absolutely charming **Le Petit Bistro** (631 North La Cienega Boulevard; 310–289–9797; moderate). It's just a few blocks away, and with its excellent (and low-priced) menu of authentic French bistro fare—black mussels mariniere, frogs' legs, crisp pommes frites, veal sausage—beveled leaded glass windows, and French waiters, you'll think you're in Paris. And what could be more romantic than that?

In the nearly eight years **Club Brasserie** (at the Bel Age Hotel, 1020 North San Vicente Boulevard at Sunset; 310–358–7776 for club) has been around, it's secured a well-deserved reputation as a classy spot for some top-rate jazz, having welcomed such artists as Buddy Montgomery, Black Note, Kevin Eubanks, Teddy Edwards, and Harold Land. A wall of windows takes advantage of the view and makes the small space seem larger than it is. Although dinner is served until 11:00 P.M., you can just stop in for the music. The first of three sets goes on at 9:00 P.M., Wednesday through Saturday. There's a two-drink minimum, but no cover charge.

A stroll together down neon-lit **Sunset Boulevard** at this hour will reveal a high-octane street scene pulsing with youthful energy. As Saturday night traffic rumbles by, older teens might be congregating in front of the Sunset Strip Tattoo parlor near the Argyle Hotel, while lines of comedy lovers are forming to get into the Comedy Store (8433 Sunset Boulevard; 213–656–6225). Trendsetters, both real and imagined, are vying to get past the velvet rope at ultracool clubs like The Whiskey Bar at the Sunset Marquis Hotel or the Sky Bar at the Mondrian. At **Book Soup** (8818 Sunset Boulevard; 310-659-3110), the ever-growing bookstore-cafe-gathering spot, a book signing might be under way. South of Sunset, on **Santa Monica Boulevard,** the action at the city's burgeoning scene of gay and lesbian clubs is just beginning to heat up.

DAY TWO: *Morning*

BRUNCH

OK, so a hand-clapping, foot-stomping, high-cholesterol Sunday gospel brunch at the **House of Blues** isn't for everybody (8430 Sunset Boulevard; 323–848–5100; $29 for an all-you-can-eat buffet and gospel show). That's what we thought the first time, too. At first, everything about it seemed contrived, starting with the Disneylandish facade of a weathered delta roadhouse. At night the House of Blues is a smokin' music club. Come Sundays, though, Range Rovers and BMWs fill the parking lot, and people wait half an hour or more to gain admittance to one of three gospel brunch shows (9:30 A.M., noon, and 2:30 P.M.). The brunch buffet consists of barbecued chicken, eggs, sausage, fried catfish, and grits. Symbols representing the world's religions are mounted across the proscenium of the stage, along with a sign, UNITY IN DIVERSITY. The interior of the club is a gallery of African-American folk art. Walls and staircases, ceilings and bars, all are covered with a staggering, eye-popping conglomeration of colors and textures: portraits and icons made from glass and stones, bottle caps embedded in the wooden bar, a bas-relief mural of blues artists. By the time the gospel group comes on, it's hard not to succumb to the joyfulness of the occasion. We clapped and sang and had a wonderful time, and you probably will too. And if you leave feeling uplifted in spirit, what could be better?

DAY TWO: *Afternoon*

End your romantic West Hollywood escape quietly with a casual **walking tour of historic apartment buildings.** A sophisticated residential neighborhood grew up on side streets off the Sunset Strip in the 1920s and 1930s. The buildings that you'll see on the self-guided tour were home to a long list of movie stars, directors, and writers. Using the Los Angeles Conservancy self-guided map and brochure (see Practical notes), you can start off on Havenhurst Drive. Off the main drags, West Hollywood feels almost like a small town. People say "hello" as they pass on the sidewalk, and nobody seems to mind if you stop to peek into cool, leafy courtyards of complexes named Andalusia (1471 Havenhurst Drive) and Patio del Moro (8225 North Fountain Avenue). Bette Davis lived at the white-brick Colonial House (1416 Havenhurst Drive), and Katharine Hepburn and James Dean once resided at Villa Primavera (1800-08 North Harper). As you stroll, look for fountains, colorful decorative tiles, and lacy iron grillwork.

FOR MORE ROMANCE

To add some Hollywood history and glamour to your getaway, see Itinerary 14, "Hurray for Hollywood!" West Hollywood is also next door to Beverly Hills, so if world-class shopping suits your plans, take a look at Itinerary 3, "Faraway in Beverly Hills."

Faraway in Beverly Hills

S PENDING A COUPLE OF DAYS IN BEVERLY HILLS is a bit like being carried off to a fairy-tale kingdom, a golden enclave, where the flowers are always in bloom, the blessings of life are abundant, and everyone is a prince or princess. It's sort of like a theme park, where fantasy magically becomes reality. The theme in Beverly Hills, of course, is money, privilege, prestige; the fantasy, for most of us, is that we really can afford to buy those jewels in the window of Tiffany's on Rodeo Drive. The reality is that despite its carefully cultivated "exclusive, rich" image, Beverly Hills is quite an affordable destination. As you'll discover with this itinerary, you and your partner don't need to spend an arm and a leg. Besides that, you can park your car at the hotel and walk just about everywhere you want to go.

PRACTICAL NOTES: Although completely surrounded by Los Angeles, Beverly Hills is an independent community. At its **Visitors Bureau** (239 South Beverly Drive; 310-248-1010 or 800-345-2110; Web site: www. beverlyhillscc.org), you can pick up the current visitor guide. It contains useful maps noting parking locations and a detailed self-guided walking tour of the city. Casual dress is just fine in Beverly Hills, but leave the fanny packs and pink running suits at home. Only "tourists" wear shorts and T-shirts here. Women can take this opportunity to dress up a bit, and men will probably feel more comfortable in a jacket at most restaurants. The **Beverly Hills Inn** (125 South Spalding Drive; 310-278-0303 or 800-463-4466) is often booked on spring weekends because of the wedding party overflow from the

Bel-Air and other hotels, so book accommodations as early as possible. The **Virginia Robinson Gardens** (1008 Elder Way; 310–276–5367), one of Beverly Hills's most well-known attractions, is open for tours on weekdays by appointment only. Admission is about $7.00.

DAY ONE: *Afternoon*

Even if it's too early to check into the Beverly Hills Inn, as guests you two can park your car at the hotel if you wish and then walk back the few blocks into the Golden Triangle of Beverly Hills. Otherwise you can easily find parking in at least a dozen lots and structures in the Golden Triangle; most offer one or two hours' free parking. After lunch and a little window-shopping, you can return to the hotel to check in.

Shopping is the lifeblood of the section of Beverly Hills known as the **Golden Triangle,** the wedge-shaped retail-commercial core of the city bordered by Wilshire and Santa Monica Boulevards and Rexford Drive. The heart and soul of Beverly Hills, the Golden Triangle is one of the most expensive tracts of real estate anywhere in the world. At the center is **Rodeo Drive,** which has been called the "platinum vein" of the Golden Triangle. Here's where you find the big guns in the world of high fashion, jewelry, fragrance, leather goods, gifts, you name it: Bottega Veneta, Frette, Harry Winston, Fendi, Gucci, Hermès, Loewe, Cartier, Tiffany, and

Romance

AT A GLANCE

✳ *Book one of the deluxe rooms in a separate cottagelike building next to the lushly landscaped pool at the intimate* **Beverly Hills Inn** *(125 South Spalding Drive; 310–278–0303 or 800–463–4466). Then walk the few blocks to* **Rodeo Drive** *for an afternoon of window-shopping. Later hop aboard a trolley tour of the city ($5.00 per person; Dayton Way and Rodeo Drive; 310–285–2438).*

✳ *For a romantic dinner for two, reserve a table on the secluded patio of* **Il Cielo** *(9018 Burton Way; 310–276–9990; moderate to expensive), with its trickling fountain and canopy of small white lights. Later, the evening takes on a nostalgia at the only nightclub in town—the* **Coconut Club** *at the Beverly Hilton Hotel, where swing and 1940s cafe society have resurfaced (9876 Wilshire Boulevard; 310–285–1358).*

✳ *Spend the morning shopping for high-quality produce and fresh baked goods at the Sunday* **Beverly Hills Farmers Market** *on Canon Drive, between Dayton and Clifton (310–285–2535).*

✳ *Privately view an episode of your favorite television show or attend a special screening at the* **Museum of Television & Radio** *(465 North Beverly Drive; 310–786–1000). Then drive up into the hills for a look at the grand historic estate called* **Greystone Mansion** *and stroll the grounds (905 Loma Vista Drive; 310–550–4796).*

many more prestigious merchants. The two of you can stroll hand in hand and admire all the finery in the windows, your money tucked safely away in your wallets.

On the corner of Rodeo Drive and Wilshire Boulevard is the fairly new **2 Rodeo,** a Beverly Hills version of a shopping center disguised to look like a European shopping street. More tony retailers are found along this cobblestoned pedestrian lane called Via Rodeo, which bisects the corner. There is a sort of international air about the place. You'll hear many languages spoken here, notably Japanese and Spanish but also German, French, and Italian. The cobblestones do lend an old-world touch, as does the flower vendor, his white cart practically hidden behind bouquets of roses, tulips, and mums and potted azaleas, who's usually found at the top of the steps that lead up from Wilshire Boulevard.

More moderately priced retailers, such as Banana Republic, Williams-Sonoma, The Limited, The Gap, and Victoria's Secret, can be found on **Beverly Drive,** just 1 block east of Rodeo. A 4-block stretch of **Wilshire Boulevard,** from Roxbury Drive to Camden Drive, is headquarters for upscale department stores: **Neiman Marcus** (9700 Wilshire Boulevard; 310-550-5900), **Barneys New York** (9570 Wilshire Boulevard; 310-276-4400), and **Saks Fifth Avenue** (9600 Wilshire Boulevard; 310-275-4211).

LUNCH

For all its opulence, Beverly Hills offers several small, low-key restaurants where you won't spend an arm and a leg for lunch. The actress Cathy Moriarity keeps transplanted New Yorkers and other pizza lovers happy with her two **Mulberry Street** pizzeria locations (240 South Beverly Drive; 310-247-8100; and 347 North Canon Drive; 310-247-8998; inexpensive). The small, stylish trattoria **Prego** (362 North Camden Drive; 310-277-7346; moderate) is part of a chain, but that hasn't compromised the better-than-average quality of the food (baby lamb chops, broiled veal chop, pastas, and crisp-crust pizzas). It's classy but comfortable.

If you'd like to see more of Beverly Hills than glitzy storefronts, then walk over to the northwest corner of Dayton Way and Rodeo Drive for a trolley tour. From May through December, the **Beverly Hills Trolley** departs from this corner for two different tours of the city. The forty-minute

"Sights and Scenes" tour takes you through the Golden Triangle and past the Beverly Hills Hotel before heading off into the residential area to go by former homes of Hollywood luminaries, such as Edgar Bergen (Candice's father), Doris Day, and Mel Blanc (the voice of Bugs Bunny and Daffy Duck). The "Art and Architecture" tour lasts ninety minutes. It cruises by the I. M. Pei–designed offices of Creative Artists Agency and makes short stops at some of the fine arts galleries in Beverly Hills. Tours cost $5.00 per person for adults. The schedule varies, but generally Saturdays, on the hour, between noon and 4:00 P.M. May through December. (The trolley can also be rented for a private version of either tour; the cost is about $221; call 310–285–2438 for more information.)

There are a few small, reasonable hotels in Beverly Hills, but I think the nicest by far is the newly refurbished **Beverly Hills Inn** (125 South Spalding Drive; 310–278–0303 or 800–463–4466; $145–$300). It's tucked just off Wilshire and Santa Monica Boulevards, on a quiet, tree-lined residential street. Yes, the lobby is done up tastefully in marble, and a full complimentary breakfast is served in the cozy Garden Room every morning. But it's other special touches that make this fifty-room inn so appealing: Sofa accent pillows that are fluffed and pinched, goose down bed pillows, and small floral arrangements and little tabletop baskets of potpourri add fresh, welcoming touches. Floral draperies and bedcovers enhance the warm tones of maple armoires, bedside tables, and other room fixtures. Ask for one of the four deluxe rooms in a separate cottage next to the pool. They each feature a small sitting area, a king-size bed, and French doors that lead to a private terrace, and they offer a very romantic sense of privacy. The small pool area, secluded behind a lush stand of banana trees and birds of paradise, could be found at a tropical resort. There's also a tiny fitness room with two saunas. Guest parking is free, and the property is patrolled around the clock.

DAY ONE: *Evening*

DINNER

Il Cielo (9018 Burton Way; 310–276–9990; moderate to expensive) is a place to gaze lovingly into each other's eyes and hold hands without feeling the slightest bit uncomfortable—because you won't be alone. *Il cielo* in Italian means "the sky"; in this case, inside it's a trompe l'oeil sky, flickering candles, and flowers; outside, a stone patio with a trickling fountain and the twinkling of real starlight and strings of small white lights in the trees. More than one starry-eyed couple has succumbed to the utterly romantic setting. It's a wonder anybody pays attention to the food—try risotto with seafood in a spicy tomato sauce, salmon with champagne and tarragon, or grilled sea bass with fresh herbs. The tiramisu is lush and captivating.

Beverly Hills is not known for its nightlife, although a few of its hotel bars are legendary—for instance, the **Polo Lounge** at the Beverly Hills Hotel (9641 Sunset Boulevard; 310-276-2251) and the **Club Bar** at the Peninsula Hotel (9882 Santa Monica Boulevard; 310-551-2888). The swing dance craze of recent years arrived in Beverly Hills in 1998 with the **Coconut Club** at the Merv Griffin's Beverly Hilton Hotel ($20 cover charge per person; 310-285-1358). Before he became a television star, Griffin, you may recall, was a crooner who sang at the legendary Coconut Grove supper club back in the 1950s. Well, the big band sound is back, at least on Friday and Saturday nights when the Grand Ballroom of the Hilton is transformed into a 1940s supper club, where you can dance to a big band orchestra. (If you don't know how to dance, your $20 cover charge includes a few quick dance lessons for the asking.) Access to the adjoining Mango Bar, Chimps Cigar Lounge, and Coco Bar is also included in the cover charge. Dinner reservations can be made for a $20 minimum per person, guaranteed by a credit card. So dress up a bit and "get hep."

Light theater fare is what usually turns up at the **Cañon Theater** (205 North Cañon; 310-859-8001), one of the busier small theaters in the Los Angeles area. A. R. Gurney's *Love Letters* ran here for more than a year, with a revolving cast of popular television and film stars in the lead roles. Stuart Ross's hit musical *Forever Plaid*, about a fictitious 1960s musical group's comeback from beyond, also had a successful run here twice.

DAY TWO: *Morning*

After breakfast—take advantage of the complimentary continental breakfast provided at the Beverly Hills Inn—stroll over to Cañon Drive. On Sundays from 9:00 A.M. to 1:00 P.M., Cañon Drive is closed to vehicles between Dayton and Clifton Ways for the weekly Farmers Market. Small in comparison to some of the other markets in the area, the **Beverly Hills Farmers Market** (310–285–2535) nevertheless offers a select bounty of fresh produce, baked goods, olive oil and honey, potted plants and fresh flowers, gourmet pastas, and live entertainment. There's no jostling from too many people, and vendors are friendly enough to answer questions and even give you some tips, for instance, for grilling mushrooms. Of course there's the occasional celebrity resident who stops by to pick up fresh herbs or snack on gourmet tamales filled with rock shrimp or green chiles and smoked gouda.

DAY TWO: *Afternoon*

A 2-block walk north on Cañon to Little Santa Monica Boulevard and west 1 block to Beverly Drive will bring you to the **Museum of Television & Radio** (465 North Beverly Drive; 310–786–1000; open Wednesday through Sunday from noon to 5:00 P.M., Thursday until 9:00 P.M. Admission is about $6.00). If elements of the building look familiar—white metal panels, pale travertine marble, and lots of glass—it's because the luminous structure was designed by Richard Meier, the architect responsible for Atlanta's High Museum, Barcelona's Museum of Contemporary Art, and, of course, Los Angeles's new Getty Center. The West Coast building of the New York–based MT&R, the Beverly Hills museum opened in 1996 with a collection of more than 75,000 clips of radio and television programs and advertisements available for

Gifts of Love

The jeweler Cartier may have just the little love token you've been looking for: the famous gold wristband "love bracelet" which is fastened with a little gold screw by the giver. The price is a mere $3,625; no extra charge for the tiny 18K gold screwdriver. Puffed heart pendants come in two sizes: the larger is encrusted in diamonds ($11,500); the smaller is of white gold ($4,150). To really say "I love you," there's the double-heart necklace of alternating gold and diamond hearts for $16,700.

the public to see and hear. After a look in the main gallery at the current exhibit of television- and radio-related art and artifacts (a recent exhibit displayed animation cels from *Peanuts* TV specials, for instance), you can go upstairs to the Hubbard Library and use a computer to search, find, and view an episode of your favorite TV program or hear an old radio broadcast. Special screenings are also scheduled; check at the information desk about these and other events.

When you leave the museum, take yourselves north on Rodeo Drive toward **Santa Monica Boulevard** and the residential flatlands of Beverly Hills. As you cross Santa Monica, you'll first come to **Beverly Gardens,** a slender strip of a park planted with trees, shrubs, and flowers. It parallels Santa Monica Boulevard for 14 blocks, a sort of buffer between the busy thoroughfare and the residential area. One of the more interesting private residences in Beverly Hills is on Rodeo Drive just north of Santa Monica Boulevard. You shouldn't have any trouble finding it on the west side of the street, especially if you're familiar with the fanciful style of Spain's Catalan architect Antonio Gaudi. Gaudi had nothing to do with this home, but we're sure he'd get a kick out of it. Several more blocks north, about ¾ mile, is **Sunset Boulevard** and the legendary **Beverly Hills Hotel,** recently reopened after a $100-million-plus renovation.

LUNCH

Retrace your route to Beverly Drive to one of the best-known delis in the country, **Nate 'n' Al's** (414 North Beverly Drive; 310–274–0101; moderate), for typical no-frills delicatessen fare. But along with your corned beef and pastrami sandwiches, brisket, chicken livers, or matzo ball soup, you might be served a healthy portion of celebrity sightings, especially on weekends.

Before ending your stay in Beverly Hills, leave the flatlands of the city for a trip up into the hills above Sunset Boulevard and a look at **Greystone Mansion** (905 Loma Vista Drive; 310–550–4796). This grand estate was constructed in the 1920s by the oil magnate E. L. Doheny. It's now owned by the city and listed on the National Register of Historic Places. Although the mansion is closed to the public, the grounds, the courtyard, and the terrace are open daily from 10:00 A.M. to 5:00 P.M. (in winter) or 6:00 P.M. (in summer), and admission is free. You can walk around the estate, with its manicured formal garden. Below the broad south terrace of the mansion, a large lawn slopes down to the road. Couples, by themselves and sometimes with young children, come to sit in the shade of a tree, read a book, or enjoy the general peaceful atmosphere and gaze out over the vista of that faraway land of Beverly Hills.

FOR MORE ROMANCE

If you have an extra morning or afternoon, you could combine this itinerary with a visit to one or more of the museums on Museum Row (see Itinerary 16). For an unusual tour of Beverly Hills—a personalized jogging tour—call **Off 'N Running Tours** (310-246-1418). The owner, Cheryl Anker, combines sight-seeing with a 4- to 10-mile run and throws in a T-shirt and snack for about $80 per couple.

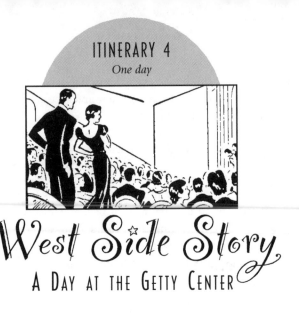

West Side Story
A Day at the Getty Center

THE BILLION-DOLLAR GETTY CENTER GLEAMS white and bright atop a Brentwood hill, a spectacular monument to an incredible $4.2 billion endowment fund and cultural largesse. Since its opening in December 1997, the Getty Center has become *the* cultural destination in Los Angeles. The Getty lacks the breadth and depth of the art treasures at, say, New York's Metropolitan Museum of Art or the Art Institute of Chicago, but that means visiting the Getty isn't overwhelming. Despite its almost fortresslike presence high on that hill and the crowds of visitors, the Getty Center is an ideal romantic West Side interlude, providing just the right combination of cultural stimulation and ordinary diversion. Besides the art collections—European paintings (including Van Gogh's *Irises* and three works by Monet), drawings, sculpture, illuminated manuscripts, decorative arts, and American and European photographs—there's a lovely central garden, fountains, spectacular views of the city and two offshore islands, gorgeous sunsets, a fine restaurant, gallery talks, and Friday evening concert performances in the summer. Best of all admission to the Getty is free. The only hitch? The limited parking, which means you have to plan well in advance and make a parking reservation to guarantee admittance to the museum (there's a $5.00 parking fee).

PRACTICAL NOTES: Planning is the key to visiting the **Getty Center** (1200 Getty Center Drive at the San Diego Freeway/I–405; 310–440–7300 for parking reservations, TTY 310–440–7305; Web site: www.getty.edu). Parking reservations are essential to guarantee admittance. Call to make them at least six to eight weeks beforehand. The cost for parking is $5.00. Visitors may also arrive by public bus (MTA 561 and Santa Monica Big Blue Bus 14), taxi, or one of the shuttle services. Holiday weekends and school vacations are the worst times to go to the Getty without a parking reservation because you'll certainly face long lines and may even be turned away. The Getty Center is open Tuesday and Wednesday, 11:00 A.M. to 7:00 P.M.; Thursday and Friday, 11:00 A.M. to 9:00 P.M.; and Saturday and Sunday, 10:00 A.M. to 6:00 P.M. It's closed Mondays and major holidays. The Getty Center has two cafeterias, a fine-dining restaurant, and several food and beverage carts that serve espresso, soft drinks, bottle water, and snacks. There's also a picnic area at the lower tram plaza. If you want to have dinner at the **Restaurant at the Getty Center**, make reservations when you call for parking reservations.

DAY ONE:

Afternoon

If it is possible, plan to visit the Getty Center in the afternoon and evening, the most romantic parts of the day to be there (the Getty is open until 9:00 P.M. on Thursday and Friday). Besides strolling through the art galleries, you can take a walk in the garden or linger on one of the terraces to watch the sun set and the

Romance
AT A GLANCE

✳ Visit the billion-dollar **Getty Center** (1200 Getty Center Drive at the San Diego Freeway/I-405; 310–440–7300 for parking reservations, TTY 310–440–7305; www.getty.edu; parking, $5.00), arriving in the afternoon and staying into the evening. Reserve parking in advance to guarantee admittance or be spontaneous and arrive by bus, taxi, or shuttle van.

✳ View a short introductory film about the $4.2 billion institution, then join a guided walking tour of the complex and learn more about the Getty Center's architect, Richard Meier.

✳ Wander leisurely through the galleries, being sure to see the illuminated manuscripts, the decorative arts collections, and the paintings, especially the Impressionist works. Pause on the terrace of South Pavilion for spectacular views of Los Angeles—from the mountains to the Pacific Ocean.

✳ Have lunch cafeteria-style in **The Cafe**, where you can sit outside, surrounded by a canopy of bougainvillea. Then follow the winding walkway down to the **Central Garden**, where you can stroll or relax on a garden bench.

✳ As afternoon gives way to evening, find a spot on one of the terraces to watch the sunset. Then have dinner in the contemporary, fine–dining **Restaurant at the Getty Center**, and afterward enjoy a concert or gallery talk.

sky become a kaleidoscope of pinks and oranges, blues and purples. You can have dinner in the restaurant and attend a concert or gallery talk.

As you'll see when you arrive at the Getty Center main gate, nothing about the place is ordinary. After you park the car at the bottom of the hill, you'll board a tram for a ¾-mile, winding ride to the Getty Center at the top. The specially designed, driverless trams are emission free and glide on a cushion of air. During the five-minute ride, you can catch glimpses of Century City, downtown Los Angeles, Westwood and UCLA, the surrounding residential neighborhoods of Bel-Air and Brentwood, and Mount St. Mary's College. There's also a paved sidewalk paralleling the service drive, which you may use to walk up the hill if you prefer.

The Getty Center rises in all its white travertine majesty like a castle in the sky. This cultural institution had its beginnings in the very personal collecting preferences of one man, J. Paul Getty, the billionaire oil magnate. Getty began collecting Greek and Roman antiquities and French decorative arts in the 1930s. In 1954, he opened the J. Paul Getty Museum at his Malibu estate. Then, in the 1970s, he built a re-creation of an ancient Roman villa on the estate to house his treasures. When Getty died in 1976, the museum received an endowment of $700 million, which has grown, reportedly, to more than $4 billion. The Malibu villa was closed in 1997; it will be renovated, and when it reopens in 2001, it will house only the antiquities. The new Getty Center in Brentwood unites the museum and various institutes for research, conservation, and philanthropy. The museum is the principal destination for most visitors.

In the arrival plaza and on the walk up the stairs or ramp to the Entrance Pavilion, you'll get your first up close look at the travertine stone tiles that cover much of the outside walls of the Richard Meier-designed complex. Often assumed to be marble, travertine is actually a kind of limestone. The travertine blocks that were used as pavement and to tile the walls of the Getty were quarried in Bagni di Tivoli, Italy. The rough-cut effect was achieved through a special guillotine process. This stone was formed between 8,000 and 80,000 years ago. In the process organic matter—leaves, branches, fish, even a deer antler—was trapped in the rock, and the fossilized remains are visible in the rough-cut wall tiles. There's plenty of Meier white metal to please aficionados, but the architect had to scale back his original design to appease neighbors who thought too much white created a jarring presence. (Architectural tours of the complex are offered periodically during the day and are free; look for the signs designating the meeting spot in front of the Entrance Hall.)

At the large, glass-walled Entrance Hall, you'll have to check backpacks or other bags, but you are permitted to take a camera into the museum. Here you can also view a short introductory film about the Getty Center, rent audio tour headsets, and pick up a map and a guide to the center. If your time is really limited, look for the brochure that outlines a quick museum tour; the tour takes in fifteen of the collections' highlights. Staff, of course, are there to answer questions about the museum and the day's special programs, including evening Gallery Talks and concert performances.

LUNCH

For a cafeteria-style selection of sandwiches, hot and cold entrees, salads, pizza, desserts, and beer and wine, try **The Cafe** (west side of Arrival Plaza, lower level; inexpensive). The dining room has glass walls that create an open airy space and provide lovely views of the surrounding hills. Outside, tables have been placed in a small arbor terrace that's surrounded by pink bougainvillea.

Architect Meier designed a cluster of five two-story pavilions to house the museum, building them around a central courtyard, and linking them together with bridges and walkways. What's nice about this arrangement is that you can follow a chronological path from one pavilion to the next, or you can wander indoors and out naturally, making your own route, and pausing in the courtyard to sit by a fountain or have a cup of coffee.

Because the Getty's collection is not encyclopedic, you can take your time wandering from one gallery to the next to suit your fancy. Paintings are displayed in the upper-level galleries, which are lighted by computerized louvered skylights, allowing daylight to illuminate the pictures during most of the day. This kind of lighting approximates the conditions in which artists painted and brings out subtleties of color and texture that artists could see in their studios. Notable among the paintings are two by Rembrandt: his *Portrait of Marten Looten* was among the first of the paintings J. Paul Getty bought in 1939, which became the start of the museum's collection, and *The Abduction of Europa*. The paintings of the Impressionists are always popular, and the Getty satisfies the public appetite with works by Renoir (*La Promenade*, 1870), Manet (*The Rue Mosnier with Flags*, 1878), Monet (*Wheatstacks, Snow Effect, Morning*, 1891, and the recently acquired *Sunrise*, 1873), Van Gogh (*Irises*, 1889), and Cézanne (*Still Life with Apples*, 1894). James Ensor's bold scene of *Christ's Entry into Brussels in 1889* (1888) was a shocking vision of the future that couldn't be publicly displayed until 1920. Works by Titian, Rubens, Poussin, Goya, and Turner are also on display.

One of J. Paul Getty's passions was eighteenth-century French cabinetry. Since his death the decorative arts collection has grown tremendously. The museum now has fourteen courtyard-level galleries to display this showy collection of furniture and decorative arts. A paneled early eighteenth-century Regence salon, a late eighteenth-century neoclassical salon, tapestries, and Sevres and Vincennes porcelain only hint at how a class of cultivated and wealthy people lived in the past. Such decorative display seems opulent and excessive by contemporary standards, but it does demonstrate an astonishing craftsmanship that can still be appreciated today.

Another strength of the Getty Museum is its collection of illuminated manuscripts, books from the Middle Ages that were written and richly decorated entirely by hand. Displayed in softly lighted, courtyard-level galleries, the manuscripts present an extraordinary record of scripture and liturgy, as well as history, philosophy, law, and science. Elaborate initials, framed paintings (called miniatures), and other decorations were executed on the pages of these manuscripts in gold, silver, and other brilliant colors.

The other courtyard-level galleries are devoted to sculpture, drawings, and photographs. If you're really interested in finding out more about a particular artwork, or perhaps the materials used to paint an illuminated manuscript, go into one of the Art Information Rooms, which are located in the four major pavilions. The Getty has an interactive multimedia resource, Art Access, to help visitors retrieve information on more than 1,500 objects and 700 artists and craftspeople. Besides all the high-tech computers, there may also be hands-on displays of materials artists use.

Outside, as you wander around the Getty complex, notice how architect Meier exploited the magnificent hilltop location, using wall angles to architecturally frame different views, and wrapping terraces around corners of pavilions. From the terrace off the South Pavilion, for example, clear days afford views far to the east, to Mt. Wilson, Mt. Baldy, and San Gorgonio. To the south Catalina Island and even tiny Santa Barbara Island, 40 miles southwest, may be visible.

In a ravine between the museum and the research institute, the artist Robert Irwin designed the 134,000-square foot **Central Garden** as an ever-changing experience. Depending on the time of year and day, different plants and shrubs will be in bloom, shadows shift and lengthen, changing the garden's appearance. A tree-lined walkway traverses a stream, which is planted on each side with a variety of grasses. The walkway descends to a plaza of bougainvillea arbors. The stream continues through the plaza and ends in a cascade of water over a stone waterfall into a pool, in which floods a maze of azalea. A semicircle of gardens surrounds the pool, offering a peaceful retreat in which to stroll or relax on a bench. In contrast to the more static nature of the buildings, the garden is always in flux.

DAY ONE: *Evening*

DINNER

When you make parking reservations, also book your dinner reservation at the **Restaurant at the Getty Center** (west side of Arrival Plaza; 310-440-7300; moderate). If you plan to attend the Friday evening concerts (summertime), which begin at 7:00 P.M., then reserve a table for 5:30. If for some reason you arrive at the Getty Center without a dinner reservation, go immediately to the restaurant and inquire about one. Chances are that the restaurant will be able to accommodate you. Besides boasting one of the best views in the city, the Restaurant at the Getty Center has earned high praise for its menu, which blends California cuisine with Mediterranean and Asian influences. Although the dinner menu changes monthly, dishes such as seared salmon with orange-braised endive and crispy potatoes, grilled free-range chicken breast with wild rice risotto and garlic sauce, and slow-roasted pork loin with butternut squash bread pudding and fried apples give a good indication of what you can expect. The room itself is quite contemporary, with walls of glass to let in the view.

Now is the perfect time to linger on one of the terraces and watch the fading light of day deepen the shadows across the city below. If you visit on

Thursday or Friday night, when the Getty Center is open until 9: 00 P.M., you can attend a free gallery talk or lecture, which begins at 7:00. The theme of the talk or lecture varies but might focus on manuscript painting or how sketching a painting can change the way we see the painting. "Friday Nights at the Getty" is a concert series presented most Friday evenings year-round. The concerts—which may be of sixteenth-century Italian music, French court music, or dance—also begin at 7:00 P.M. With some exceptions, the concerts are also free. Check the specifics for the day you plan to visit when you call for parking reservations.

FOR MORE ROMANCE

Add a chapter to your West Side Story with a visit to Santa Monica (see Itinerary 7), Playa del Rey (see Itinerary 21), or Malibu (see Itinerary 8).

Pasadena Pas de Deux
HISTORIC PASADENA

ISTORY IS ONE OF THE VEILS OF ROMANCE. And in the Los Angeles area, it's hard to get more historical than Pasadena. At the end of the nineteenth century, sun-starved Midwesterners began vacationing in this San Gabriel Valley location. They built mansions, cultivated gardens, and established a community that's still rooted in their conservative legacy. That is not to say Pasadena is staid or boring—far from it. The city fairly crackles with a new, youthful vigor. That energy is particularly evident in the Old Town district, where many fine restaurants and shops have taken up residence in restored and renovated historical buildings. And despite the high profile of the annual New Year's Day broadcast of the Tournament of Roses Parade, Pasadena has the look and feel of a small town, too well-bred perhaps to toot its own horn, as you should discover after a couple of romantic days exploring the city that took its name from the Chippewa Indian word that means "crown of the valley."

PRACTICAL NOTES: **Old Town Pasadena** is the 12-block historical district anchored along Colorado Boulevard, between Pasadena Avenue and Arroyo Parkway. Small-scale vintage buildings have been renovated and now house dozens of cafes, restaurants, and shops. Most business-es in Old Town open by 11:00 A.M. Parking is plentiful and reasonable, and the streets are safe. **Touring Eden** (818–769–2304) offers small-group and private guided tours of Pasadena's Gamble House, a historical

Romance
AT A GLANCE

✻ Settle in to a quaint cottage suite or a deluxe room at the historical **Ritz-Carlton Huntington Hotel** (1401 South Oak Knoll Avenue; 626–568–3900 or 800–241–3333), once the winter resort of vacationing Easterners. Stroll around the landscaped grounds, especially the Japanese Garden.

✻ Fall in love again with paintings and sculpture of Degas at the **Norton Simon Museum**, a gem of a small museum (411 West Colorado Boulevard; 626–449–6840).

✻ Linger over a candlelit dinner at a cozy table at the **Raymond Restaurant** (1250 South Fair Oaks Avenue at Columbia Street; 626–441–3136), a converted Craftsman-style bungalow. After dinner, take in a performance at the State Theater of California, the **Pasadena Playhouse** (39 South El Molino at Green Street; 626–356–7529).

✻ Explore Pasadena's historical past on a driving tour that takes you by the Italian Renaissance-style **Wrigley Mansion** (391 South Orange Grove), the **Fenyes Mansion** (470 West Walnut Street), the famous Arts and Crafts-style **Gamble House** (4 Westmoreland Place), and the baroque-looking **Pasadena City Hall** (100 North Garfield Avenue).

Craftsman-style bungalow; historic mansions; and gardens. If you're even thinking about attending the **Tournament of Roses Parade,** it's never too early to call and find out about parking, reserved seating, and ticket prices; call Sharp Seating Company at (626) 795–4171. Flea market lovers should try to plan a visit to Pasadena around the **Rose Bowl Flea Market** (323–560–7469), held the second Sunday of the month. With hundreds of vendors on hand, you'll find something that you, or your sweetheart, can't live without.

DAY ONE: *Afternoon*

Pasadena's **Ritz-Carlton Huntington Hotel** (1401 South Oak Knoll Avenue; 626–568–3900 or 800–241–3333; $245–$2,000) is one of the most romantic hotel properties in Southern California. You'll sense that as soon as you pull into the curved driveway that sweeps up to the entrance of what looks more like a grand turn-of-the-century country estate than a hotel. The present hotel, which sits on a hill amid twenty-three acres of grounds and gardens, was built in 1914 as a winter resort for the vacationing wealthy Midwesterners and Easterners who flocked to Pasadena at the time. There's still plenty of the old-world elegance and clubby atmosphere in the public rooms: the thick Oriental carpet in the lobby, the white-gloved bellman, the fireplace and horse paintings in the bar, the rich wood paneling of the Grill restaurant. Of course tea is served every afternoon in the Lobby Lounge, with classical music accompaniment. The original historic building and the new addition contain deluxe rooms and suites, while on the grounds are six charming cottages with names like *Wisteria, Gardenview,* and *Shamrock.* (The one-bedroom cottage suites generally cost more than $500 a night, but you may be able to land one of these at a considerable discount; ask about the "Special Occasion" package. The "Bed-and-Breakfast" package includes deluxe, not cottage, accommodations with breakfast for two for about $250.)

By all means take a stroll through the exquisitely landscaped grounds. The Japanese Garden, with its gentle cascades of water, dreamy willows, and meandering path, is so romantic that more than one marriage proposal has been offered here. California history is traced in some forty mural paintings on the Picture Bridge that spans the Japanese Garden.

The **Norton Simon Museum** (411 West Colorado Boulevard; 626–449–6840) is small enough to comfortably fit into your afternoon schedule. It's open from noon to 6:00 P.M. Thursday through Sunday; currently admission is $4.00. This really is a gem of a museum, and you'll probably want to come back another time. Everybody does. So to get the most of a short visit, be sure to buy one of the pocket-sized "Brief Guides" to the museum; it expertly covers all the highlights. As you stroll through the galleries, keep in mind Norton Simon's philosophy behind the collection: History and tradition are conveyed in the visual arts. Business executive Simon spent more than two decades of his life, not to mention countless millions of dollars, to gather a collection of Western and Asian art masterpieces that span 2,000 years. Besides the poetic beauty of Botticelli's fifteenth-century *Madonna and Child with Adoring Angel,* or the delicately erotic eighteenth-century *Reclining Nude* by Jean-Antoine Watteau, look for such romantically themed works as the hauntingly seductive *The Transportation of Psyche by Zephyrus to the Palace of Eros,* an oil sketch by Napoleon's court painter Pierre Paul Prud'hon. In this depiction of the Greek myth, the west wind (Zephyrus) brings Psyche, the personification of the human soul, to Eros, god of love. *The Happy Lovers* by Jean-Honoré Fragonard is typical of the kind of playfully sentimental French Rococo–style paintings popular during the reign of Louis XV. Among the most popular works in the collection are those of Impressionist Edgar Degas, including his best-known sculpture, *The Little Fourteen-Year Old Dancer.* If it's hard to imagine the kind of wealth it took to amass an art collection like this, remember that Simon built a multinational corporation that included Hunt-Wesson Foods, McCalls Corporation, and Canada Dry.

DAY ONE: *Evening*

DINNER

Pasadena can probably boast of having more restaurants per capita than just about anywhere else in the Los Angeles area. If you don't believe that, head up to Old Town and count its eateries. Of course quality varies, and not all are ideal for a cozy or romantic night out. (In fact you don't even have to go out. You could call Ritz-Carlton room service and ask to have dinner for two sent up to your room or set out on your cottage patio.)

But if you'd like to spend the evening exploring the 12-block Old Town district, with its abundant shops and cafes, the Cuban-Asian restaurant **Oye!** (69 North Raymond Avenue; 626–796–3286; expensive) is exotic and intimate, and very small. The whole place is swathed in white—white tablecloths, gauzy white draperies, a white stone floor. To get to Oye!, walk straight through **Xiomara** (also an excellent restaurant). Oye! is tucked away in the back. Its fusion of Cuban and Asian influences is masterfully blended in dishes like mango- and rum-glazed giant prawns with Chinese black bean sauce and a boneless half-duck smoked with tea leaves, served with tamarind sauce. For dessert try the chocolate bread pudding with a Cuban coffee and Kahlua sauce. After dinner, you're just a block from Colorado Boulevard if you want to join the promenade of families, friends, and lovers who nightly throng the boulevard and fill the cafes. Many of the shops are open late on the weekends.

Pasadena is full of darling little bungalows. In the commercial districts many of them house shops and galleries, even hair salons. One has been handsomely converted into a fine little restaurant: **Raymond Restaurant** (1250 South Fair Oaks Avenue at Columbia Street; 626–441–3136). Brides-to-be love to have their showers at the Raymond. Just about everyone I know who's been here succumbs to the charms of the place—polished wood, Tiffany lamps, and fireplace—and the straightforward menu choices like grilled king salmon or Pacific sea bass, Provimi veal, lamb shank, roast Long Island duckling, or a grilled breast of chicken with mango mint chutney, served with couscous. Outside something's always in bloom—

wisteria, bougainvillea, azaleas, poppies, and geraniums—and dining on the patio on a warm summer night can be intoxicatingly
romantic.

For my money there's nothing more romantic than an evening at the theater,
especially when the history and architecture of the theater itself lend so much
to the occasion. The **Pasadena Playhouse** (39 South El Molino at Green
Street; 626–356–7529) moved to this site in 1925 and became the State
Theater of California in 1937. Later it was the training ground for actors like
Kim Stanley, William Holden, Raymond Burr, and Elaine May. Don't miss a
chance to spend an evening at this richly decorated theater, one of the most
charming venues in Southern California. It presents a year-round season of
plays. The other historical auditorium in town is the **Pasadena Civic
Auditorium** (300 East Green Street; 626–793– 2122 or 626–449–7360 for
the box office), where the **Pasadena Symphony Orchestra** performs
(October through May; 626–793–7172), and touring Broadway musicals
like *Damn Yankees*, *Kiss of the Spider Woman*, and *Ain't Misbehavin'* are also
presented.

When you finally return to the hotel after your evening out, make a
point of strolling through the Japanese Garden. If you're not holding
hands when you start your stroll, you will be before you finish. On a
balmy night, with lights softly illuminating the path and the gentle play
of water on the rocks in the stream, the effect is positively enchanting.

DAY TWO: *Morning*

BREAKFAST

Sunday brunch at the Ritz-Carlton is an event, and a pricey one at that:
more than $40 per person, with champagne. Certainly as popular,
though not nearly such a production, is the **Old Town Bakery** (166 West
Colorado Boulevard, at Pasadena Avenue, in Tanner Market, 626–
793–2993), where scrumptious things like Tahitian vanilla-infused waf-
fles, blueberry pancakes blended with ricotta, and cinnamon French
toast are served on a sunny patio.

Paradise on Wheels

A more instructive garden sight-seeing tour of Pasadena is offered by **Touring Eden** *(12358 Ventura Boulevard, 354, Studio City; 818–769–2304), a guided architecture-garden tour of Pasadena conducted by Liz Steinfeld, a landscape design professional. The tours, which can be individually customized, go out in small groups or can be arranged privately.*

DAY TWO: *Afternoon*

Much of the history of Pasadena is right there in front of you in the architecture of the homes of its early residents. Many elegant mansions once lined South Orange Grove Boulevard, which was known as **Millionaire's Row** at the turn of the century. Using a free map provided by Pasadena Visitor Information Center (171 South Los Robles Avenue; 626–795–9311), you can take a self-guided driving tour of Millionaire's Row and Arroyo Seco, another district rich with architectural landmarks. (The hotel can also provide you with a photocopied map pinpointing the way to these treasures.)

Two remaining Millionaire's Row mansions are open for public tours, but their hours are limited. The Italian Renaissance–style **Wrigley Mansion** (391 South Orange Grove; 626–449–4100) now serves as Tournament of Roses headquarters and is open for tours on Thursdays only, February through August, from 2:00 to 4:00 P.M. Admission is free. The gardens, however, are open daily. The eighteen-room **Fenyes Mansion** now houses the Pasadena Historical Museum (470 West Walnut Street; 626–577–1660). The public may visit from 1:00 to 4:00 P.M. Thursday through Sunday. There is a $4.00 admssion fee.

Probably the best-known example of Pasadena's architectural heritage is the **Gamble House** (4 Westmoreland Place; 626–793–3334), a masterpiece of the turn-of-the-century Arts and Crafts movement. Pasadena architects Charles Sumner Greene and Henry Mather Greene used nature, rather than tradition, as their guide in designing the home for the Gamble family in 1908. They incorporated wide terraces, sleeping porches, and cross ventilation to capture the breezes, along with custom-designed furniture, leaded stained glass, paneling, and landscaping. Public tours are given from noon to 3:00 P.M. Thursday through Sunday; $5.00 admission.

One of the surprises on the tour is the **Pasadena City Hall** (100 North Garfield Avenue; 626–744–4000 or 744–4755), a baroque domed edifice, enclosing an old-world courtyard and garden lined with cloistered arches. On the weekends this lovely, romantic courtyard is a popular spot to shoot bridal party photos; sometimes a mariachi band enlivens the proceedings. With or without the wedding parties and mariachis, you'll feel as if you've been transported to Mexico or the Mediterranean.

LUNCH

Across the plaza from the City Hall, in an ivy-covered red-brick building next to an old chapel, is one of Pasadena's most charming restaurants, **Holly Street Bar & Grill** (175 East Holly Street; 626–440–1421; moderate). Sitting under a white canvas umbrella outside in the enclosed courtyard, where a solo guitarist might be playing, can only add to the enjoyment of pan-roasted salmon with pancetta risotto in a Maine lobster broth or chicken and spinach ravioli with a sweet garlic tomato sauce.

End your Pasadena getaway more or less where it began. Just a few blocks from the hotel, an authentic bit of California history is tucked away at **El Molino Viejo** (1120 Old Mill Road, San Marino; 626–449–5458). The distance is short enough to walk from the hotel: Walk south on South Oak Knoll 1 long block, then turn left at Old Mill Road. You'll see the entrance to the Old Mill on the left. Built in 1816 as a gristmill for the San Gabriel Mission, the Old Mill is one of the last examples in Southern California of Spanish Mission architecture. Once bustling with activity, the mill is quiet today, surrounded by a peaceful garden, where pink coral bells grow under old oak and sycamore trees and, in the breeze, Lady Banks roses dance up a trellis. It's an ideal spot to reflect on the past two days and the perfect opportunity to speak words of love to each other.

FOR MORE ROMANCE

If you have an extra day, you could combine this two-day itinerary with the one-day visit to the nearby Huntington Library, Art Collections, and Botanical Gardens in San Marino (see Itinerary 17).

Romancing the Coast

Island of Romance
AVALON, SANTA CATALINA ISLAND

I F TIME OR BUDGET WON'T PERMIT A TRIP TO THE MEDITERRANEAN, how about a quick, romantic escape to Avalon on Santa Catalina Island? This picturesque village, just 22 miles off Long Beach, has romance written all over it—a small, picture-perfect yacht harbor, waterfront restaurants, European-style hotels. What's more, the air is clean, the water is clear, and there's no traffic, because the number of vehicles is strictly regulated. Most people get around on golf carts, bicycles, or their own two feet. That Avalon is favored by couples in love is evident almost immediately on arrival. Couple after couple stroll hand in hand along the streets, ride tandem bicycles, or linger over lunch in the cafes. Catalina seems to appeal to everybody—youngsters still in their teens over from the mainland just for the day; honeymooners, unmistakable in their devoted attention to each other; thirtysomething marrieds who've managed to grab a few days away from the kids; and mature partners, relaxed and comfortably synchronized after years of companionship.

PRACTICAL NOTES: Catalina, like any resort, has seasons. The high season generally runs from June through September. But Catalina is such a popular destination year-round that almost all hotels on the island require a two-night minimum stay on weekends (three nights on holiday weekends). If you're after romance as well as some peace and quiet, then plan to escape to Avalon during the off-season (October through May), when visitor numbers are lower. Avoid high-season summer weekends, when thousands of day-trippers descend on the tiny town of Avalon, overrunning hotels and restaurants. The suggested hotel for this itinerary, Hotel Villa Portofino, offers some midweek and off-season packages that include round-trip boat transportation from San Pedro, Long Beach, Newport, or Dana Point; accommodations; and amenities like champagne and chocolates. There's no freeway to Catalina, so the way to get to there is by boat or helicopter. **Catalina Express** (reservations and information: 310–519–1212 or 800–995–4386; $38 per person, roundtrip) operates daily scheduled passenger ferry service between San Pedro or Long Beach and Avalon on Catalina. For boat service from Newport, contact **Catalina Passenger Service** (714–673–5245; $36 per person, roundtrip), which has one round-trip daily. The crossing from any of the three ports takes about seventy-five minutes. Helicopter service is faster —about fifteen minutes to cross from San Pedro or Long Beach—but quite a bit more expensive (about $120 round-trip). Call **Island Express Helicopter Service** for more information at (310) 510–2525. The **Santa Catalina Island Company** operates several Discovery Tours of the island in addition to the ones mentioned in this itinerary. Call (310) 510–8687 for recorded information. The **Catalina Visitors Bureau and Chamber of Commerce** can provide brochures and additional information on tours, packages, special events, and the island; call (310) 510–1520 or go to the Web site: www.catalina.com.

Romance
AT A GLANCE

✻ Journey across the 22-mile ocean channel on a high-speed boat (Catalina Express, 310–519–1212 or 800–995–4386; Catalina Passenger Service, 949–673–5245) from the mainland to picturesque **Avalon** on Santa Catalina Island. After you settle into a harbor-view room at the European-style **Hotel Villa Portofino** (111 Crescent Avenue; 310–510–0555 or 888–510–0555), have lunch at one of the village's waterfront restaurant.

✻ Rent bicycles and spend part of the day exploring some of the local land attractions. Then get a peek at the underwater show in Avalon Bay on a narrated **Undersea Tour** (Discovery Tours,; 310–510–8687).

✻ After a romantic dinner of Mediteranean-Continental-inspired cuisine at **Ristorante Villa Portofino** (310–510–0508), take a walk along the waterfront to enjoy the evening's balmy breezes and harbor lights.

✻ Explore something of the island's interior on a two-hour guided coach tour (**Discovery Tours,** 310–510–8687). Back in Avalon, walk along Via Casino to the art deco Casino building (Discovery Tours, 310–510– 8687) and a stop at the tiny gallery of the **Catalina Art Association** (310–510–0808).

DAY ONE: *Morning*
Try to plan your arrival on Catalina around noon; that will mean making a

morning boat crossing. (There are several morning departures from either San Pedro or Long Beach, but there's only one daily departure from Newport, at 9:00 A.M.) These high-speed ferries travel about 25 knots per hour and are fairly comfortable, with airline-style seating in the cabins and bench seats on the open decks. There are rest rooms and a snack bar in the main cabin.

Of course there's absolutely nothing romantic about feeling seasick, but chances are that won't happen, unless the crossing is particularly rough for some reason. But here are a few recommendations for ways to minimize the possibility: Don't get on the boat with an empty stomach. Eat something, but avoid coffee and other foods high in acid. You can take an anti-motion-sickness preparation, such as Dramamine, and bring along some soda crackers to munch on. If you start to feel queasy, take off your sweater or jacket so that your body can cool down a bit. Go outside and let the wind blow in your face and look at the flat horizon, not the rolling sea. You can also ask one of the crew to bring you a beverage called Smooth Sailing. It contains ginger, which helps calm upset stomachs.

Sailing into **Avalon Bay** will calm any queasiness you might have experienced. The picturesque little village of Avalon, tucked into a canyon beside this blue-water gem of a bay, has been compared to a Mediterranean village along the coast of Italy or Greece. Yachts, cabin cruisers, and sailboats moored in the small harbor bob in the gentle tide. People stroll along Crescent Avenue, the 6-block pedestrian waterfront promenade, ducking in and out of shops and cafes. Sunbathers and frolicking children share two tiny beaches that straddle a pier.

On the landing dock, collect your luggage and walk up to the taxis waiting above the dock. It's about a five-minute ride to Hotel Villa Portofino. The cost should be about $5.70 for two. If you prefer to walk into town, have your luggage sent over to the hotel instead for a $2.00 per bag service charge. (The hotel will send you information about these services when you make your reservation.) Driving into Avalon or walking, you'll notice a profusion of attractive cottages and cascades of bougainvillea—and an absence of neon signs and traffic lights.

The small, European-style **Hotel Villa Portofino** (111 Crescent Avenue; 310-510-0555, -0556, or 888-510-0555; $65-$335) gets high marks in the romance category for good reasons. First, it's just across the street from the beach and has lovely harbor views from the rooftop sundeck and a few of the rooms. The location is at the quieter Casino end of Crescent Avenue. You couldn't find a friendlier staff, who take their cue from the inn's charming proprietor, Thomas Cappannelli. All rooms have private baths and furnishings that reflect a Mediterranean influence. But Cappannelli has tried to give each of the thirty-four rooms a unique touch. The oceanfront Villa D'Este suite, for example, has a large, luxurious sunken bathtub. From the Portofino minisuite, you don't even have to get out of bed for a glorious view of the ocean (it's also the room in which a well-known Los Angeles newscaster proposed to his wife). My favorite, though, is the Bella Vista, a smaller corner room with a gas fireplace, marble bath, and wraparound oceanfront balcony. Cappannelli's efforts have garnered the hotel AAA's three-star rating. Although checkout time at the hotel is 11:00 A.M., your room may not be ready. If not, leave your bags with the front desk and walk across the street for lunch.

DAY ONE: *Afternoon*

LUNCH

Located in a white-stucco Mediterranean-style courtyard building called El Encanto, the **Landing Bar and Grill** (101 Marilla Street; 310–510–1474; inexpensive) is a typically casual Catalina restaurant. You can sit out on the bilevel deck, which overlooks the harbor, to enjoy the view and a fresh fish lunchtime special or order from the menu of salads, burgers, sandwiches, and pizzas.

After lunch, stroll back along Crescent Avenue toward the boat dock. Midway, at Sumner Avenue, are **Wrigley Plaza** and a fountain faced with colorful Catalina tiles, which were once manufactured on the island. The serpentine wall that winds along the beach is also decorated with the now-rare tiles, as are some of the storefronts, notably C. C. Gallagher. Reproductions of the tiles are sold in some of the gift and souvenir shops.

Visiting Bermuda, everybody rents scooters to zip around on and explore. Well, in Avalon, it's a bicycle or a golf cart. For a six- or twenty-one-speed mountain bike or tandem, try **Brown's Bikes** (107 Pebbly Beach Road; 310–510–0986), about 100 yards from the landing dock. Hourly rates for bike rentals range between $5.00 and $10.00, $12.00 for a tandem. Golf carts at **Island Rentals** (125 Pebbly Beach Road; 310–510–1456; cash or traveler's checks only, no credit cards) go for about $30.00 per hour, with a refundable $30.00 deposit (but be sure to ask about any special rates that day). Bring a valid driver's license and be over twenty-one to rent golf carts. To find your way around, just follow the color-coded map showing the various (flat, slight hills, steep hills) routes around Avalon. It's impossible to get lost.

One popular route is up to the **Wrigley Memorial and Botanical Garden,** not quite a 2-mile ride into Avalon Canyon. On a bicycle the incline is slight, but steady, so unless you've been practicing, you'll probably have to walk the last quarter mile or so. William Wrigley, the chewing-gum magnate, loved Catalina Island and was buried here in a handsome memorial after his death in 1932. From the memorial, which is sited in a beautiful garden planted with indigenous California and Catalina plants, the view of blue Avalon Bay is commanding and has inspired many an affectionate moment. If you're concerned about disturbing Mr. Wrigley, fret not. He was relocated to the mainland during World War II, when it was feared that Catalina would fall into enemy hands during an invasion.

DAY ONE: *Evening*

DINNER

Ristorante Villa Portofino (101 Crescent Avenue; 310–510–0508; moderate) is in a class by itself when it comes to restaurants in Avalon. Though the overall mood is still casual, a peach-and-cream ambience sets the *ristorante* apart as the romantic spot for dinner. Windows are thrown open on balmy evenings, and candles flicker gently in a breeze's caress. Here's a place to linger over fine food and wine; nobody will rush you to finish before you are ready. But ambience alone isn't enough, and chef-proprietor Roberto Marino pays careful attention to what's going on in the kitchen as well. That should be clear when you start off with the carpaccio of Hawaiian ahi (tuna) with capers and drizzled with lemon and olive oil, or the bluepoint oysters Rockefeller, flown in fresh from the mainland. For tagliolini pasta Portofino, Marino marries sun-dried tomatoes, asparagus, and chicken with just a touch of cream. Among the main courses, the Chilean sea bass flakes into tender, sweet morsels. Marino likes to use fresh herbs and wine to braise his meats, like rack of lamb and filet mignon, for rich and satisfying flavor.

Everything changes at night in the ocean when sea creatures who hide from daylight come out. You can get a peek at some of what's going on down there in Avalon Bay during a forty-five-minute narrated **Undersea Tour** (Discovery Tours; 310–510–8687). The tour vessel is really a semi-submersible craft that looks like a submarine. From the viewing area, which has large underwater glass windows, you get a pretty good up close view of night-feeding sea creatures, such as spiny lobster, California moray eel, and abalone. The nighttime tour leaves from the green Pleasure Pier between 7:00 and 8:00 P.M. year-round. In the summer an additional nighttime tour is scheduled for 9:00 P.M. An adult ticket costs about $25. (The Undersea Tour is also scheduled several times during the day.)

DAY TWO: *Morning*

Avalon is on the eastern side of Catalina Island, and if the night hasn't brought a thick cloud bank, one of the most brilliant moments of your day will be watching the sun rise over the ocean. A walk along Via Casino Way or over to Lover's Cove provides an excellent vantage point. Take advantage of the in-room coffeemakers at Villa Portofino and make a cup of coffee or tea to take along. The complimentary muffins and fruit that the hotel provides won't be set up in the reception area until 8:00 A.M.

BREAKFAST

The **Busy Bee** (306 Crescent Avenue; 310–510–1983; inexpensive) sits right on the waterfront in the middle of town. A table on the deck is a good place from which to watch Avalon Bay come to life as boat dwellers, who've spent the night sleeping on their boats, arise and motor to shore in their little rubber dinghies.

The rugged hills of Santa Catalina Island must have been a welcome sight in 1542 to the Portuguese-born navigator Juan Rodriguez Cabrillo and his weary crew, who had sailed from Baja California in search of a mythical northern passage connecting the Pacific and Atlantic oceans. They rested on the island, ap-

Dance and Romance

For the past few years, as a sort of salute to the romantic history of the Avalon Ballroom in the Casino building, a Valentine's Dance has been held at the legendary ballroom. During its heyday in the Big Band era, the huge circular ballroom (its diameter is 158 feet) used to hold up to 3,000 couples dancing to the music of Benny Goodman, Stan Kenton, or the Dorsey brothers. Mariachi bands would greet revelers as they arrived in Avalon by boat from Long Beach, and the walkway to the Casino was arched in lights. Call the Catalina Island Chamber of Commerce for information about the Valentine's Dance and other special events (310–510–1520).

parently enjoying a hospitable welcome from the native Gabrielino Indians. Cabrillo named the island San Salvador. Another explorer, Sebastian Vizcaino, arrived sixty years later and renamed the island Santa Catalina in honor of Saint Catherine. Many nonnative plants and animals were introduced to the island over the centuries since its "discovery," and the Santa Catalina Island Conservancy, which owns more than 85 percent of the island, is working to restore the environment to what Cabrillo and Vizcaino saw when they "discovered" Catalina. The best way to learn more about Catalina's unique ecology (and the only way to get a glimpse of the island's famous buffalo herd) is via one of two tours: the **Skyline Drive tour** (approximately two hours; $19 per person for adults) or the longer Inland Motor Tour (approximately three and three-quarter hours; $35 per person for adults). Both tours, which depart at 9:00 A.M., are operated year-round by **Discovery Tours** (310–510–8687). You can find ticket booths at the Boat Landing, the green Pleasure Pier, Discovery Tours Center at Crescent and Catalina, and at Island Plaza, a half block from Crescent, between Catalina and Sumner.

DAY TWO: *Afternoon*

LUNCH

Enclosed on the street side by a glass partition and by an exposed brick wall on another, the courtyard patio of **Channel House Restaurant** (205

Crescent Avenue; 310-510-1617; inexpensive) is a friendly, cheerful spot for lunch. A pair of trees—a huge palm and a ficus—dominate the courtyard, where potted chrysanthemums, geraniums, and other flowering plants lend color and personality. Inside, a huge wooden bar and skylights give this restaurant a New England feel. Try one of the sandwiches —the San Franciscan, a prime rib sandwich with Monterey Jack cheese and Ortega chiles is served, of course, on grilled sourdough; the grilled swordfish burger is served with all the trimmings—pasta, or the ample salads.

The north end of Avalon Harbor is dominated by a large circular structure called the Casino. If you walk toward it, at the end of Crescent Avenue you'll pass through Via Casino Arch and enter a walkway that leads to the building. (As you stroll toward the casino, look for bright orange male Garibaldi fish in the clear water.) Built in 1928, the Casino never was a gambling hall, but rather a theater and ballroom (*casino* in Italian means "place of entertainment"). A fifty-minute **Casino Walking Tour** (Discovery Tours; 310-510-8687; $9.00 per adult) lets you see all the highlights, such as the fabulous art deco murals, the movie theater with its 1929 pipe organ, and the wooden ballroom dance floor. During the Big Band era of the 1930s and 1940s, couples crowded the dance floor when live broadcasts were carried by CBS radio. Go ahead, take a turn around. That era may be over, but when you're in love, there's always music.

On the bay side of the Casino, the **Catalina Art Association** art gallery (310-510-0808) may be open. Hours vary seasonally, but it's generally open from about 10:30 A.M. to 4:00 P.M. It's a good place to pick up work by local artists, such as paintings, photography, cards, and jewelry.

DAY TWO: *Evening*

DINNER

It's less than a minute's walk from the hotel to **Armstrong's Fish Market and Seafood Restaurant** (306 Crescent; 310-510-0113; moderate), where dining is a decidedly relaxed, casual affair on a waterfront deck at tables covered with checkered plastic cloths. The restaurant is set on the beach; the bay laps at the shore right under the deck. Lights from the small boats moored in the harbor twinkle and reflect in the ripples cutting the surface of the water. An altogether appropriate setting, considering fresh fish is the specialty at Armstrong's, where mesquite adds a distinctive Southwest touch to grilled swordfish and other seafood.

After dinner, take a moonlight stroll along Via Casino or, during the summer when shops stay open later, along Crescent Avenue. By now the daytime crowds have departed, and Avalon takes on a more tranquil nature.

DAY THREE: *Morning*

The hotel will set you up with towels and beach chairs if you just want to walk across the street and spend the morning basking in the sun. Decidedly more secluded and infinitely more romantic is the private **Descano Beach,** just past the Casino. A modest tariff (about $1.50) will gain you admittance to a pretty little beach, where there's also an outdoor shower and changing rooms, a bar and restaurant, even a small souvenir store. You can rent a kayak for a paddle around the clear waters, or just relax. Checkout time at the hotel is 11:00 A.M., so you'll want to make arrangements with the front desk beforehand about changing and storing luggage before your afternoon departure.

If you're like most of us who've spent an idyllic few days on Catalina, you'll stand on the deck of the boat as it pulls away from the dock for a last look at Avalon. Chances are you'll also make a promise to yourself and each other to return soon.

FOR MORE ROMANCE

The day before you arrive on Catalina, call one of the two island florists— **In Paradise** (310–510–9616) or **Catalina Floral Design** (310–510– 0529)—and have flowers waiting in your room at Hotel Villa Portofino.

Seaside Serenade
SANTA MONICA

EVERYTHING OLD IS NEW AGAIN, so the song goes. In the late nineteenth century, Santa Monica was known to Easterners as the quintessential California beach town. As more wealthy Easterners summered in Santa Monica, grand hotels sprang up, beach facilities took shape, and the city became a hot property in California real estate. By the mid-twentieth century, things had mellowed and Santa Monica was more a quiet suburb than a trendy destination. Now Santa Monica is hot once again. It all comes together here on the end of the continent—the ocean and beaches, the fresh air cooled and cleaned by sea breezes, celebrity residents, artistic creativity, and the hedonistic rewards offered by a ton of good restaurants and expensive shops. Santa Monica also has a salty, seaside facet to its personality, just to keep things a bit more intriguing.

PRACTICAL NOTES: Santa Monica is an easy-going city where a casual wardrobe is fine, although "casual" can also carry a connotation of "chic" at some of the more expensive restaurants and hotels. Otherwise, you should get by with clothing that's comfortable for walking or bike riding. Ocean breezes can be cool, especially in winter months, so bring a jacket or sweater as well. For more information about Santa Monica, visit the Web site: www.santamonica.com. It offers plenty of helpful information about restaurants, events, and activities. When you arrive in town, real time, stop at the Santa Monica Visitor Center to pick up maps and other information you may need. You'll find it at 1400 Ocean Avenue at Santa Monica Boulevard; 310–393–7593. It's open daily in the winter from 10:00 A.M. to 4:00 P.M. and until 5:00 P.M. in the summer. It's not open on rainy days (no kidding).

DAY ONE: *Morning*

Romance

AT A GLANCE

✻ Begin a day trip to Santa Monica at the historic **Santa Monica Pier** *(Ocean Avenue at foot of Colorado Boulevard). Enjoy all the sights and sounds of this historic pier, perhaps taking a ride on the 1922 carousel, or having your handwriting analyzed or your photo taken next to a cardboard cutout of a Hollywood star. Walk to the ocean end of the pier for a margarita and Mexican food at Marisol (310–917–5050; inexpensive).*

✻ *After lunch, rent bikes or skates and spend the afternoon pedaling or skating along the bike path that parallels the beach. If you make it as far south as Venice (about 2 miles), you can rent a canoe for an hour or two and paddle around the canals. Call 310–822–7172 for directions to the launch site.*

✻ *Sunset is one of the most romantic times at the beach, so find some high ground for the best viewing—the pier, the cliff-top* **Palisades Park** *(Ocean Avenue, north of the pier), the third-floor* **Ocean Bar** *at Hotel Oceana (849 Ocean Avenue; 310–393–0486)—as the afternoon gives way to evening and the sun sinks lower in the sky over the ocean.*

✻ *Take advantage of the ocean breezes and dine alfresco on the patio at* **Il Fornaio** *(1551 Ocean Avenue; 310–451–7800; moderate),* **Rebecca's** *(101 Broadway at Ocean Avenue; 310–260–1100; moderate), or* **Ocean Avenue Seafood** *(1401 Ocean Avenue; 310–394–5669; moderate).*

✻ *After dinner, return to the pier for a ride on the Ferris wheel or roller coaster at* **Pacific Park.** *End the day with a stroll along* **3rd Street Promenade** *or attend a performance at* **McCabe's Guitar Shop** *(3101 West Pico Boulevard, at 31st Street, 310–828–4497) or* **Highways** *at the 18th Street Arts Complex (310–453–1755).*

Don't wait for a bright sunny day to make a day of it in Santa Monica. Summer weekends, especially, can bring a million people from all over Los Angeles to the city's wide beaches, crowding the pier, the bike path, and the Santa Monica's other facilities as well. A nice day any other time of the year is just as pleasurable, more so perhaps, because you won't be fighting hordes of other people.

Part of the character of Santa Monica is to relax and take it easy, so please don't feel that you have to follow every suggestion here. Pick and choose what appeals to you; lingering longer at one spot may mean having to skip another destination all together. That's just fine.

We like to begin a visit to Santa Monica at the pier. If the city has one landmark attraction, it's the **Santa Monica Pier** located at Ocean Avenue at the foot of Colorado Boulevard. Built in 1908, it recently was renovated at a cost of $45 million. You can drive your car onto the pier and park (for about $5.00). For those who remember seaside piers and boardwalks from their youth, the smells of tar and wood, popcorn, and cotton candy will surely trigger memories. So will the sight of forty-four handcrafted prancing horses on the carousel in the Hippo-drome, going 'round and 'round to the sounds of a mighty Wurlitzer. The **Hippodrome** has housed a carousel since 1916. The carousel that's currently operating there was built in Philadelphia in 1922 and brought to the pier in 1946. Forty-four of the original hand-painted wooden horses were restored in the 1980s. (Visit the **Carousel Giftshop** in the Hippodrome to purchase small,

Big Wheel Keep on Turnin'

Head to Santa Monica Pier's new Big Wheel, where for $3.00 you can soar 9 stories over the sea on the new Ferris wheel. The views of Catalina Island (26 miles away), Malibu, and the coast are stunning. In summer, the best time to fly is around 7:45 P.M., when the green flash hits the horizon.

framed limited-edition prints of the Santa Monica pier and the carousel. Prices range from about $18 to $70.) Robert Redford and Paul Newman fans will remember the carousel scene from the movie *The Sting.*

Save the small amusement park, **Pacific Park,** for later in the evening when the sun sets and the lights come on. Now just take a stroll around the pier, which is the oldest pleasure pier on the West Coast. Strolling the pier is a different experience each time you do it. An acrobat may be performing handstands and other balancing feats on top of an arrangement of plastic trays, supported by ordinary kitchen glasses. Fortune-tellers may be there to analyze your handwriting; you may encounter a photographer who will take your picture next to a cardboard cutout of Cindy Crawford, Leonardo De Caprio, or the TeleTubbies; musicians may be entertaining a small crowd gathered 'round. And everywhere people fish from the pier, couples promenade hand in hand or sit on one of the benches, families on outings walk together, and young people giggle and flirt.

DAY ONE: *Afternoon*

LUNCH

Walk to the end of the pier to **Marisol** (310–917–5050; inexpensive), not so much a place to go for great food as for great ocean views and people-watching. Sit outside on the deck if possible. As you've already surmised from the name, the food is Mexican. The best recommendation for ordering is to stick to the basics—quesadillas, tamales, enchiladas, or tostadas, for example—along with a beer or a margarita. The two of you can sit back and enjoy the ocean views and the passing parade of people.

After lunch, walk back down the pier toward the carousel again. As you pass the carousel, look for signs to direct you to Ocean Front Walk and the **UCLA Ocean Discovery Center**, one of the newer pier attractions (1600 Ocean Front Walk; 310–393–6149; adult admission, $5.00). The small aquarium, which is open on weekends only from 11:00 A.M. to 5:00 P.M., includes tidepool exhibits and other "wet labs" that explain the ecology of the Pacific Ocean.

If it's still early in the afternoon, there's time for a bike ride on the paved path along the beach. From the pier, turn south on the beach path, and you'll come across rental stands almost immediately where you can rent bicycles, skates, and Rollerblades. (Bike rentals run between $3.50 and $7.50 per hour; locks cost an additional $1.00; a deposit will probably be required, as will a valid driver's license or other identification.) Altogether the beach path extends 22 miles along the coast, providing a front-row seat to the local beach culture: hip skaters moving to a high-speed beat, Spandex-clad bikers as colorful as exotic tropical birds, joggers and volleyball players, and bicycling seniors carrying pet dogs around in front baskets.

Remember Jack LaLanne and Vic Tanny, the midcentury gurus of physical fitness? Those bodybuilders and other gymnasts and stunt actors used to work out on a stretch of Santa Monica sand that became famous as **Muscle Beach**. It's in front of what is now the Loew's Santa Monica Beach Hotel. A restoration project is underway to restore Muscle Beach to something that more resembles what it was in the 1950s. But you can still impress your partner with a quick workout on the rings and bars.

You could pedal, skate, walk—or drive—all the way to **Venice**. It's just about 2 miles south of the Santa Monica Pier along the bike path. Venice, of course, is that earthy, bohemian community that's come to epitomize the hip and free-spirited California beach culture, where tattooed and pierced street performers juggle chainsaws, walk on broken glass, and otherwise entertain the weekend crowds along the famed boardwalk.

In Venice, about 2 blocks from the beach between Venice and Washington Boulevards, is a picturesque remnant of Los Angeles history, the **Venice Canals.** Venice was developed as a resort, replete with canals, in the 1920s by Abbot Kinney, who took his inspiration from the city in Italy. Most of the canals of the California Venice were filled in in 1929. The few that remain today are flanked by a tony enclave of expensive historic bungalows, quarters for successful artists, writers, and other well-paid types. Residents and tourists stroll along the footpaths that are laid out alongside the canals, using the occasional arched footbridge to cross the canals. Quacking ducks paddle along the narrow channels, and strains of music drift across the water. For a duck's eye view of the canals, **rent a canoe** for an hour. Call 310–822–7172 for canoe rentals and for directions to the launch site.

Sunset is one of the most romantic times at the beach, so find some high ground—the pier, the cliff-top **Palisades Park** (Ocean Avenue, north of the pier), third floor Ocean Bar at Hotel Oceana (849 Ocean Avenue; 310-393-0486)—as the afternoon gives way to evening, and the sun sinks lower in the sky over the ocean.

DAY ONE: *Evening*

DINNER

After a stimulating day, it's time to stimulate the palate at one of Santa Monica's many restaurants. Within 2 blocks of the pier along Ocean Avenue are several choices, starting with the Italian chain restaurant, **Il Fornaio** (1551 Ocean Avenue; 310-451-7800; moderate), which has a patio facing the ocean. The food is consistently good here (try the simple, thin-crust pizzas, rotisserie chicken, mesquite-grilled veal chops), the atmosphere striking, and the prices, for Santa Monica, reasonable. Next door **Ivy at the Shore** (1541 Ocean Avenue; 310-393-3113; expensive), which you'll find to be spacious and airy, with rattan seating and an outdoor terrace. It buzzes with the sort of stylish informality that's come to define the Los Angeles "lifestyle." Romantic in a hip, sexy way, not at all demure or cozy, Ivy at the Shore is known as much for outstanding new American cooking—knockout crab cakes, fried chicken, meat loaf and *tarte tatin*—as it is for its beautiful clientele. If you enjoy people-watching, come early and have a tropical drink at the bar. Definitely one of the "in" spots in the Los Angeles area.

Try the patio at **Rebecca's** (101 Broadway at Ocean Avenue; 310-260-1100; moderate) for sizzling sunsets, a wrap-around tequila bar, and a menu of Mexican standards—tamales, tacos, chile rellenos. **Ocean Avenue Seafood** (1401 Ocean Avenue; 310-394-5669; moderate) is the most formal of the restaurants along this stretch of Ocean Avenue. Everything about the place is first-rate, including the oyster bar. Ocean Avenue Seafood has patio dining.

After dinner, you can return to the pier for a turn through Pacific Park for some fun at the arcade games and a ride on the Ferris wheel or roller coaster. As cornball as they are, try the ball tosses and other games of skill at which you can win a little stuffed animal for your honey. (Admission to the park is free; you just pay for the rides and games. Park hours vary with the season; call 310-260-8744 for information.)

Two blocks inland is **Third Street Promenade,** a 3-block pedestrian strip of shops, restaurants, and multiplex theaters. Popularly described as an "urban village," Third Street Promenade draws an interesting mix of moviegoers, college students, street musicians, upscale residents, young people, and tourists. The retail mix ranges from the lowbrow ("Hollywood madam" Heidi Fleiss has a boutique here) to the highly evolved **Midnight Special Bookstore** (1318 Third Street Promenade; 310-393-2923), which specializes in politics, sociology, and literature.

If Third Street Promenade sounds just a bit too pedestrian for your liking, there are several performance possibilities in Santa Monica. You'll just have to plan your dining schedule a bit differently to accommodate the usual 8:00 or 9:00 P.M. show times. **McCabe's Guitar Shop** (3101 West Pico Boulevard, at 31st Street; 310-828-4497), for example, was into the "unplugged" format long before MTV got hip. Well-known musicians frequently turn up in the back room here. In the 18th Street Arts Complex is **Highways** (310-453-1755), where performance artists like Tim Miller and Annie Sprinkle and such comics as Lea DeLaria tackle issues of gender, sexuality, politics, and other contemporary themes.

When it's time to call it a day, or night, you can leave Santa Monica knowing full well that there's plenty to discover about this coastal city to keep you coming back time and again.

ᚠOR MORE ROMANCE

If it's the beach you're after, then you'd better look to Malibu (see Itinerary 8). Santa Monica's beach, though as wide as 100 yards in some places, can be incredibly crowded on warm summer evenings. You could combine a daytrip to Santa Monica with a getway in Playa del Rey (Itinerary 21).

Beach Blanket Romance
MALIBU

HO WOULDN'T LOVE TO MORPH into a privileged Malibu beach dweller for a day or two? Well, here's your chance. Pack a bathing suit, some shorts, a couple of T-shirts, and a comfortably casual after-dark outfit, and head for Pacific Coast Highway. Don't stop until you get to the Malibu Beach Inn, about 25 miles due west from downtown Los Angeles. With the J. Paul Getty Museum villa closed until 2001 and the Malibu Pier boarded up because of storm damage, there's not much to do here except walk on the beach, watch the surfers, marvel at the sunsets, and gaze up at wildflower-draped mountains that seem to tumble (literally, sometimes) to the sea. Couple nature's awesome gifts with the temporal wonders of movie stars who live here in megamillion-dollar oceanfront homes, and it's easy to leave the city behind for a couple of days.

PRACTICAL NOTES: Small hotels like the Malibu Beach Inn usually require a two-night minimum stay on weekends. Don't wait until the last minute to book a room; weekends are often sold out. If you want to have lunch or dinner at Geoffrey's (310–457–1519) or Wolfgang Puck's Granita (310–456–0488), call in advance to make a reservation; these restaurants are too popular to just walk into without risking disappointment (or a long wait). For more information about Malibu, call the **Malibu Chamber of Commerce** at (310) 456–9025.

DAY ONE: *Afternoon*

If you just dropped your luggage onto the cool Mexican paver stones of the lobby of the **Malibu Beach Inn** (22878 Pacific Coast Highway; 310–456–6444, 800–462–5428, 800–255–1007; www.malibubeachinn.com; $145–$275) and ran right out to the beach, nobody would blame you. The forty-seven-room inn sits on a wide, sandy beach and has a 180-degree view of the coastline, from the Malibu Lagoon, Surfrider Beach, and Malibu Pier on the right as it sweeps off to the south past Santa Monica to the Palos Verdes Peninsula. Sometimes Catalina is visible on the horizon. This is what a beach hotel should be: oceanfront rooms, most with fireplaces, all with private balconies, that are simply, but comfortably, decorated with attractive furniture.

Third-floor rooms have vaulted ceilings, and Jacuzzis have been installed on the decks of seven rooms on the first floor. Canvas drapes can be drawn closed across the deck for privacy. Here and there are decorative touches, such as wave-painted tiles in a bathroom or a small flower painted in a niche above a fireplace. Honor bars, coffeemakers, VCRs, in-room safes, and hair dryers are among the amenities. At this writing, there's no restaurant

Romance

AT A GLANCE

✻ Check into your oceanfront room with a Jacuzzi at the **Malibu Beach Inn** (22878 Pacific Coast Highway; 310–456–6444, 800–462–5428, 800–255–1007), then take a walk along Surfrider Beach and Malibu Point, playgrounds for surfers and pelicans, respectively.

✻ Admire the lavish homes along the beach of exclusive Malibu Colony. Then check out the **Adamson House and Malibu Lagoon Museum** (23200 Pacific Coast Highway; 310–456–8432), which will enlighten you with a bit of Malibu history. Afterward meander the grassy area around Malibu Lagoon, one of the few remaining coastal wetlands in the region.

✻ Have a sumptuous dinner at **Geoffrey's** (27400 Pacific Coast Highway; 310–457–1519), located in the cliffs of Malibu overlooking the ocean, considered one of the best restaurants in the region. After dinner return to the inn for a soothing time in the Jacuzzi or a walk in the moonlight along the beach.

✻ After breakfast at **Coogie's Beach Cafe** (23700 Pacific Coast Highway; 310–317–1444) take a drive up into the hills above Malibu for spectacular coastal views. Then return to the inn, order a "Beach Blanket Picnic," and spend the afternoon relaxing on the beach.

✻ Splurge for dinner at **Granita**, Wolfgang Puck's Malibu restaurant, a favorite with local celebrity residents (Malibu Colony Plaza, 23725 West Malibu Colony Road; 310–456–0488).

on the premises, but the hotel does provide a limited room service menu consisting of snacks and sandwiches, as well as continental breakfast, which is served on the patio or in the lobby each morning (7:00–10:30 A.M.) or can be sent to your room.

Do you sense the spirits of Moon Doggie and Gidget or Frankie and Annette hovering about? Walk west on the beach toward the Malibu Pier. (The pier, sorry to say, was closed to the public in 1997 because of severe storm damage.) As you walk under the pier, you'll come to an arc of a beach divided by a stream that flows from the Malibu Lagoon. This is the famous **Surfrider Beach** (also known as Malibu Lagoon State Beach). This beach and all those surfers in the water and their pals on the sand were the inspiration for that string of 1960s *Beach Blanket* and *Gidget* movies that starred the perennially young Frankie Avalon, Annette Funicello, and Sally Field.

At the bend, **Malibu Point**, a spit of sand is a playground for pelicans and other shore birds. Just around the bend is the playground of the rich and famous—**Malibu Colony.** The exclusive enclave is or has been home to celebrities like Bruce Willis, Demi Moore, Donna Karan, Larry Hagman, and Shirley MacLaine. Having movie star neighbors is nothing new in this neck of the woods. Dolores Del Rio was one of the first stars to build a home in Malibu decades ago.

Celebrity confers certain privileges, one being the wealth to afford a home here, where a simple beach "bungalow" along this strand can cost millions. But privilege and privacy only extend down to the median high water mark, so as long as you keep to the wet sand, you can walk along this "private" beach, admiring the homes all you like.

Inveterate museum lovers know that Malibu was home to one of the world's richest and best-known museums, the **J. Paul Getty Museum**, a re-creation of an ancient Roman country house that's set in a lush canyon. Unfortunately, the villa is closed until at least 2001 for renovation. Its priceless collection of Greek and Roman antiquities, European paintings, and illuminated manuscripts has been relocated to the new Getty Museum in Brentwood (see Itinerary 4, "West Side Story"). When the villa does reopen, only the antiquities will once again be housed in it. Another Malibu museum, however, the **Adamson House and Malibu Lagoon Museum** (23200 Pacific Coast Highway; 310–456–8432) is open Wednesday through Saturday from 11:00 A.M. to 3:00 P.M. The artifacts, photographs, and maps assembled make a good introduction to Malibu history. Flanking the grounds is **Malibu Lagoon,** where Malibu Creek meets the ocean, one of the few remaining coastal wetlands in the region. The unique environment supports a population of plants and animals adapted to fresh and salt water. A trail through the grassy areas leads to the beach. Access to the trail is from the parking lot on the west side of the lagoon.

Probably the best place for the two of you to be, though, as the afternoon wanes is back at the inn, on the lobby terrace or the deck of your room, with a glass of mineral water or wine. With the sure, steady sound of the surf rolling onto the beach and the sky taking on a paintbox of color as the sun sets, the world seems a friendlier place, where everyone has privilege and there's time to listen to what they have to say.

DAY ONE: *Evening*

DINNER

Location, location, location. That's what makes **Geoffrey's** (27400 Pacific Coast Highway; 310–457–1519; expensive) a totally Malibu experience. Set on a cliff about 4^1/$_2$ miles north of Pepperdine University, Geoffrey's overlooks the Pacific and a row of expensive beachfront homes. The restaurant is designed as an indoor-outdoor terrace. The bar and some tables are under a roof, while the open terrace area is warmed by heaters and protected from night wind by a glass windbreak. Ask for one of the tables at "the Point," perched right on the edge, where you'll feel a bit cozier, and order grilled fish, free-range chicken, or stuffed Colorado lamb chops from the eclectic menu. If the

A Marriage
Made in Malibu

Even by Hollywood standards, the Malibu wedding of pop star Madonna and actor Sean Penn on August 16, 1985, was one of the events of the century. Reporters, tipped off to the top-secret location on Wildlife Road, commandeered a squadron of helicopters that hovered over Malibu in an effort to photograph the couple as they took their vows during the outdoor cliff-top ceremony.

high cost of dining at Geoffrey's doesn't suit your plans, consider stopping in for just a drink and the view.

By and large, Malibu is a bedroom community, albeit an exclusive one, and doesn't offer much in the way of nighttime entertainment. Neighbors here might get together for a private screening of a film that may well star a local resident or that has been written or produced by one. You could watch a video on the in-room VCR at the hotel or see the real thing at **Malibu Theatre** (3822 Cross Creek Road; 310–456–6990). For music, dance, or theater, turn to Pepperdine University's **Smothers Theatre** (24255 Pacific Coast Highway; 310–456–4522) for performances by visiting performing artists.

DAY TWO: *Morning*

BREAKFAST

If you end up slipping into the Malibu lifestyle easily enough to miss the 10:30 A.M. cutoff for continental-style breakfast in the lobby terrace at the inn, or if you just want to pull yourself away for a possible celebrity sighting, then go to **Coogie's Beach Cafe** (in Malibu Colony Plaza, 23700 Pacific Coast Highway; 310–317–1444; inexpensive). Even if no stars show up, the Coogie's cakes (whole wheat pancakes with strawberries and bananas) and french toast Malibu style (oat-nut bread) taste just as good.

A walk past the arcaded storefronts of Malibu Colony Plaza will reveal the obvious: This would be just another ordinary, albeit upscale, strip mall shopping center but for two things: its Malibu location and the presence of Wolfgang Puck's Granita restaurant. After all, even movie stars have to buy groceries somewhere, and a celebrity-chef restaurant close to home means they don't have to drive miles into West Hollywood or Beverly Hills on the weekends.

After breakfast, drive up into the hills and canyons above Malibu, where **Pepperdine University** (24255 Pacific Coast Highway at Malibu Canyon Road; 310–456–4000) commands spectacular coastal views, and where many of Malibu's movie-star residents have owned homes (Barbra Streisand's former estate is on Ramirez Canyon Road, about 6 miles north on PCH). These chapparal-covered hills pose a major fire hazard each year. In 1993, a devastating wildfire tore through the hills above Malibu.

DAY TWO: *Afternoon*

LUNCH

One of the reasons you came to Malibu was to relax on the beach. So keep lunch a simple affair today. Order something from the inn's "Beach Blanket Picnic" menu—a peanut butter and jelly sandwich, a salad, buffalo wings, lox and cream cheese, hot dogs, or a tuna or chicken salad sandwich.

The hotel will provide you with towels (complimentary) and deck chairs ($6.00 per day) if you just want to plant yourself in the sand for the afternoon. Depending on whether the day is hazy or not, you may be able to see Catalina Island on the horizon. You may also see dolphins just offshore. You may even notice a famous face or two among the other hotel guests on the beach with you. The inn's proximity to Pepperdine University makes it attractive as lodging for Supreme Court justices, politicians, and business leaders who visit the campus to give speeches.

DAY TWO: *Evening*

DINNER

To say you've been to Malibu but not Wolfgang Puck's restaurant **Granita** (in Malibu Colony Plaza, 23725 West Malibu Colony Road; 310–456–0488; expensive) is like going to a Dodgers game without having beer and a

Dodger dog. Puck's restaurant is part of the Malibu experience. The decor of Granita has been described as *"The Little Mermaid* on acid," but the food—for example, Chinese duck with pomegranate plum sauce, wood-fire-roasted salmon with Swiss chard, and Puck's California pizzas—is consistently delicious. Besides that, the people-watching is unparalleled; Puck himself shows up occasionally to cook, and celebrity neighbors drop by often enough. Don't forget to try one of the daily changing *granitas* (fruit ices). Granita has recently added casual seating in the bar area where you can order from a limited bar menu.

Dinner at Granita should be entertaining enough so that all the two of you really need to do is return to the inn, sit together out on the deck, and let your gaze drift up to the stars or along the coast, where a ridge of lights traces its way from Malibu to Santa Monica and beyond.

DAY THREE: *Morning*

After breakfast at the inn and one last walk on the flat, broad, sandy beach at Malibu, drive north on the Pacific Coast Highway, beyond Zuma Beach, to one of three "pocket" beaches for a completely different experience. These secluded rocky coves—El Matador, La Piedra, and El Pescador—are narrow strips of sand tucked below 50-foot cliffs. Signs mark the turnoffs into tiny gravel lots, where you're on an honor system to pay the parking fee or risk a costly fine. Steep, rocky paths and wooden steps lead down to the beaches, which may be "hidden" but hardly unknown: On summer weekends they can get very crowded. Still, there's a feeling of having discovered something special when you visit these beaches.

FOR MORE ROMANCE

Include a miniexpedition paddling a kayak through Malibu's waters. See Itinerary 29, "Ocean Kayaking Adventure in Malibu," or call **Malibu Ocean Sports** (310–456–6302) for more information. If you'd like a little more adventure with your romance, see Itinerary 27, "Sweethearts in the Saddle," for information about horseback riding in the Santa Monica Mountains above Malibu.

Starry Nights and Seaside Seduction
OXNARD

O XNARD MAY NOT BE ON EVERYONE'S SHORT LIST of getaway spots, but it's hard to beat this coastal town for a place to unwind and take long walks on the beach under a starry nighttime sky. Only about 60 miles north of Los Angeles, Oxnard has a beautiful, broad beach bunkered by sand dunes and an unobstructed "backyard" view of the offshore Channel Islands. Oxnard lives by a slower pace, especially for anyone used to a big-city rhythm of life—you'd be hard-pressed to find a restaurant open past 9:30 P.M., even on the weekends. And that's the beauty of the place, because a little ocean air and plenty of R and R can work restorative wonders, romantically speaking.

PRACTICAL NOTES: **Embassy Suites Mandalay Beach Resort** is an all-suite oceanfront property. Oceanfront suites are almost always sold out on weekends, so reserve yours as soon as possible; otherwise, ask for gardenside accommodations in Building 2 or 3. The courtyard garden enclosed by these buildings is more secluded than other areas of the resort, making suites that face it pleasant. The resort offers a Romance Package, which generally requires a two-night minimum stay.

DAY ONE: *Afternoon*

For all the images of the Southern California good life that involve the beach, there are very few hotels actually right on the sand. The **Embassy Suites Mandalay Beach Resort** (2101 Mandalay Beach Road; 805–984–2500 or 800–362–2779; $179–$399) is an all-suite property located right on a wide beach. It's a popular spot for beachfront weddings. It's also a favorite of families with children, who seem to gravitate to the pool. But look out the window of your oceanfront suite to the beach—a broad clean sweep of sand surrounded by lovely, rolling dunes that drift practically right up to the lawn. Waves, white and foamy, slip onto the beach as sunlight sparkles on the ocean. In the distance is a view of Anacapa Island, the closest of the Channel Islands, and to the north, you can see the coastline curving off toward Santa Barbara.

LUNCH

Capistrano's Restaurant (at Mandalay Beach Resort; 805–984–2500, ext. 569; moderate) is a casual, yet interesting, spot for lunch. The restaurant is large, and part of it is set in a colonnaded patio that has an Old Mexico atmosphere. The other section is set under a thatched roof ceiling and faces the pool, so it has a more sunny, tropical feeling. The lunch menu offers the usual: sandwiches, salads, pastas, all well done, and served by a friendly, accommodating staff.

After lunch you may find the sunny, warm beach enough of a lure to wish only to idle away the afternoon draped in a chair or playing in the surf. So be it. The pool attendant can fix you up with a towel. For some unexplained reason the hotel doesn't provide beach chairs, but since you've been forewarned, you can bring your own.

Perhaps, though, your idea of afternoon fun is riding a bike or in-line skating. There's a little concession stand next to the pool from which you can rent a two-person surrey bike (about $15.00 per hour) or regular bike ($8.00 to $10.00 per hour). In-line skates are also available for rent (about $8.00 per hour), but those are not really recommended unless you've tried them before. A cement-paved trailway extends along the beach for about ½ mile in either direction of the hotel. Bicyclists, skaters, runners, and walkers all share the path quite harmoniously.

DAY ONE: *Evening*

Dinner tonight will be a unique experience—a dine-around at three or four restaurants at **Channel Islands Harbor.** Turn right when you leave the resort and follow Harbor Boulevard for about ½ mile to the harbor. The postcard setting is splendidly picturesque: The hundreds of sailboats and yachts moored at the slips in the harbor's marinas create what looks like a spindly forest of masts, tall and short. Along small canals and private docks stand multimillion-dollar homes. Shops and restaurants occupy Fisherman's Wharf and Harbor Landing commercial centers.

DINNER

The **Harbor Hopper Water Taxi** (805-985-4677) provides a fun way to get around the harbor for one of the most enjoyable dining experiences in Southern California. Rather than having dinner at just one restaurant, you can have a cocktail at one, an appetizer at another, move on to a third for the entree, and, if you're game, yet a fourth for coffee and dessert. The little Harbor Hopper, which looks like a tiny tugboat, is enclosed and has a smile painted on its bow. Captain Lou or Bill or Vic will pick you up at a designated spot and ferry you around the harbor to each of your restaurant stops. The hotel concierge can help you arrange a harbor dine-around, and each restaurant can call for the ferry when you're ready to move on. (The fare is about $1.00 per person per "hopp," and operating hours vary by season and weather conditions.) Don't wait too late to get a start on your dine-around. Remember that this is an early-to-bed sort of town; most restaurants are ready to close by 9:00 or 9:30 P.M.

All the restaurants mentioned here feature seafood, of course; have harbor views; and are fairly casual spots. A dine-around evening could look something like this: Start out with a cocktail at the **Lobster Trap** (Casa Sirena Hotel & Marina, 3605 Peninsula Road, Channel Islands Harbor; 805–985–6311; moderate). The bar area gets pretty lively. The restaurant is replete with captain's chairs and plank-thick wooden tables, and it serves hearty portions of seafood, prime rib, and steak if you decide to stay for dinner. "Hopp" over to the enormously popular **Whale's Tail** (3950 Bluefin Circle, Channel Islands Harbor; 805–985–2511; moderate) for a starter of freshly shucked oysters or clams, or order a full dinner such as swordfish grilled and served with a ginger-lime butter sauce, lobster linguini with a light cream sauce, or a top sirloin. (And don't miss a peek at the tugboat salad bar.) Next door to Whale's Tail is **Port Royal** (3900 Bluefin Circle, Channel Islands Harbor; 805–382–7678; moderate), the least casual and, therefore, the most so-phisticated, dining spot in the harbor area. Here waiters wear white shirts and ties, and tables are set with white linen and fine tableware. You can linger as long as you like in a cozy booth by the fireplace and look out over the harbor. A couple of the signature dishes at this young restaurant are halibut filet Juneau with sweet onion marmalade wrapped in cabbage leaves and finished with a lemon-vodka cream, filet mignon and fresh lobster, and prime rib of beef roasted with garlic and rosemary. If you still have room, make a last stop at **Tugs Restaurant** (3600 South Harbor

The Case of the Lawyer in Love

Before he got famous as the author of the Perry Mason mysteries, Erle Stanley Gardner was a lawyer who lived in Oxnard. He met his wife, Natalie Francis Talbert, in Oxnard, and in 1912 eloped with her to San Diego. The couple returned to a small house in Oxnard, and the following year, their daughter, Grace, was born.

Boulevard, Channel Islands Harbor; 805–985–8847; inexpensive) for a heavenly bite of the classic Key lime pie or the sinful chocolate cake.

It would be a shame to end the evening without a stroll on the beach to be alone with each other and the stars. If the moon is bright, waves sliding onto the sand catch the glint of moonlight, and all is right with the world in that moment.

DAY TWO: *Morning*

BREAKFAST

Embassy Suites Mandalay Beach Resort handsomely lives up to its promise of a full complimentary breakfast served in the poolside Surf Room and adjacent lanai. Light eaters can head right to the buffet table, which is laden with an assortment of fresh fruit, cereals, yogurt, mini-muffins, and croissants. For a cooked breakfast you'll have to join the cafeteria-style line for a cooked-to-order meal of eggs, pancakes, or French toast. Even though breakfast is served from 7:00 to 10:30 A.M. weekends (6:00 to 9:30 A.M. weekdays), super-early risers will find the in-suite coffeemaker a blessing.

Head over to Channel Islands Harbor later in the morning to stroll along the dockside **farmers market** (Sundays from 10 A.M. to 2 P.M.). Local farmers sell plenty of fresh produce, flowers, nuts, herbs, and other items (remember that Oxnard is a major strawberry-growing region).

Before you venture off on an afternoon excursion, remember that check-out time at the resort is noon. You can leave your luggage with the bell captain and reclaim it at the end of the day.

DAY TWO: *Afternoon*

Here's a romantic finish to your weekend getaway: a **private harbor cruise** aboard a canopied Bay Cruiser vessel, which looks a bit like a miniature

African Queen. Only this boat is electric, you pilot it yourself, and it's rented by the hour from Electra Craft (3600 South Harbor Boulevard, Channel Islands Harbor; 805-382-1924 or 800-221-2083). There's nothing to it—it's like driving a car, only on water. After a quick safety drill, in which you learn that a double toot of a horn is a warning from a larger vessel, and that sailboats under sail have the right-of-way, you're off on your own private cruise around the harbor and the residential section of canals called Mandalay Bay. The canopied boats come equipped with a CD player so you can bring your favorite music. They're quiet and fumeless because they're electric. The water of the harbor is calm, so even first-time skippers won't have any trouble. Bring along coffee and croissants or champagne and Brie, a bouquet of flowers from the farmers market, or ask Sydney McFarland, one of Electra Craft's proprietors, to arrange a catered meal if the occasion is particularly special. According to Sydney, one of the best time to cruise the bay is before noon, when all is calm. She also advises that she's usually booked up on summer and holiday weekends, so it's best to make reservations a month in advance. The hourly rental on a 17-foot boat is about $45 for the first hour, $35 for each additional hour. (Most couples find that an hour isn't quite enough time and rent the boat for two hours.)

LUNCH

After your harbor cruise, stop in at **Le Petit Cafe Bakery** (2810 South Harbor Boulevard, Channel Islands Harbor: 805-985-4334; inexpensive) for a baguette sandwich, salad, or a bowl of French onion soup. (You could also reverse the order of your outing: Stop in here before the harbor cruise, order something to go, like the huge "French Quickie"—ham, scrambled eggs, and cheese on a croissant or baguette.)

FOR MORE ROMANCE

Combine a visit to Oxnard and the Channel Islands with a stopover in Ventura, about 5 miles north along Harbor Boulevard. See Itinerary 11, "Ventura Adventure."

You could also incorporate a cruise out to the Channel Islands. **Island Packers** (3600 South Harbor Boulevard, Channel Islands Harbor; 805-642-1393 for reservations; 805-642-7688 for recorded information; Web site: www.islandpackers.com) runs half- and full-day excursions from Oxnard Harbor to Anacapa, one of the islands, from April through November, and whale-watching cruises from July through September. If you plan to go on one of the excursions, pack so that you can dress in layers, and don't forget suntan lotion, a hat, and a pair of binoculars. See Itinerary 11, "Ventura Adventure," for more information about these excursions.

ITINERARY 10
Three days and two nights

Jewel of the Coast
SANTA BARBARA

RIVING INTO SANTA BARBARA along Highway 101 is one of those purely magical Southern California experiences: the Santa Ynez Mountains on one side, the Pacific Ocean on the other, and sunlight melting through the wispy watercolor haze of mist that can hang over the red-tile roofs of the city late into the morning. Here is a painter's landscape if ever there was one. Subtropical and Mediterranean foliage flourish in the climate, lending Santa Barbara a year-round mantle of color and greenery. Long a favorite getaway spot of movie stars, Santa Barbara is also an ideal coastal destination for mere mortals looking for a few days' retreat. It's about 90 miles from downtown Los Angeles, close enough to be convenient but far enough to bring you and your loved one a change of scenery, climate, and attitude.

PRACTICAL NOTES: Get your bearings in Santa Barbara with a stop at the **Santa Barbara Visitors Center** (One Garden Street, off Highway 101; 805-965-3021), where you can pick up brochures and other information about the city and its attractions. Ask for a free copy of the area map that highlights fifteen points of interest on a scenic drive and a 12-block "Red Tile" walking tour through downtown. To have visitor information mailed to you, call the Santa Barbara Visitors Bureau (the city's marketing agency) at 800-927-4688 or visit the Web site: www.santabarbaraca.com. Parking in downtown Santa Barbara is plentiful, with some nine public parking lots offering the first ninety minutes free. There's also a cheap (25 cents) and convenient **MTD shuttle route** (805-683-3702) between downtown and Stearns Wharf. If your romantic getaway is planned for a weekend, be prepared to spend at least two nights here. Most hotel properties require a two-night minimum stay on the weekend during summer months. Some hotels, especially those near the beach, require the two-night minimum as early as May. And almost all hotels require a minimum stay on three-day holiday weekends. Santa Barbara falls into the "resort casual" category of dress, although once the sun goes down, the air can get cool, so a sweater or light jacket is a good thing to bring along. Restaurant reservations for dinner are always recommended, especially on weekends.

DAY ONE:
Afternoon

LUNCH

Plan to arrive in Santa Barbara early in the afternoon for lunch at **Citronelle** (at the Santa Barbara Inn, 901 East Cabrillo Boulevard; 805–963–0111; moderate), a restaurant that a lot of people think is one of the best in the country. That seems a somewhat suspicious claim at first, when you discover that Citronelle is located in a hotel, or more accurately in what we used to call a motel. But this is no hotel restaurant. First of all, chef Michel Richard's Santa Barbara outpost sits atop the three-story waterfront motel and has a wall of windows that open it up to sweeping views of the Pacific Ocean. Ceiling fans, white linen tablecloths, and rattan chairs suggest a tropical

Romance
AT A GLANCE

* Begin a visit to Santa Barbara with lunch and a beachfront view at **Citronelle,** one of the best restaurants in town (Santa Barbara Inn, 901 East Cabrillo Boulevard; 805–963–0111; moderate). Then check into a cozy room with a fireplace and garden view at the **Villa Rosa Inn** (15 Chapala Street; 805–966–0851), a small European-style hotel just a block from the waterfront.

* If time permits, take a walk along the **West Beach esplanade** on Cabrillo Boulevard or rent bicycles and peddle your way around. Later in the afternoon, after 5:00 P.M., head back to the inn for wine and cheese.

* Enjoy a candlelit dinner and Santa Barbara wines at **Emilio's Ristorante & Bar** (324 West Cabrillo Boulevard; 805–966–4426; moderate). After dinner, on Saturday evenings, there's dancing in the lounge of the **Four Seasons Biltmore Hotel** (1260 Channel Drive; 805–969–2261) until midnight.

* Attend the **sidewalk art show** on Sundays under the trees of Chase Palm Park along Cabrillo Boulevard, just east of Stearns Wharf. Then take the trolley to the **Santa Barbara Museum of Art** and follow the **Red Tile tour** through downtown Santa Barbara.

* Dinner at the **Wine Cask** (813 Anacapa Street; 805–966–9463; moderate) is an atmospheric affair in front of a grand fireplace or outdoors on the terrace.

* Before leaving town visit **Mission Santa Barbara** (2201 Laguna Street, at Los Olivos; 805–682–4713), the queen of California's eighteenth-century missions.

setting. Then there's the food, considered to be just about the finest in Santa Barbara: moist and tender scallops, for example, perfectly seared and dressed with a citrusy glaze and thin, crisp Maui onion rings. Citronelle's most popular dish may be the thin filets of baby salmon, served with a chardonnay cream sauce. Call ahead and ask to reserve a table for two along the window. It will be hard to pull yourselves away long after lunch is over.

What She Did for Love

By the time she arrived in Santa Barbara in 1941, Madame Ganna Walska, a Polish-born opera singer, was on her sixth husband. He persuaded her to buy an estate in Montecito in order to establish a spiritual center for Tibetan scholar-monks. When that idea—and the marriage—failed, Madame turned to horticulture. The result was Lotusland, a magnificent private garden that nonmembers may tour on a very limited, reservations-only basis; call (805) 969-9990 several months in advance for reservations.

From Citronelle head west on Cabrillo along the waterfront to Chapala Street, 1 block past State Street and Stearns Wharf. Turn right onto Chapala. Ahead, you'll see a two-story, light-mauve stucco, Spanish Colonial-style building. The **Villa Rosa Inn** (15 Chapala Street; 805-966-0851; $100-$230, two-night miniumum on weekends) is one of those finds that puts a whole new spin on a familiar place like Santa Barbara. The small, eighteen-room inn has plenty of coziness and charm, but minus any bed-and-breakfast preciousness. Even the lobby seems more like a living room, with its beamed ceiling, tiled fireplace, coffee table laden with magazines and newspapers, and French doors that open onto a swimming pool, Jacuzzi, and tree-shaded courtyard. Ask for a second-floor room with French doors that open onto the courtyard. (Number 16 is a small, but cozy, choice, with a sitting area, no TV, but a bargain at $140.) Keeping with the small inn tradition, the Villa Rosa serves a continental breakfast in the lobby each morning, as well as afternoon wine and cheese. In the evening between 9:00 and 11:00 P.M., and on request, sherry and port are served by the fireplace. Villa Rosa nicely fills a niche between the deluxe amenities of the Four Seasons Biltmore or the Montecito Inn and the impersonal comfort of the larger resort motels on, and just off, Cabrillo Boulevard. Besides that, Villa Rosa is only 2 blocks from Stearns Wharf and the beach.

You may have to find a parking spot on the street; the inn's lot is too tiny to accommodate all guests. Even if it's too early to check in (3:00 P.M. is the check-in time at Villa Rosa), leave your luggage with the hotel, which will secure your bags until you return, and walk the 2 blocks over to **Stearns Wharf** at the foot of State Street. Follow the esplanade along West Beach. A fountain with three bronze dolphins leaping marks the entry to the pier, built in 1872, reportedly the oldest working pier on the West Coast. Once the site of cargo ship and passenger ferry activity, the pier today is mainly a landmark visitor attraction. There are marine exhibits at the **Sea Center** (805–963–1067), Channel Islands habitat exhibits at the **Nature Conservancy** (805–962–9111), seafood restaurants, souvenir shops, and great views of the small boat harbor and the mountains. (A fire destroyed a portion of the pier in 1998, so some of the attractions may not be accessible as repairs continue.)

One way to see more of the Santa Barbara waterfront—and to get some exercise—is to rent a pair of bikes for a ride along **Cabrillo Beachway,** a 2³/₄-mile paved trail that begins at the small boat harbor and extends east through Chase Palm Park and on to the Andree Clark Bird Refuge. Pick up six-speed beach cruisers, twenty-one-speed mountain bikes, surrey bikes, or a tandem at **Cycles for Rent** (101 State Street at Mason; 805–966–3804, 888–405–2453; www.cycles4rent.com). It's just 1 block up from Stearns Wharf and is generally open from 8:00 A.M. to 8:00 P.M. during the summer (hours vary during the winter). Bike rental rates range from $4.00 to $10.00 an hour.

After the bike ride, head back to the inn. Between 5:00 and 7:00 P.M., wine and cheese will be served in the lobby. The occasion is a relaxed, informal way to meet other guests or to just take advantage of the courtyard setting and enjoy the balmy evening air.

DAY ONE: *Evening*

DINNER

Walk the 2 blocks to **Emilio's Ristorante & Bar** (324 West Cabrillo Boulevard; 805–966–4426; moderate) for dinner in an ivy-covered beachfront trattoria. Somewhat of a neighborhood spot, Emilio's prepares a seasonal menu—like butternut squash tortellini, pistachio-crusted albacore, and glazed pork tenderloin—using herbs, organic vegetables and fruit from local farms, plus local line-caught fish. For reasonably priced Santa Barbara wines to accompany your dinner, ask about the Au Bon Climat 1995 Chardonnay ($30), the Coupe 1995 Syrah ($23), Brander 1996 Sauvignon Blanc ($23), and Foxen 1994 Cabernet Sauvignon ($37). The five or six tables at the window are coveted spots for romantic, candlelit dinners.

Dancing—the kind in which couples actually touch and hold each other—to live music has become something of the rage on a Saturday evening at **La Sala,** the lobby lounge at the **Four Seasons Biltmore Hotel** (1260 Channel Drive; 805-969-2261). The music varies each week, and you don't even have to be up to speed with your dance steps to enjoy watching other couples take their turn. The fun usually lasts until midnight. During the week, a pianist or guitarist entertains.

Later, when you return to your room at the Villa Rosa, a long-stemmed rose and pieces of dark Belgian chocolate will be waiting on your pillows.

DAY TWO: *Morning*

BREAKFAST

You only need to throw on a robe, slip down to the lobby, and fill up a tray with coffee, croissants and Danish pastry, juice and fresh fruit, and yogurt that you can bring back up to your room. Of course the courtyard, with its potted geraniums and other flowers and plants, makes a cheerful spot to sip coffee or tea, read the paper, and plan the day's activities.

Every Sunday morning, and occasionally on Saturdays of holiday weekends, starting around 10:00 A.M., the East Beach section of Chase Palm Park along Cabrillo Boulevard becomes an outdoor arts and crafts gallery where dozens of regional artists, photographers, glassmakers, potters, and jewelers exhibit their wares. As it goes with these shows, the quality varies, but there's the occasional "find" that makes attending one of them a tempting proposition. And you couldn't ask for a better setting—palm trees and ocean breezes.

DAY TWO: *Afternoon*

Drive your own car or take the trolley from Stearns Wharf up State Street. Get off at the Museum of Art (at Anamapu Street) for a stroll back down State Street, what may well be the most attractive main street you'll find anywhere. This is the **Red Tile district,** a descriptive explained by the ubiquitous red-tile roofs of the uniform "Spanish" look of buildings erected after a 1925 earthquake destroyed much of the downtown area. One block east, on Anacapa, is the **County Courthouse** (1100 block of Anacapa Street; 805–962–6464), a palatial Spanish-Moorish–style building built in 1929. Although a glimpse at ornately carved doors, imported tiles, and hand-painted murals gives reason to visit, the real draw is the panoramic view of Santa Barbara from the 70-foot clock tower. (The Red Tile district is bounded by Victoria, Santa Barbara, De la Guerra, and State Streets. The Visitor Center has a walking tour map; see Practical Notes.)

The Spanish theme is carried out especially convincingly at **El Paseo** (15 East De la Guerra Street), a shopping arcade between State and Anacapa Streets. Winding walkways, adobe walls, and wrought iron railings and balconies evoke a picturesque street in Spain. Here you'll find art galleries, gift shops, and a few cafes and restaurants. Stop by the Wine Cask (813 Anacapa Street; 805–966–9463) while you're in the area to make a reservation for dinner later in the evening.

LUNCH

There are plenty of perfectly fine restaurants and cafes in the Red Tile district. The **Chase Bar & Grill** (1012 State Street; 805–965–4351; inexpensive), for example, is known for its New York-style Italian food: fried calamari, steamed shellfish, homemade sausage, and a great meatball sandwich. There are always several lunch specials to choose from. Or you could stick with the Mexican-Spanish theme by traveling a few blocks east to a little Mexican restaurant that even New Yorkers know about. It could be described as a "hole in the wall," but **La Super-Rica Taqueria** (622 North Milpas at Alphonse; 805–963–4940; inexpensive) serves up simple, well-prepared Mexican food that's good enough to attract customers like part-time resident Julia Child. (Everybody raves about the stuffed chili peppers and corn tortillas and homemade salsa.) You order and pick up at the counter, and then take your paper plates and plastic cutlery to a bare-bones dining room, protected from the elements by a tented ceiling. The location for this cash-only operation, open daily from 11:00 A.M. to 9:00 P.M. (until 9:30 on Fridays and Saturdays), is east of the main downtown State Street district, but worth the detour.

Before rushing back to the inn for late-afternoon wine and cheese, take a walk on the beach or along the paved walkway. There will probably be a beach volleyball game or two still going on. Surfers and sailboarders won't have called it quits yet, and out in the ocean, sailboats will begin heading back to the harbor.

DAY TWO: *Evening*

DINNER

Hand-painted beamed ceilings and a grand fireplace are the set pieces for the romantically atmospheric **Wine Cask** (813 Anacapa Street; 805–966–9463; moderate). The restaurant also has an outdoor terrace, another atmospheric spot, especially on warm summer evenings. The cooking here is best described as Californian, as evidenced by such offerings as peppercorn-crusted seared ahi tuna, ginger risotto, chicken breast with garlic mashed potatoes, and a grilled filet mignon with truffle mashed potatoes and roasted vegetable timbale with a Bordelaise sauce. With its own retail wine shop, the restaurant has an extensive wine list, with an emphasis on Santa Barbara County wines.

DAY THREE: *Morning*

Save Santa Barbara's most famous landmark, **Mission Santa Barbara** (2201 Laguna Street, at Los Olivos; 805–682–4713), for last. The mission opens daily at 9:00 A.M., so you can get as early a start as you wish. You've probably already seen the mission's twin towers in a postcard photo, so it should be immediately recognizable when you come upon it on a hill at the upper end of Laguna Street (follow State Street to Mission; turn toward the mountains; continue to Laguna). Built in 1786, and known as the Queen of the Missions for its graceful beauty, it was the tenth of twenty-one Franciscan missions built in California. For an admission fee of about $3.00, visitors can follow a self-guided tour through rooms displaying historical items, including manuscripts and embroidered vestments, and on through a lovely landscaped garden, the chapel, and finally a serene cemetery. Fronting the mission is a wide expanse of lawn with a rose garden below. A few hundred feet north of the mission, across Los Olivos Street, are the remains of tanning vats, a pottery kiln, and parts of an early water system.

FOR MORE ROMANCE

If you want to extend your visit by another half or full day, you can set out on a Wine Country tour of the Santa Ynez Valley, about 35 miles north of Santa Barbara. Pick up a map and guide at the Visitors Center, or call the Santa Barbara County Vintner's Association (800-218-0881). One rather romantic possibility for traveling to Santa Barbara from Los Angeles is to take the train. Call Amtrak (800-872-7245) for information and rates. Santa Barbara Sailing Center (805-962-2826 or 800-350-9090) offers summer weekend dinner and sunset champagne cruises that sail along the coast. For two other romantic itineraries in Santa Barbara, see Itinerary 22, "Hills of Enchantment," and Itinerary 28 "Set Sail."

Ventura Adventure
VENTURA

I t doesn't take long to discover that Ventura—San Buenaventura, more precisely—was made for a day trip for romantic urban explorers. The coastal city is about 60 miles north of Los Angeles off the 101 Freeway, so it's easy to get to. A slow-growth profile makes Ventura easy on the nerves too. Congestion is minimal, free parking is plentiful, and sea breezes keep the temperature at bay. The downtown core has been renovated and revitalized, the harbor is picturesque, and there are lovely unobstructed views of and easy access to the offshore islands that make up Channel Islands National Park.

PRACTICAL NOTES: **Island Packers** (1867 Spinnaker Drive, Ventura Harbor; 805–642–1393 for reservations, 805–642–7688 for recorded information; Web site: www.islandpackers.com) operates half-day and full-day excursions year-round to Anacapa Island, one of the offshore Channel Islands. Dress in layers for one of these excursions, and don't forget suntan lotion, hat, camera, and a pair of binoculars.

If you've made plans to take an excursion out to Anacapa Island in the afternoon, or if you're more interested in the natural history of the area than shopping, visit the **Channel Islands National Park Visitors Center and Park Headquarters** at Ventura Harbor (1901 Spinnaker Drive; 805–658–5730). Here you'll get a quick orientation about the islands, the original Chumash inhabitants, and wildlife. A simulated tide pool is part of the exhibit, and a park ranger is on duty to answer questions.

DAY ONE: *Afternoon*

LUNCH

Like a garden courtyard hidden behind the thick walls of an Italian villa, **Nona's Courtyard Cafe** (in the Bella Maggiore Inn, 67 South California Street; 805–641–2783; inexpensive) produces a feeling of cool sanctuary, induced in part by vine-covered walls, a fountain, and trees and plants. The homemade minestrone, salads, and sandwiches (like a garlicky grilled chicken breast sandwich with tomato, eggplant, and mozzarella, served on focaccia bread) are tasty and generous. If you've worked up a heartier appetite, maybe one of the daily pasta or risotto specials would be a better choice.

Romance
AT A GLANCE

✶ Explore the historic downtown district of Ventura, including a visit to one of the California missions, **Mission San Buenaventura** (211 East Main Street; 805–648–4496) and the **Ventura County Museum of History and Art** (100 East Main Street; 805–653–0323; closed Mondays).

✶ Browse the antique and vintage shops along **Main Street.** Then have an early lunch in the plant-filled **Nona's Courtyard Cafe** (in the Bella Maggiore Inn, 67 South California Street; 805–641–2783; inexpensive).

✶ Depart from Ventura Harbor for an afternoon boat excursion to **East Anacapa Island,** 11 miles offshore (Island Packers, 1867 Spinnaker Drive, Ventura Harbor; 805–642–1393 for reservations, 805–642–7688 for recorded information; Web site: www.islandpackers.com).

Centuries ago the Chumash, the original inhabitants of this part of California, had villages on some of the offshore Channel Islands, which lie between 11 and 40 miles off the coast in the Santa Barbara Channel. The first European explorers in the region landed on the islands in the sixteenth century. Of the eight Channel Islands that make up Channel Islands National Park, Anacapa, about 11 miles away, is the closest to Ventura. And for lovers with a sense of adventure, it's an ideal destination as part of a day trip to Ventura.

Because the island is a national park, access to it by commercial outfits is limited. **Island Packers** (1867 Spinnaker Drive, Ventura Harbor;

805–642–1393 for reservations, 805–642–7688 for recorded information; Web site: www.islandpackers.com) operates about four different half- and full-day trips to the island, depending on the time of year. Afternoon excursions to Anacapa leave at about 1:30 P.M. Don't forget to dress in layers to protect against weather changes and wetness, and wear sturdy shoes if you're going to hike on the island. The adult cost for an excursion ranges between $21 and $37.

The crossing from Ventura Harbor to the island takes a little more than an hour, and if you're lucky, on the way you'll get to see blue sharks or dolphins. Depending on the excursion you choose, the boat will dock at a cove for a landing, or you'll cruise along the island's rugged north shore. You'll observe seals, sea lions, and various bird species, as well as beautiful, mysterious sea caves—a great way to discover this unique natural environment without going ashore. The boat's skipper narrates the cruise.

A landing on the island means you'd better be prepared to get a bit wet from water sloshing against the pilings as you climb a rung ladder onto the dock. From the dock you climb up 153 steps to Anacapa's plateau (there is no wheelchair access to the island). Even though Ventura and Oxnard are clearly visible on the mainland 11 miles away, there's a peaceful sense of isolation on Anacapa. You'll have time for a picnic lunch if you wish (bring your own or Island Packers can help with arrangements). You can go off by yourselves to explore the 2 miles of trails or tag along on a guided nature walk with a park ranger or the trained naturalist among the Island Packers' crew. From vantage points atop the island's steep cliffs, which are havens for seabirds and marine mammals, you look down to Cathedral Cove on the north shore, where you can spot an occasional kayaker. From south-facing cliffs, you can see sea lions basking on the rocky outcroppings. Just be sure to be back at the dock at the appointed hour for departure. There's nothing romantic about being stranded here without the proper gear.

On the mainland, Ventura's downtown historic district along Main Street is compact enough to explore on foot in a couple of hours. Before setting out to explore, however, get your bearings at the **Ventura Visitor & Convention Bureau** (89 South California Street, Suite C; 805–648–2075 or 800–333–2989). You can leave your car in the parking structure across the street; otherwise, street parking is limited to two or three hours, which should be enough time to take in most of what downtown Ventura has to offer.

From the visitors center, you can take the trolley (Wednesday–Sunday; $1.00 for all day, unlimited use) to the **Ventura County Museum of**

History & Art (100 East Main Street; 805–653–0323; closed Mondays) for a digestible introduction to the historical coastal community. Artifacts trace the history of human settlement in the region, from the Chumash era centuries ago to the Spanish mission and rancho periods of the eighteenth and nineteenth centuries to subsequent European and American settlements. The museum also houses a remarkable collection of the miniature Historical Figures of George Stuart. These three-dimensional, quarter-life-size figures of popes, kings and queens, Aztec warriors, and American patriots are uncannily lifelike, with tiny eyelashes, veined hands, and face wrinkles.

Across Main Street, the **Albinger Archeological Museum** (113 East Main Street; 805–648–5823) sits on an excavation site where objects from thirty-five centuries of human settlement, from prehistoric Native Americans to Chinese immigrants who arrived in the early twentieth century, were uncovered.

Next door is the star historical attraction of Ventura, **Mission San Buenaventura**. Begun in 1792, it was the ninth and last of Father Junipero Serra's chain of California missions. Entrance to the mission and its grounds is through the small gift shop a few steps to the east at 211 East Main Street (805–648–4496). The mission is open to visitors Monday through Saturday, 10:00 A.M. to 5:00 P.M, and on Sunday until 4:00 P.M. A donation of $1.00 for adults is requested.

At this point **Main Street** turns into a sort of antiques row, with several thrift stores and bona fide antiques shops, at least two antiques "malls," and a couple of rare-book stores. If you keep heading east on Main Street, you'll come back to California Street.

FOR MORE ROMANCE

If you want to extend your visit to Ventura, book a room at the charming, European-style **Bella Maggiore Inn** downtown (67 South California Street; 805–652–0277, 800–523–8479; $75-$130). You might want to take a look at the Oxnard itinerary (Itinerary 9, "Starry Nights and Seaside Seduction") and combine some of its elements. For a third option, the beautiful Ojai Valley lies less than 20 miles northeast of Ventura. Spend a lazy, romantic afternoon having lunch on the terrace under the oak trees at the Ojai Valley Inn. (See Itinerary 26, "Ojai Idyll," for a description.)

The Art of Allure
LAGUNA BEACH

OU'D NEVER KNOW IT ON A SUMMER WEEKEND, when traffic on the Coast Highway is a bumper-to-bumper mess, but Laguna Beach is practically a village, barely 8 miles square, with a population of only 24,000. Despite flocks of visitors, Laguna Beach, just 50 miles south of Los Angeles, manages to keep its village character. Whole neighborhoods of bungalows from the 1920s, when half the population of 300 were artists, remain intact. Shaggy eucalyptus trees, not billboards and blinding neon signs, line the main street, Forest Avenue. The trees cover the hillsides, too, planted in the nineteenth century by the early homesteaders. Urban development encroaches, yet artists are still inspired by the landscape around Laguna Beach—rocky cliffs, tranquil coves, rugged coastal canyons. Sitting on the sunny, windswept patio of a blufftop restaurant, the surf crashing onto the sandy beach below, you and your partner will see how easy it is to succumb to the lure of Laguna Beach.

PRACTICAL NOTES: If at all possible, visit Laguna Beach during the week. Weekends year-round are busy; in the summer months, the high season, traffic is very heavy, restaurants are crowded (reservations are a must), and hotels and inns require minimum stays of at least two or three nights. Parking is metered (bring lots of quarters). Laguna Beach's year-round calendar of special events includes the famous **Sawdust Festival** (July through August; information, 949–494–3030) and the **Festival of Arts/Pageant of the Masters** (July through August; information, 949–494–1145). Both events draw enormous crowds. The **Laguna Beach Visitors Bureau and Chamber of Commerce** (252 Broadway, Laguna Beach; 949–497–9229 or 800–877–1115) also has a Web site: www.lagunabeachinfo.org. Stop by the visitor center to pick up a copy of the current visitor guide and other information.

DAY ONE: *Afternoon*

Try to time your arrival in Laguna Beach just as lunchtime is beginning, around 11:30 A.M. or noon, especially if you're visiting on a weekend. Parking will be a little easier to come by, and restaurants will not yet be crowded. After lunch and before checking into your hotel, there will be time to stroll through the village center, amble along the boardwalk at Main Beach, gallery hop, or visit the local art museum. On your way into town, stop at the oceanside **Heisler Park** (call 949–497–0716, ext. 6, for information about city parks). It's atop a promontory on Cliff Drive, just behind the Laguna Museum of Art and Las Brisas restaurant. Turn toward the ocean at Cliff Drive at the museum. From the wooden gazebo atop the bluff, you can look out at the arc of Main Beach and down at the rocky cove below, where tide pools fascinate children and adults alike. From this vantage point, or as you follow the pathway through the park, you'll get an idea of what attracted painters and movie stars to live here and

Romance AT A GLANCE

* Arrive in Laguna Beach around midday and have lunch on the sunny terrace of **Village Market & Cafe** (Laguna Village, 577 South Coast Highway at Laguna Street; 949–494–6344; moderate), where you can survey the Pacific and Laguna's beaches. Then check into the **Carriage House**, a bed-and-breakfast inn (1322 Catalina Street at Cress Street; 949–494–8945; $95–$150), or the beach-chic **Surf & Sand Hotel** (1555 South Coast Highway; 949–497–4477 or 800–524–8621; $235–$900).

* The galleries and shops along Forest Avenue and Coast Highway offer an afternoon's worth of browsing and shopping. Or visit the **Laguna Beach Museum of Art** (307 Cliff Drive at Coast Highway; 949–494–8971), where the focus is on California artists. In the evening, have dinner in the lyrically romantic setting of **Ti Amo Ristorante** (31727 South Coast Highway; 949–499–5350; moderate).

* The following day, rent bikes and peddle around the quaint historic neighborhood of 1920s bungalows, picnic at the cliff-top Heisler Park overlooking the beach, or explore some of Laguna's picturesque little coves. End the day with sunset cocktails and dinner on the terrace of **Splashes** restaurant (Surf & Sand Hotel, 1555 South Coast Highway; 949–497–4477; moderate).

why Hollywood movie producers have used Laguna Beach to stand in for the rocky cliffs of England, Polynesian beaches, the French Riviera, and the coasts of Italy and Greece.

Laguna's Hollywood Heyday

Since its establishment as an artists' colony in 1917, Laguna Beach has enjoyed a romantically colorful history. Along with the community of artists drawn by the striking natural beauty of the area, Hollywood began noticing Laguna Beach in the 1920s. Stars like Charlie Chaplin, Mary Pickford, Douglas Fairbanks, and Rudolph Valentino built vacation homes in Laguna Beach. During Prohibition legendary parties were thrown by Gilbert Roland and Ramon Navarro, and rum runners, finding shelter in Laguna's coves, kept the booze flowing. Bette Davis owned a home at Woods Cove, and one of Hollywood's most famous couples, Humphrey Bogart and Lauren Bacall, frequented the Hotel Laguna during its heyday in the 1930s and 1940s.

LUNCH

Sit on a sunny, windswept patio high above the emerald and turquoise waters of the Pacific Ocean at the **Village Market & Cafe** (Laguna Village, 577 South Coast Highway at Legion Street; 949–494–6344; moderate). Park in the lot where an attendant will keep an eye on your car. The cafe is the only restaurant in Laguna Beach that sits right on the edge of a bluff overlooking the ocean. If it's not hazy over the ocean, Catalina Island is visible. It's a glorious spot for the two of you to enjoy a salad (fresh crisp greens are topped with tender jumbo shrimp or avocado, for example, and garnished with sprouts, cucumber slices, golden raisins, and pistachios), one of several pasta or fresh seafood entrees (including abalone), or a sandwich served on nice dark bread.

After lunch, take a quick turn through the artisans' booths in Laguna Village. We left the car in the lot after checking with the attendant and walked the few blocks to **Forest Avenue** to check out some of the shops and galleries. Laguna Beach has about ninety art and craft galleries, gift shops, and boutiques. Several are located on eucalyptus-lined Forest Avenue, along with the ubiquitous T-shirt shops and ice cream parlors. As you walk along, notice the red public phone booth, more commonly seen in Britain than along the California coast, and the brushed aluminum sculpture fountain in front of the fire department. Then, after you've strolled in a loop up and down Forest Avenue, you can cross Coast Highway to Main Beach for a walk along the boardwalk or the ocean's edge or to watch a game of beach volleyball.

For more serious-minded gallery hopping, head a few blocks north from Main Beach to a section of Coast Highway called **Gallery Row** (roughly bounded by Aster and Hawthorne). You should even have time to stop by the **Laguna Museum of Art** (307 Cliff Drive at Coast Highway; 949–494–8971), where the focus is on the art of California and the role of art and artists in the United States.

In keeping with the village feel, Laguna Beach has several bed and breakfasts. The **Carriage House** (1322 Catalina Street at Cress Street; 949–494–8945; $95–$150) is a bit different from most B&Bs because it was converted from a small apartment building in 1981. Each of the six suites has a private entrance, so there's a feeling of privacy so often lacking in a B&B. The gray, two-story Colonial building wraps around a secluded brick courtyard that's shaded by a big, old cottonwood tree and giant birds of paradise. It's something you might expect to find in the French Quarter of New Orleans. Bathrooms are small and standard, but each suite has a sitting room, a dining room, and a new TV with a VCR; five suites have kitchens. Not luxurious, but quaint, very comfortable, and homey, a bit like a visit to Grandma's, where you half expect to find a cookie jar filled with home-baked goodies. You will find, however, a complimentary carafe of wine and a basket of fruit and cheese to welcome you. An expanded continental breakfast is served in the dining room, out on the patio, or in your room from 8:30 to 10:00 A.M. Smoking is permitted only outside in the courtyard.

At the opposite end of the spectrum is the casually beach-chic **Surf & Sand Hotel** (1555 South Coast Highway; 949–497–4477 or 800–524–8621; $235–$900), which sits right on the beach. Wear silk or linen and understated jewelry here, where tones of white and sand beige are translated olfactorally through vanilla-scented pillar candles placed at both ends of the check-in counter. All 164 rooms have ocean views; casual yet distinctive white-washed furnishings; marble and sandstone bathrooms, with separate showers and tubs (some spa tubs); terry robes; honor bars; and plantation shutters opening to a private balcony. Consider booking a deluxe corner king room ($325–$350), which has a 180-degree view of Laguna's sand and surf. The corner kings also have a tape/CD player. Guest services and amenities include a swimming pool, complimentary beach umbrellas, chairs, and towels, and on-site or in-room massage therapists. Ask about the two-night "Romantic Getaway" package the hotel offers, which includes champagne on arrival, breakfast in the restaurant, and an in-room dinner. During the summer, Surf & Sand imposes a three-night minimum stay during July and four nights during August.

At the foot of **Ruby Street** (about the 2000 block of South Coast Highway), next to a big old stucco house above Woods Cove that Bette Davis used to own, there's a tiny pocket park, with steps that lead down to a wooden deck and a single park bench. All the initials and the "so-and-so loves so-and-so" carved into the redwood railing of the deck testify to this spot's romantic seclusion. Hedges obscure any view while you're sitting on the bench—but then, you two didn't come for the view, did you? If another couple has beat you to the punch, walk west on Ocean Way for a block to Diamond Street and the public access steps down to **Woods Cove.** It's a dramatically picturesque spot.

DAY ONE: *Evening*

DINNER

How could you miss with a restaurant named "I Love You" in Italian? **Ti Amo Ristorante** (31727 South Coast Highway; 949–499–5350; moderate) has been divided into several rooms and is decorated in a lyrically romantic fashion: A hand-painted mural of an early Roman scene covers one wall; gauzy swags of fabric are draped over windows; menus are glued to boards that have been decorated to resemble stone tablets. Everybody loves the place, from Barbara and George Bush to Paula Abdul, whose autographed tablets are mounted on a wall at the entrance. The main room upstairs has a fireplace and one or two tables with what loosely can be described as an ocean view (over the roofs of neighboring houses). But the menu is enticing: Besides traditional homemade pastas, look for special dishes like swordfish with braised purple cabbage, garlic mashed potatoes, and roma tomato compote; rack of lamb with caramelized shallots and roasted mushroom-herb sauce; or a mixed grill with pancetta-wrapped filet mignon and roasted garlic demiglaze. A good wine list enhances the experience.

DAY TWO: *Morning*

Spend the morning together at the beach. All of Laguna's beaches, particularly Main and Sleepy Hollow, are popular and can get pretty crowded on summer weekends. To get away from the crowds, travel about 3 miles north of downtown on the Coast Highway and you'll come to **Crystal Cove State Park** (8471 Pacific Coast Highway; 949–494–3539). Beaches here, which lie at the foot of coastal bluffs against a backdrop of chaparral canyons and hillsides, are less crowded than Main and some of the other popular beaches in Laguna. Beach access at Crystal Cove State Park is available at three entrance areas (Reef Point, Los Trancos, and Pelican Point). Trails and stairways lead from parking lots on the bluffs to the beaches below. Parking costs about $6.00 per car. Laguna has several picturesque coves worth exploring, too, including the protected **Divers Cove** just north of Main Beach next to Heisler Park, and the picturesque **Woods Cove** at the foot of Diamond Street. Call (949) 497–9220, ext. 0, for beach information.

DAY TWO: *Afternoon*

BRUNCH *or* LUNCH

Cottage Restaurant (308 North Coast Highway at Aster Street; 949–494–3023; inexpensive) is exactly the sort of place you'd expect to find in Laguna: a turn-of-the-century beach bungalow with a garden patio. The cooking is hearty and home style, and champagne brunch is served every day until 3:00 P.M. Another lunchtime option is to pack along whatever suits your fancy for an impromptu picnic at one of Laguna's beaches or coves. **Crescent Bay Point Park** (Coast Highway at Crescent Bay Drive) comes highly recommended for its splendid ocean vistas.

Rent bicycles this afternoon (**Laguna Beach Cyclery,** 240 Thalia Street; 949–494–1522) and spend part of the afternoon exploring a historic neighborhood of 1920s bungalows in a section of town called Laguna-North (when you stop at the visitor bureau, pick up a brochure with a self-guided map). Laguna-North is tucked away east of the Coast Highway and north of Broadway, between Cedar and High Drives and Hill and Hawthorne Streets. These homes, almost all from the 1920s, were humble interpretations of the Craftsman style popularized by the Pasadena architects Charles and Henry Greene. Home owners individualized their modest dwellings by adding a colonial entry, columns, a pyramidal roof, and special window treatments. Several represent other styles, including Pueblo Revival and Spanish Mediterranean Revival popular in the late 1920s and early 1930s. The homes were owned mostly by year-round Laguna Beach residents—merchants, carpenters, plumbers, and other tradespeople—who worked in town to serve the seasonal visitors.

DAY TWO: *Evening*

DINNER

In the evening, with the setting sun painting a colorful Pacific panorama and the surf breaking on the beach 25 feet below, **Splashes** (Surf & Sand Hotel, 1555 South Coast Highway; 949-497-4477; moderate) is on the short list of the most delightful dining spots in Laguna Beach. Pristine linens cover the tables, but Splashes is relaxed and friendly, though not overly casual. Don't miss the chance to dine outside on the sheltered terrace, warmed on cool evenings by gas heaters. The menu is Mediterranean-inspired, with preparations changing to incorporate seasonal ingredients: baby *frisee* salad of greens with gorgonzola cheese, crispy potatoes, toasted walnuts and caramelized onions; braised shank of veal or lamb; ahi tuna in a veil of crushed morel mushrooms; grilled salmon with spicy lentils, grilled endive, and roasted eggplant; filet mignon with Port wine sauce. The wine list includes California, French, and Italian labels.

Laguna is a laid-back village, not given to abundant nightlife. But it does have a very fine regional theater, the **Laguna Playhouse** (6060 Laguna Canyon Road; 949–497–2787; Web site: www.lagunaplayhouse.com), where you might see a revival of a Eugene O'Neill classic, *A Moon for the Misbegotten,* or the premiere of a new musical, *Gunmetal Blues.* Of course, on a balmy evening, with moonlight shimmering on the ocean, there's nothing like a walk on the beach to bring the evening to a close.

DAY THREE: *Morning*

More than its quaint bungalows or the preponderance of art galleries, it's geography that defines Laguna Beach. Sandwiched between the Pacific Ocean and a range of chaparral-covered hills and tucked into narrow coastal canyons, Laguna Beach seems to many an ideal spot. For a look at the big picture, drive up to the section of town known as **Top of the World.** Follow Park Avenue up to Alta Laguna Road. Turn left and drive to the end of the road, where you'll come to **Alta Laguna Park.** To the west, Laguna Canyon cuts its way to the ocean. To the north and northeast, the urban sprawl of Orange County is laid out, stopped on its march to the ocean by the San Joaquin and Sheep Hills.

FOR MORE ROMANCE

Make a side trip to the historic Mission San Juan Capistrano (949–248–2048), about 5 miles south in San Juan Capistrano. The swallows return to the mission every year in mid-March and depart in October on their annual migration to Argentina, some 6,000 miles away.

Theme Itineraries

Romance Afloat
THE *QUEEN MARY*, LONG BEACH

IN THIS AGE OF THE BIG RED BOAT, KATHIE LEE, and "fun" cruises to Ensenada, most of us can only imagine what it must have been like to sail across the ocean on a *real* luxury liner during the golden age of travel from the 1920s through the 1950s. Built by Cunard to be the world's largest ocean liner and launched in 1936 by its royal namesake, the *Queen Mary* was, and still is, a real luxury ocean liner. The only thing is, the *Queen* hasn't sailed an ocean since 1967, when it made its final voyage from Southampton, England, to the Port of Long Beach, where the ship's been berthed as a floating hotel. Today, a stay aboard the *Queen* is about as close as you'll get to the golden age of travel, when movie stars and kings crossed the ocean in style and luxury. Practically the only difference is that today the *Queen* never leaves port.

PRACTICAL NOTES: The *Queen Mary* (1126 Queens Highway, Long Beach; 562-435-3511 or 800-437-2934; $75-$400) is located at the south end of the 710 (Long Beach) freeway. Just follow the signs, which will lead you right to the parking lot for hotel guests. Accommodations on the *Queen* range from inside cabins (for $75, no porthole, no view, no nothing) to super luxurious parlor suites that cost up to $400. The best advice for planning a stay on the *Queen Mary* is to ask for a water view when booking a room and to inquire about one of several special packages. The price of a one-night Romance Package ($185–$210), for example, includes a deluxe stateroom, champagne toast, and breakfast for two in the Promenade Cafe. The Bed and Brunch ($225, Saturday only) includes Sunday brunch. More information about the *Queen Mary* is available at the Web site: www.queenmary.com.

DAY ONE: Morning

If aquariums hold your interest, then give yourselves about ninety minutes to wander around the new **Long Beach Aquarium of the Pacific** (100 Acquarium Way; 562-590-3100) before making your way to the *Queen Mary*. As the name suggests, the focus here is the Pacific Ocean: Southern California and Baja, the northern Pacific, and the tropical Pacific. A huge full-scale model of a blue whale, the largest living creature on the planet, is suspended above the entrance hall. Adult admission is about $14.

DAY ONE: Afternoon

As you pull into the parking lot for the *Queen Mary*, you should be immediately impressed with the size of the ship that lies docked at Pier J, just ahead of you. The *Queen* is grand, indeed, in size and in history. Three huge funnels (smokestacks) tower above the decks of the 81,000-ton ship. In 1936 the *Queen Mary* sailed on its maiden voyage from Southampton, England, to New York, filled with

Romance
AT A GLANCE

* Arrive in Long Beach with enough time to visit the new **Long Beach Aquarium of the Pacific** (100 Aquarium Way; 562–590–3100). Then let your imaginations set sail when you board the historical luxury ocean liner **Queen Mary** (1126 Queens Highway; 562–435–3511 or 800–437–2934; $75–$400). Take a guided tour of the vessel, which sailed its maiden voyage from Southhampton, England, to New York in 1936.

* After dinner at **Sir Winston's** (Sun Deck; expensive), the Queen's elegant restaurant, watch fireworks from the deck on summer evenings, dance with your partner in the lounge, or take a moonlight stroll around the deck.

* Begin the day with Sunday brunch in the **Grand Salon,** a famously elaborate event. Later, when it's time to disembark the ship, pretend you're on a shore excursion in an exotic port of call by visiting the **Museum of Latin American Art** (628 Alamitos Avenue at 7th Street; 562–437–1689).

nearly 2,000 passengers and 1,200 crew members. The wine cellar aboard the ship could hold 15,000 bottles of wine, and the first-class dining room, the largest of any ship ever built, could serve all 800 first-class passengers at once. Until World War II interrupted the *Queen's* service as a luxury liner, the ship could sail between England and New York in four days, a world record it held for fourteen years. During the war, it was refitted as a troopship and, camouflaged with gray paint, was called the *Gray Ghost*. The *Queen* transported thousands of troops and served as Winston Churchill's seaborne headquarters. Plans for the invasion of Europe were orchestrated aboard the *Queen*. At war's end, the ship carried thousands of European war brides and their children to join their husbands in the United States and Canada. Once again known as Queen of the Atlantic, the *Queen Mary* transported the rich and famous across the sea, until 1967, when it arrived in Long Beach.

From the parking lot, it's a short elevator ride up to the registration deck, where you "come aboard" the ship rather than merely register at a hotel. As the steward escorts you to your cabin, you'll begin to see why today, retrofitted once again as a luxury liner, the *Queen Mary* is the perfect setting for a time-altering holiday. Throughout the ship, the custom woodwork and 1930s-style art deco furnishings make it easy to see why the *Queen* is listed on the National Register of Historic Places. The hotel now comprises three decks of the original first-class staterooms and suites, of which no two are alike.

Two steps into the Queen Mary Suite, for example, and I immediately felt the old-world charm and elegance. The ample foyer, which had enough room for me and my partner, the steward, and our luggage cart, had thick wall-to-wall carpeting and rich, burl paneling. The ceilings in the suite were high, so we never felt claustrophobic. Throughout the suite, warm woods were used for cabinetry, a desk and dressing table, and bookcases. Despite the silk, not real, flowers in a vase in the foyer, there were other luxe touches to remind me of the golden past: an etched-glass disk with a laurel leaf design in the sitting room and the hand-carved wooden headboard in the bedroom. A gentle sea breeze blew in from the open portholes, and the soft diffused lighting from table lamps and art deco wall sconces created a subtle atmosphere of romance and elegance.

You may decide not to leave your stateroom or suite, and that would be quite understandable. In any event, take a moment now to make a dinner reservation at Sir Winston's on the Sun Deck. Request a table for two overlooking the water.

If you do venture out, take a stroll on the Promenade Deck. Along the way you'll encounter a series of enlarged photographs of some of the ship's more famous passengers. Spencer Tracy leans casually against the railing in one of the photos, his overcoat flapping in the ocean breeze. American divorcee Wallis Simpson is seen sauntering arm in arm with the Duke of Windsor, the man who gave up the throne of England for her. On nearly every voyage throughout its long history, the *Queen* carried notable passengers: diplomats and dignitaries, ambassadors and kings, film stars and moguls—all knew the ship well. Marlene Dietrich graced its decks, Fred Astaire danced in the ballroom, and Bob Hope practiced his golf swing from the upper decks. Elizabeth Taylor and Nicky Hilton sailed aboard the *Queen* in the 1950s on the first leg of their honeymoon trip to Europe.

Make your way toward the bow of the ship to the Passenger Information desk on the Promenade Deck. There you can pick up a map for a self-guided tour of the ship, but the one-hour guided tour is much more interesting and brings you to some parts of the ship not accessible on the self-guided tour. You can make a reservation for a guided tour (the cost is reasonable, about $7.00 per person for adults) when you book your stay or when you come on board. Guided tours leave from Passenger Information and are scheduled during the day from 10:30 A.M. to at least 4:00 P.M. Our guide, Joe, led us from stem to stern, filling us in on the history of the ship, facts and figures, as well as revealing some of the *Queen*'s secrets. The ballroom mirrors, for example, were faintly tinted pink to fool seasick passengers into believing they didn't look as dreadfully green-tinged as they felt. We got a look at the indoor swimming pool (no longer in use), a tiled monument to art deco styling, with walls and columns gracefully arched to expose tucked-away areas with deck chairs and tables. The pale yellow color scheme, coupled with vibrant red and turquoise, was echoed in the furniture and wall sconces. It was easy to imagine the laughter of children and adults who had once upon a time splashed their way across the Atlantic.

At the end of the tour, retrace your steps to the bow of the ship and the Observation Bar. Above the sleekly curved bar, a parade of 1930s-dressed characters promenades in a stylized mural that spans half the room. From this vantage point, especially seated outside, the two of you can watch a parade of sailboats weave around the jetty, and if, like many couples, you get lost in a hand-holding reverie, you'll still be there to watch the setting sun.

DAY ONE: *Evening*

DINNER

As a semiformal dining spot, **Sir Winston's** (Sun Deck; expensive) is the most elegant of the ship's restaurants, so you can enjoy the occasion to dress up a bit. Plenty of windows afford open vistas of the bay and Long Beach skyline. The wood-paneled room is decorated with tapestries, tables are properly dressed with thick linen cloths, the service is attentive, and the clink of silverware on fine china adds to the old-world style. The menu is a fusion of Continental and California. You might try an appetizer of warm goat cheese in a crisp potato basket with grilled vegetables, pistachio nuts, and red pepper coulis. Follow that with a romaine salad with Boursin cheese and hazelnuts. For main courses, you'll find venison and rack of lamb on the menu, as well as swordfish niçoise (grilled and served with tomato and basil olive oil) and beef tenderloin wrapped in phyllo. Outside, harbor lights twinkle, and with a bit of imagination, they could be the city lights of New York or Southampton or some other port not quite forgotten from the *Queen's* past.

I Do, I Do, Since '72

The Queen Mary Royal Wedding Chapel was originally the second-class smoking lounge. Converted to a wedding chapel in 1972, it's decorated with British brown oak burl and walnut pillars. Today, the chapel hosts about 400 weddings a year. In June 1997, to celebrate the twenty-fifth anniversary of the chapel, a special vow-renewal ceremony was held for couples who had been married aboard the Queen Mary.

After dinner, there's music and dancing in the Observation Bar on the Promenade Deck, although the bar can get quite crowded, especially on a Saturday night when guests from onboard wedding receptions spill over into the bar. In the summer, Saturday evenings include a fireworks display around 9:00 P.M. In any case, there's a moonlight stroll on the deck or the time-warp cocoon of your stateroom to consider instead.

DAY TWO: *Morning*

BRUNCH

The *Queen Mary*'s Sunday champagne brunch is legendary in Southern California. It's held from 10:00 A.M. to 2:00 P.M. in the Grand Salon, the ship's original first-class dining room. The room, of course, is magnificent, but it was designed to accommodate 800 people, so you can expect a big, hungry crowd. The array of food, set out buffet style, is spectacular —some fifty different dishes are presented, from made-to-order omelettes, Mexican and Chinese dishes, and roast beef to skyscrapers of fresh fruit, pastries, and make-your-own sundaes. A plucky harpist does her best to be heard over the conversation, which can rise to an intense level. Despite the commotion, we quite enjoyed the brunch, as much for the spectacle of all that food as for the grandness of the room itself.

DAY TWO: *Afternoon*

Before disembarking, stroll through the Main Hall, the original first-class shopping arcade. Small, boutiquelike shops display historic periodicals, scrimshaw, jewelry, crystal, china teapots, and chocolates. One of the more intriguing items for sale is the book *A Guide to the Haunted Queen Mary*. In chronicling the ship's history, it reveals a number of chilling tales, ghost stories, and unexplained events that reportedly occurred aboard the ship. I opted instead for a souvenir deck of playing cards. Each card, portraying the *Queen* in all its dignity, would long remind me of this weekend voyage that never left the pier.

Though you've never left port, it's easy enough to pretend you've come ashore for an excursion in an exotic port of call with a visit to the exuberant **Museum of Latin American Art** (628 Alamitos Avenue at 7th Street; 562–437–1689). It's about ten minutes from the *Queen* (from Queensway Bridge, turn right on Shoreline Drive, which turns into Alamitos). A renovated 10,000-square-foot skating rink now houses the museum's permanent collection of contemporary art from Mexico and Central and South America, as well as temporary exhibits. Look for textiles, jewelry, carved masks, and the work of local and Latin American artists in the gift shop.

LUNCH

If you get hungry while you're visiting the museum, there's a friendly little restaurant with an outdoor patio, **Viva** (562–435–4048; inexpensive), right across the courtyard. The Latin American theme is carried out here too, with dishes like *tamal de pollo* (a Bolivian dish), *enchilada de espinaca y ajo* (El Salvador), and the traditional Mexican *torta*, or sandwich, of marinated beef, lettuce, and avocado.

FOR MORE ROMANCE

With some careful planning (and reservations made well in advance), you can take a one-hour cruise through the canals of Naples Island, an affluent neighborhood in Long Beach, aboard a gondola. Cost is about $55 per couple and includes a basket of bread, cheese, salami, and wine glasses. Go at sunset and bring a bottle of wine; call **Gondola Getaway** (562–433–9595) for reservations and further details.

Extend your stay aboard the *Queen Mary* by a day and combine it with a day trip to Catalina Island. You can make arrangements through the *Queen Mary*; ask about the *Queen Mary*–Catalina Getaway package. (For more information on Catalina attractions, see Itinerary 6, "Island of Romance".)

Hurray for Hollywood!

ollywood, it seems, has always been there to inform us of love and romance. The silver screen has served as our classroom for the subject for nearly a century—from the flickering images of the silents to the black-and-white art deco glamour of the 1930s to the Technicolor brilliance of the 1940s and 1950s to the digitally mastered kisses of the 1990s. And an evening at the movies is still the classic first date. This itinerary will guide you toward unlocking a bit of the romance and glamour of Hollywood.

You can have lots of fun with this itinerary, if you remember a couple of things: Hollywood the place can be drab and somewhat seedy, nothing like the glossy image of Hollywood the legend. The romance of the screen is manufactured through an elaborate technical process, which is the magic of Hollywood. But if the two of you use your imagination, you can create your own Hollywood magic with props and wardrobe that will add to your experience—rent a vintage or luxury car for the day, wear rhinestone-studded sunglasses or fabulous faux jewelry, buy an outrageous little cocktail hat at a vintage clothing store, or dress up in elegant evening clothes for a night out at a Hollywood cabaret.

PRACTICAL NOTES: Pick up a good map of Los Angeles that shows more than just the major streets and freeways. A couple of the locations suggested in this itinerary are not on major thoroughfares.

To rent a sexy vintage car, such as a 1969 Cadillac Coupe de Ville white convertible, a 1965 Mustang GT convertible, or the Ferrari convertible Al Pacino drove in *Scent of a Woman*, try **Beverly Hills Rent a Car** (310–337–1400). Cabaret performances at the Cinegrill in the Hollywood Roosevelt Hotel (323–466–7000) and the Gardenia Club (323–467–7444)

Romance

AT A GLANCE

❊ Rent a classic or vintage car, preferably a convertible (Beverly Hills Rent a Car; 310–337–1400), and cruise up into the hills above the movie colony for an upclose look at the landmark HOLLYWOOD sign. Later take a few souvenir snapshots of each other in front of the gate of **Paramount Studios** (5555 Melrose Avenue at Bronson; 323–956–5575), the only working movie studio still in Hollywood.

❊ When it's time for lunch, **Musso & Frank Grill** (6667 Hollywood Boulevard at Cherokee; 323–467–7788; moderate) offers an historic old-Hollywood setting, while **Chasen's Hollywood Cafe** (in the Hollywood History Museum; 1660 North Highland Avenue at Hollywood Boulevard; 323–464–7776) is a new version of legendary Hollywood eatery.

❊ Spend part of the afternoon checking out a few Hollywood landmarks, such as the **Capitol Records Tower** (1750 North Vine Street), the **Hollywood Walk of Fame** of pink terrazzo stars embedded in the sidewalks, the 1922 **Egyptian Theater** (6712 Hollywood Boulevard), the Chinese Theater just two blocks away, and the restored art deco landmark Max Factor building, which now houses the new Hollywood History Museum (1660 North Highland Avenue at Hollywood Boulevard; 323–464–7776). Then head out to the San Fernando Valley to **It's a Wrap** (3325 Magnolia Boulevard, Burbank; 818–567–7366), which sells wardrobe and props from television shows and movies.

❊ Relive a bit of Hollywood glamour in the evening at the intimate cabaret **Cinegrill** in the Hollywood Roosevelt Hotel (7000 Hollywood Boulevard; 323–466–7000) or the **Gardenia Club** (7066 Santa Monica Boulevard; 323–467–7444; moderate).

DAY ONE: *Morning*

are popular and can sell out. Call ahead for information and reservations.

If this chapter were a scene in a movie, it would fade in as the morning sun begins to burn off the haze of a new day in Hollywood. The white letters spelling out H-O-L-L-Y-W-O-O-D in the hills above the fabled movie capital catch the early light. Fifty feet high and visible from miles away on a clear day, they seem to glow like bright lights on a movie marquee, proclaiming a place that exists only in the imagination. If you've rented a classic convertible, then start out right by putting down the top, donning a scarf and sunglasses, and heading for the Hollywood Hills and the HOLLYWOOD sign. A drive up Beachwood Drive (off Franklin Avenue) will bring you as close to the sign as you can get without hiking through dense underbrush. The drive also brings you into a villagelike neighborhood that was used as a location in the original 1956 film *Invasion of the Body Snatchers*. Many of the screenwriters, actors, and other show business types who live in this area congregate at the homey **Village Coffee Shop** (2695 North Beachwood Drive at Westshire Drive; 323–467–5398; inexpensive) for breakfast.

For a panoramic look at Hollywood, drive over to the **Griffith Observatory** (2800 East Observatory Road; 323-664-1191), which is east of the HOLLYWOOD sign, in Griffith Park. (From Franklin Avenue or Los Feliz Boulevard, turn toward the hills at Vermont Avenue and follow the signs.) Set on a promontory, the observatory commands a stunning view of Hollywood and most of the rest of Los Angeles, extending to the Pacific Ocean. On a clear day you can see sunlight shimmering on the ocean. The observatory itself is quite famous and recognizable; it's frequently used as a movie backdrop, most notably in the 1955 classic *Rebel Without a Cause*, which starred James Dean, Natalie Wood, and Sal Mineo. It also popped up in Arnold Schwarzenegger's *The Terminator*. For pure romance, though, the observatory must be visited at night, when the lights of the city below sparkle like sequins caught in the search- lights of a movie premiere. If you two do return in the evening, bring a wrap, sequined or otherwise, to keep warm because it can get chilly in the hills when the sun goes down. The observatory is open until 10:00 P.M.

If you haven't been snapping souvenir photos of each other, now's the time to do it—in front of the **Paramount Studios** gate (5555 Melrose Avenue at Bronson; 323-956-5575). From Hollywood or Sunset Boulevards, drive south on Gower Street or Vine Street to Melrose Avenue and turn east (left). The original entrance arch is now tucked away on Marathon Street, behind the new double gate on Melrose. Paramount is the only major studio still located in Hollywood. (An excellent two-hour guided walking tour of the studio is given on weekdays only. Admission is $15 per person.)

DAY ONE: *Afternoon*

LUNCH

Even though there's absolutely nothing inherently romantic about **Musso & Frank Grill** (6667 Hollywood Boulevard at Cherokee; 323-467-7788; moderate), you wouldn't be making a bad choice to have lunch here. The oldest restaurant in Hollywood, it dates back to 1919, a classic American bar and grill. As rich in dark wood paneling as in Hollywood legend, it still attracts a notable crowd (the artist David Hockney strolled in with friends the last time we were there). The food is straightforward—steaks, classic Caesar salad, grilled lamb chops—the martinis are excellent, and

Making a Lasting Impression

In the forecourt of Mann's (formerly Grauman's) Chinese Theatre, famous "couples" have left their foot- and handprints in the cement. Paul Newman and Joanne Woodward, one of Hollywood's most enduring husband-and-wife teams, share a square signed on May 25, 1963. Other romantic legacies come to us from Yul Brynner and Deborah Kerr, who costarred in the 1956 musical The King and I. Other screen couples include Fred Astaire and Ginger Rogers, and Sophia Loren and Marcello Mastroianni. Jack Benny declared his love for his wife, Mary Livingston, on January 13, 1941, with the words, "My [Benny drew a heart here] belongs to Mary, but my feet belong to Grauman." And now it's your turn—you can't leave your footprints in the cement, but the two of you can ask another sightseer to take your picture as you kneel down to pose at the footprints of your favorite movie stars.

the jacket-clad waiters not occasionally brusque. It's also the only decent restaurant along this stretch of Hollywood Boulevard.

A new addition to the Hollywood restaurant scene is **Chasen's Hollywood Cafe**, at the Hollywood History Museum (1660 North Highland Avenue at Hollywood Boulevard; 323–464–7776; moderate). The original Chasen's was a legendary Hollywood eatery, where movie stars like Elizabeth Taylor couldn't get enough of house specialties like chili, hobo steak, cheese toast, and banana shortcake (Taylor reportedly had Chasen's chili flown to Rome while she was filming Cleopatra.) This version of Chasen's is geared to tourists, but its location next to the historic Max Factor building and the Hollywood History Museum makes it one of the few spots in town that manages to recapture a bit of the old magic. (Do call first to make sure the restaurant is open; at this writing, the opening date is scheduled for winter 1999.)

You could spend part of the afternoon cruising around Hollywood to check out a few of its more famous landmarks, testing each other's Hollywood trivia quotient. Atop the **Capitol Records Tower** (1750 North Vine Street), a blinking light spells out "Hollywood" in morse code. The first of those pink terrazzo stars embedded in the sidewalks to immortalize entertainment personalities were unveiled in 1960 at the northeast corner of Hollywood Boulevard and Highland Avenue (Ronald Colman, Joanne Woodward, and Burt Lancaster were among that first batch of honorees). The **Egyptian Theater** (6712 Hollywood Boulevard), now renovated and the new permanent home of the film preservation society American Cinematheque, was built by Sid Grauman in 1922, before his more famous **Chinese Theater** just two blocks away. And on Highland Avenue at Hollywood Boulevard, in the restored art deco landmark Max Factor building, the new **Hollywood History Museum** (1660 North Highland Avenue at Hollywood Boulevard; 323–464–7776). Scheduled for a winter 1999 opening as of this writing, the museum realizes a dream many Hollywoodphiles have long held for a permanent home for artifacts, costumes, props, posters, and other memorabilia of Hollywood's glamorous past.

One thing I like to do in a special place like Hollywood is to buy something that captures a unique aspect of the locale. A souvenir of sorts, but not the ubiquitous and unimaginative T-shirt or refrigerator magnet. Not always an easy task. But in Hollywood, all you have to do is walk into a store like **Collector's Book Store** (1708 North Vine Street; 323–467–3296) or **Larry Edmunds Cinema Bookshop** (6644 Hollywood Boulevard; 323–464–3273), where you'll find a book, publicity still, poster, or some other movie-related treasure to take home. Another possibility is to head for the San Fernando Valley (take the Hollywood Freeway north) to Burbank and **It's a Wrap** (3325 Magnolia Boulevard, Burbank; 818–567–7366). The man-eating plant, Audrey, from *Little Shop of Horrors*, watches over this big, bright store that looks like the wardrobe department of one of the nearby studios. In fact, It's a Wrap sells wardrobe and props from television shows and movies. The main floor is divided into men's and women's sections, with carousels and racks displaying jackets, dresses, sweaters, shirts, shoes, suits, belts, and hats. Each item is tagged with a code identifying the show or studio it came from. The second level is more like a specialty boutique, where you might find a three-button blue wool Donna Karan blazer ($275) or a Versace suit ($1,500). Who knows, you may find that perfect accessory to wear tonight.

DAY ONE: *Evening*

Dinner and cabaret at the **Hollywood Roosevelt Hotel** (7000 Hollywood Boulevard; 323–466–7000 or 800–950–7667) bring the day in Hollywood to a close. Built in 1927, when Hollywood was young and buoyant, the hotel is chock-full of Hollywood history. During the golden era of Hollywood in the 1930s and 1940s, it was at the center of attention in the social swirl. The Motion Picture Academy of Arts and Sciences held its first Academy Awards ceremony in the hotel's Blossom Room in 1927 and met at the hotel regularly until 1935. It was rumored that during Prohibition, Errol Flynn used to mix his gin recipe in the back of the hotel barbershop. F. Scott Fitzgerald and Ernest Hemingway would hang out at the Cinegrill cabaret, the same place where Mary Martin sang as a young actress and where Marilyn Monroe and Arthur Miller met. Monroe had a long association with the hotel. As a starlet in the 1940s, she once posed for photographs on the diving board of the hotel's pool. Years later she returned several times to room 246, overlooking the pool and now dubbed the Marilyn Monroe Suite. It's popularly said about the hotel that during those years, "every star in Hollywood was in these beds, and some of them even slept here."

Today the stars have decamped to more prestigious properties, but the hotel continues to play a role in Hollywood legend. The gallery of the mezzanine level has been given over to an exhibit of Hollywood history, and the fanciful Spanish Colonial decorative embellishments of the lobby are delightful reminders of a more glamorous, romantic era in the movie capital.

DINNER

Come to **Theodore's** in the Hollywood Roosevelt Hotel (moderate) for old Hollywood atmosphere. It's also convenient to the Cinegrill cabaret, which is just across the grand lobby. High ceilings, potted palms, well-spaced tables, and proper dining armchairs lend Theodore's just the right touches of bygone elegance. The menu offers a nice range of classic, traditional dishes—lamb chops, broiled chicken, fresh fish, and pasta.

In the old days, Hollywood would step out for the evening at nightclubs such as Mocambo and Ciro's. Those big clubs may be a thing of the past, but sophisticated cabaret entertainment still survives in this town. After dinner just walk across the lobby to the **Cinegrill**, an intimately scaled cabaret room that's a favorite stage for artists such as Shirley Horn, Maureen McGovern, Julie Wilson, Lainie Kazan, Ruth Brown, and Nancy Dussault. Shows generally begin around 8:00 P.M.; an additional show may be scheduled at 10:30 P.M. on Friday and Saturday, depending on the artist. There's usually a cover charge of between $10 and $25, with a two-drink minimum.

Another Hollywood cabaret is only a few blocks away. Not so long ago I fell in love at the **Gardenia Club** (7066 Santa Monica Boulevard; 323–467–7444; moderate) while actress-singer Andrea Marcovicci sang haunting ballads of love's angst, so this supper club is a special place for me. You don't have to have dinner to attend the show, but that's usually the only guarantee of being seated. And even if the food is not highly recommended, the quality of entertainment is always top rate. Besides the cost of dinner, there's a cover of between $5.00 and $20.00, and a two-drink minimum. Dinner service starts at 7:00 P.M.; shows begin at 9:00 P.M.

If the day were to end just as it began, like a scene from a movie, the music would swell as the two of you drive off into the night, and the picture would fade to black. The End.

FOR MORE ROMANCE

At night, from the Hollywood Hills, the view of Hollywood and Los Angeles glittering below is spellbinding. The vistas from Mulholland Drive can be spectacular. To reach Mulholland Drive, head north on Highland Avenue past the Hollywood Bowl. Keep to the left and merge onto Cahuenga Boulevard West, not the freeway, at the Bowl. At the second light (Woodrow Wilson Drive), make a sharp left onto the winding Mulholland Drive.

If you want to extend your stay overnight, the Hollywood Roosevelt Hotel offers an attractive one-night package for two that includes accommodations and breakfast at Theodore's for about $159.

No Passport Required
EXPLORING CHINATOWN, LITTLE TOKYO, AND OLVERA STREET

os Angeles's wonderfully diverse ethnic makeup can make the city seem as exotic and romantic as a foreign destination. Although the cultures of many nations make up the social pastiche of Los Angeles, it's the influences of China, Japan, and Mexico that are most widely felt. Pockets of these cultures, transplanted to Los Angeles by generations of immigrants, can be found within only a few blocks of City Hall downtown. Sampling a bit of what each has to offer in this two-day itinerary will make the two of you feel as if you've set off on a globe-trotting escape. As you explore these enclaves, notice the special character and distinctly different personality of each—the exuberance and commotion of Chinatown, the self-conscious harmony of Little Tokyo, and the colorful festiveness of Olvera Street.

PRACTICAL NOTES: Chinatown, Little Tokyo, and Olvera Street are especially appealing when a festival or traditional celebration is taking place. In Chinatown, Chinese New Year is celebrated with parades and beauty pageants; it's usually held in January or February. On the full moon of the eighth lunar month (September), the annual Chinese Moon Festival marks the end of the summer harvest. Call the **Chinese Chamber of Commerce** (213–617–0396) for more information. August brings a weeklong celebration called **Nisei Week Japanese Festival** to Little Tokyo each year with parades, folk dancing, and art exhibits (213–687–7193). The **New Otani Hotel & Gardens** in Little Tokyo offers two special Japanese experience packages. The big difference between the two, besides price, is that one includes Japanese-style sleeping arrangements on futons on the floor and the other offers Western-style beds. Olvera Street, or El Pueblo de Los Angeles, celebrates the traditional Dia de los Muertos, or Day of the Dead, on November 2; Las Posadas from December 16 to 24; and Cinco de Mayo in May. Call **El Pueblo de Los Angeles Historical Monument Authority Commission** (213–625–5045) for more information.

DAY ONE:
Morning

BRUNCH

Start off in Chinatown, which, as you'll discover, is all about sounds and tastes and aromas. A good way to begin to take in some of those tastes and aromas is at *dim sum* at **Empress Pavilion** (in the Bamboo Plaza, 988 North Hill Street at Bernard Street; 213–617–9898; moderate). Little dumplings filled with meat or fish or beans and vegetables are steamed or fried and served to you on small plates or in metal containers. What's fun about this is that the food is brought to you by servers wheeling a procession of serving carts between tables in this large restaurant. Each cart contains different selections. You make your choice —maybe deep-fried taro dumplings (my favorite), sticky rice in lotus leaf, pan-fried

*R*omance
AT A GLANCE

✳ *Set off on a globe-trotting adventure without ever leaving downtown Los Angeles. Begin your escape with dim sum and souvenir shopping in* **Chinatown.** *Then unpack your bags in one of the Japanese-style rooms at the* **New Otani Hotel & Gardens** *(120 South Los Angeles Street; 213–629–1200; California: 800–273–2294; U.S. and Canada: 800–421–8795) in Little Tokyo.*

✳ *As you explore this historic section of the city, stop for a sticky, sweet tea cake made daily at the confectionery,* **Fugetso Do** *(315 East First Street). Continue on to the outstanding* **Japanese American National Museum** *(369 East First Street; 213–625–0414), which occupies both a renovated Buddhist temple and an adjacent brand new pavilion. Before the afternoon is over, you can return to the hotel for a traditional ritual bath and massage.*

✳ *Savor the tastes of Japan at a special five-course traditional kaiseki dinner at the hotel's* **Thousand Cranes** *restaurant (moderate to expensive). Entertainment in the evening could be a performance of a play at* **East-West Players** *(120 North Judge John Aiso Street; 213–625–7000).*

✳ *In the morning, the last stop on your cultural tour is* **Olvera Street,** *the oldest section of the city, where a central plaza and a re-creation of a Mexican market street provide a colorful, festive backdrop for mariachi bands and traditional dance troupes, people-watching, and souvenir shopping.*

shrimp pot stickers—and the server stamps a card on your table, which becomes your bill. The waiters' English can be hard to understand sometimes, so if you ask what something is, you may not get an answer you understand. I've learned that it's better not to ask—if something looks or smells good, it probably is, so just point.

Chinatown is concentrated along North Broadway and Hill Street, between Ord and Bernard Streets, just north of Union Station. You'll find parking at one of several lots in the area. Then you can just stroll around. (If you have dim sum at Empress Pavilion, park in multilevel **Bamboo Plaza**, 988 North Hill Street. The restaurant will validate your parking ticket, thereby reducing the cost.) As the two of you wander around, take a look in the many shops that open to the street. You'll see baskets full of ginger and other roots, leaves and dried bark, and antlers and other unrecognizable bits used by herbalists to concoct pulverized prescriptions that are boiled into strong brews. Grocery stores are stocked with items like dried squid, shark's fins, and live fish. Chickens squawk in cages stacked up in poultry stores. And everywhere, customers bustle about, purchasing vegetables and other foodstuffs for the day. The smells are often sharp and pungent, the hand-lettered signs rarely in English, and the din of voices an aural patchwork of languages and dialects. It's a rich, stimulating environment.

Gift shops are plentiful and varied, from tacky to exceptional. Some are housed in highly decorated pagoda-style buildings built in the 1930s when Chinatown was moved from its original location so that construction of Union Station could proceed. There's a wishing well grotto in **Central Plaza** (900 block of North Broadway). We always stop here and toss in a few coins. After all it can't hurt, and the last time, I got lucky—my coin bounced right into the little cup marked "love." Across Hill Street find your way to **Chungking Court** (900 block of Hill Street) and visit **Fong's** (943 Chung King Road; 213–626–5904) to shop for tiny, delicately wrought cloisonné bowls, Chinese miniatures, textiles, and other finely detailed objects. The cloisonné fantail fish make beautiful but inexpensive gifts ($5.00–$10.00) to be put on a chain and worn as a necklace. To take home a bit of the sounds of Chinatown, buy one of the small brass bells ($5.00–$30.00). If he's not busy, Mr. Gim Fong will be happy to show you photographs of his family and talk about its history. **Ten Ren Tea Company** (Far East Plaza, 726 North Hill Street) is sedate by Chinatown standards and stocks scores of varieties of tea, all grown in Taiwan. If you'd like to shop for jade or fine Chinese antiques, ring the bell for admittance to **Jin Hing Company** (412 Bamboo Lane). The shop is tucked into the alley called Bamboo Lane behind Bamboo Plaza. You'll be tempted to peek into every shop, but don't or you'll never make it to the next port of call—Little Tokyo.

DAY ONE: *Afternoon*

You'd have to go to Tokyo to have a more Japanese experience than the one offered at the **New Otani Hotel & Gardens** (120 South Los Angeles Street; 213-629-1200; California: 800-273-2294; rest of U.S. and Canada: 800-421-8795). The New Otani's appeal for Westerners is the "Japanese Experience" package (about $599). The one- or two-night package includes a Japanese suite overlooking the hotel's beautiful garden, which is revealed when you open the *shoji* (rice paper) screens that cover the windows in the sitting room. The hotel provides cotton *yukata* (robe) for you to slip into, as well as slippers and complimentary sake. Sliding shoji screens conceal the sleeping area, which is really a raised platform, with tatami mats covering the floor. Later, the room maid will prepare the sleeping area by setting out cotton-covered foam futons. If sleeping on a futon is pushing it for you, a Western-style deluxe room can be substituted for a lower cost (ask for the "Touch of Japan" package, about $399).

The Japanese suite has a sunken tub and private sauna, which are used for ritual bathing. Basically, here's how that goes: First fill the tub with hot water and pour in a packet of bath salts provided by the hotel. In the separate shower area, sit on the stool and wash, using the handheld shower to rinse off. Then it's ten minutes in the sauna, a rinse in the shower, and a soak in the tub. The final step is another scrubbing and rinse.

Shiatsu massage, another age-old Japanese tradition, restores energy flow in your body by applying pressure to specific acupressure points. As part of your Japanese package, appointments for massages will be made for you, as will reservations for dinner in one of the hotel restaurants. Breakfast the following morning—American or Japanese—is also included. When you depart, you'll be presented with a bonsai tree as a gift.

If you don't have massages scheduled, you should have time to explore a bit of Little Tokyo, where people of Japanese ancestry have lived for more than a century. First Street, between San Pedro Street and Central Avenue, is the historic core. On the north side of the street, a row of thirteen shops and apartments has been designated a National Historic Landmark. A time line in the sidewalk notes the dates and various businesses that have occupied the site. At least peek in the window of number 315, **Fugetso Do,** a confectionery, and the oldest store in continuous operation in Little Tokyo. Better yet, try one of the delicious tea cakes, which are not like American pastries, but made instead of pounded rice and bean paste.

At the corner of First and Central is the **Japanese American National Museum** (369 East First Street; 213-625-0414). Housed in two buildings—a handsomely restored Buddhist temple and a new exhibition pavilion—the museum presents changing exhibits pertaining to the Japanese-American experience. It's a highly personal experience to visit this museum, because volunteer docents are always on hand to share their own stories and experiences, such as life in a concentration camp during the World War II internment of Japanese Americans or growing up on a coffee plantation in Hawaii. Across the street, a fire watchtower stands at the entrance to **Japanese Village Plaza.** Watchtowers like this one were hung with a bell and were used to warn Japanese villages of fire. Along the ambling walkway through the plaza, you'll find small mom-and-pop shops and restaurants.

The plaza cuts through to Second Street, where you can walk around the corner to San Pedro Street and the **Japanese American Cultural and Community Center** (244 South San Pedro Street; 213-628-2725). The monumental rock sculpture in the plaza is a tribute to the *issei,* or first-generation Japanese immigrants. It was designed by Isamu Noguchi. A "stream" runs through the adjacent sunken garden and symbolizes the "journey" of Japanese immigrants in American society.

DAY ONE: *Evening*

DINNER

Is there anything more civilized than two kimono-clad hostesses bowing to welcome you when you step off the elevator onto the Garden Level at the New Otani? But before you go into *Senbazuru,* or Thousand Cranes, the hotel's signature restaurant, for dinner, tell the hostess that you wish first to have a drink in the Genji Bar. The sleekly designed, sophisticated bar is best seen after dark, when the streak of gold against a dark blue background in the mural painting by Los Angeles artist Lita Albequerque seems to glow like a comet in the night sky.

Thousand Cranes (moderate to expensive) is not a lavish room, but rather simply designed. The main feature is a huge glass wall that separates the room from the Japanese garden and reflecting pond. At night, with the stone lanterns lighted in the garden, the effect is quite stunning. The hostess will guide you across a stone pathway to a table (ask for one by the window). Immediately, individual hot towels will be presented for you to cleanse your hands. You may order a la carte or from a special menu of *kaiseki* dinners. Designed for at least two people, *kaiseki* is an elaborate, elegant presentation of five traditional courses. You may start out with a crescent-shaped dish holding bite-size portions of squid with cod egg, seaweed stuffed with fish, and chopped monkfish liver. After soup comes a grilled dish of fish or buttery soft beef, then tempura, miso soup, and finally fresh fruit. The price of *kaiseki* can be a bit steep (about $42 to $85 per person), but it's still cheaper than flying over to Tokyo for dinner.

The Languages of Love

In a polyglot city like Los Angeles, there are plenty of ways to say "I love you." In Spanish, it's te quiero. The Japanese whisper ai shiteimasu to one another, while Chinese say wo ai ni. When a Thai man tells a woman "I love you," he says, Anh yêu em; a Thai woman says, Em yêuanh. In Armenian, the words are kez geh seerehm, and Arabic speakers say eneh beh hobbehk.

If the two of you are theatergoers, look into what's on the boards at **East-West Players** (120 North Judge John Aiso Street; 213–625–7000), one of Los Angeles's venerable small theater companies. The company, which recently moved into a restored historical building in Little Tokyo, provides a voice for Asian Pacific actors and writers.

Before you retire for the evening, return to the New Otani Hotel & Gardens and stroll through the garden. It's one of the most romantic spots in the entire city. Landscaped in traditional techniques, this half-acre oasis combines the seven Zen principles of nature in its purest form:

asymmetry, simplicity, tranquillity, naturalness, austerity, subtlety, and unworldliness. A path meanders through the garden, over a gentle stream, and around a pond. Water cascades over a stone wall into the pond, and special red rocks, found only on one island in Japan, have been carefully placed throughout the garden. The office towers of the city form a glittering nighttime backdrop. It's a beautiful spot, day or night, but the romance quotient increases considerably after the sun goes down and the lights of the city come up. Don't miss the moment.

DAY TWO: *Morning*

BREAKFAST

Of course, you can get good old American bacon and eggs for breakfast at the New Otani Hotel. But you could also follow the lead of the hotel's many Japanese guests who prefer the traditional Japanese breakfast of broiled fish, steamed vegetables, and miso soup. On Sundays, the lavish Japanese brunch buffet features these and many other Japanese specialties, as well as eggs and a few other American-style breakfast items.

After breakfast at the hotel, you'll be ready for the last stop on your culture tour—Olvera Street. This is the oldest section of the city, where the **Avila Adobe** (10 Olvera Street; 213–680–2525), which was built in 1818, is the oldest existing residence in Los Angeles. Olvera Street is a one-block re-creation of a Mexican market street. It's adjacent to a plaza and across North Main Street from **Our Lady Queen of Angels (Old Plaza) Church,** the city's oldest church (535 North Main Street; 213–629–3101). Surrounded by twenty-seven historic buildings, Olvera Street has become thought of as the city's birthplace, although it really is only near the actual founding site. The facts about Olvera Street may be somewhat mixed up, but it's still one of the most beloved spots in all Los Angeles. That's probably because the atmosphere is always colorful and festive.

We love Olvera Street in the morning, before the day is too hot and before the place gets too crowded. We like to peek in the window of **La Luz del Dia** (W-1 Olvera Street; 213–628–7495), the cafeteria-style restaurant facing the plaza at the south end of Olvera Street, to watch the women make tortillas by hand. Then, nibbling a *churro* (a long, sticklike doughnut covered with sugar and cinnamon) or *pan dulce* (a leavened sweet roll with sugar sprinkled on top) and sipping a *chocolate*, we sit in the plaza and people-watch. On Sunday mornings, churchgoers, many of them immigrants from Mexico and Central America, cross the little plaza on their way to mass at the church. Vendors, selling from little stalls set up down the center of the narrow street or from shops housed in the historic buildings, set out their wares—embroidered blouses and dresses, flags, tooled leather goods, serapes, wooden puppets—the kind of inexpensive and colorful items you might expect to find in Tijuana. Fruit vendors set up their stands, from which they sell sliced mangoes and other melons, which you can have squeezed with lemon and sprinkled with chili powder. Later, mariachis and other street performers join the scene. We usually end up poking around in **Casa de Sousa** (634 North Main Street; 213-626-7076), where more serious examples of folk art can be found. Then it's time for brunch, maybe huevos rancheros, at **La Golondrina** restaurant (W-17 Olvera Street; 213-628-4349).

When it's time to leave for home, don't just say *adios* to Olvera Street, Chinatown, Little Tokyo and Los Angeles's remarkable ethnic energy; say *hasta la proxima,* "until the next time."

ITINERARY 16
One day

Courting the Muse
LOS ANGELES'S MUSEUM ROW

*A*n art museum is one of the few public places I can think of that provides opportunity to build intimacy with another person. Great art forces us to reframe our thinking about ourselves and our perspective on the world, enriching us in ways that can be described as spiritual. Los Angeles is fortunate to have three art and cultural museums clustered together on Wilshire Boulevard in the Miracle Mile district: the large and varied Los Angeles County Museum of Art (LACMA), the small and charming Craft and Folk Art Museum (CAFAM), and the Southwest Museum at LACMA West, a satellite of the renowned Southwest Museum that's located across town.

PRACTICAL NOTES: The **Los Angeles County Museum of Art** (5905 Wilshire Boulevard, two blocks east of Fairfax Avenue, Miracle Mile; 323–857–6000; Web site: www.lacma.org) is open Monday, Tuesday, and Thursday, noon to 8:00 P.M.; Friday until 9:00 P.M.; Saturday and Sunday, 11:00 A.M. to 8:00 P.M.; closed Wednesdays, Thanksgiving, and Christmas. Admission for adults is about $7.00; seniors, $5.00. Admission is free on the second Tuesday of the month. All public areas and galleries are handicap accessible, and rest rooms have special facilities. Photography, including video recording, is permissible in many galleries without the use of flash or tripods. Paid parking is available in an adjacent structure and across the street at Wilshire and Spaulding. The **Craft and Folk Art Museum** (5814 Wilshire Boulevard, Miracle Mile; 323–937–5544) is open Tuesday, Wednesday, and Friday, noon to 5:00 P.M.; Thursday noon to

116

9:00 P.M.; and Saturday. 10:00 A.M. to 4:00 P.M. Adult admission is $3.50; admission is free Thursday from 5:00 P.M. to 9:00 P.M. and every first Tuesday. The **Southwest Museum at LACMA West** (6067 Wilshire Boulevard at Fairfax Avenue; 323–933–4510) is open daily, 9:00 A.M. to 8:00 P.M. Admission is $5.00.

DAY ONE: Morning

Because LACMA doesn't open until noon (weekdays) or 11:00 A.M. (weekends), make the first stop of the day just a few blocks north of Wilshire Boulevard at **Farmers Market** (6333 West Third Street at Fairfax; 323–933–9211) for coffee and fresh-baked pastries. A Los Angeles institution, Farmers Market has been around since the 1930s. It started out as a cooperative where local farmers could sell their produce, but today the permanent setup includes dozens of vendors selling food, produce, candy, household items, and souvenirs. You can find just about everything here, from fresh fish and fruit to gooey cinnamon rolls and intricately braided challah bread to spicy gumbo and English toffee. The best strategy is to first circle the stands to find what you want. Then find seats beneath an umbrella or awning, and while one of you holds the seats, the other can go off to get the food. Local residents from the surrounding neighborhoods, many of them immigrants often speaking foreign languages, rub elbows with tourists (the cameras and fanny packs give them away) in a never-ending parade of people.

Romance

AT A GLANCE

* Begin the day with breakfast at one of the little restaurants or food vendors at **Farmers Market** (6333 West Third Street at Fairfax Avenue; 323–933–9211). Then let art and culture be your guides and spend the day exploring Museum Row on Wilshire Boulevard in the Miracle Mile district.

* The **Los Angeles County Museum of Art**, LACMA (5905 Wilshire Boulevard; 323–857–6000; www.lacma.org), has exceptional collections of art from Asia and America. Next door, in a historical 1930s building, the **Southwest Museum at LACMA West** (6067 Wilshire Boulevard at Fairfax Avenue; 323–933–4510), a satellite location of the city's oldest museum, the art and culture of Native America is on display.

* Take a lunch break at **Callender's Wilshire** (5773 Wilshire Boulevard; 323–937–7952; moderate), then cross Wilshire for a stop at the **Craft and Folk Art Museum** (5814 Wilshire Boulevard; 323–937–5544). Continue museum hopping at the **Carole & Barry Kaye Museum of Miniatures** (5900 Wilshire Boulevard; 323–937–6464) and the **Petersen Automotive Museum** (6060 Wilshire Boulevard at Fairfax Avenue; 323–930–2277).

Newshounds will find at **Sheltam's Fine Periodicals** a mountain of domestic and international newspapers, the entertainment trades, and rows of art magazines. After breakfast, walk over to **Antique Alley,** a long, thin building on the northwest outskirts of the market area. Kitsch may occupy the low rung on the art ladder, but Antique Alley gets a top rung on the kitsch ladder: Roy Rogers lunch boxes, Bakelite bracelets, snow domes commemorating the Seattle World's Fair, and corner after corner filled with knickknacks, clothing, and furniture from decades past.

To reach **LACMA** (5905 Wilshire Boulevard; 323–857–6000) from the Farmer's Market, drive south on Fairfax Avenue to Wilshire and turn east. You'll find pay parking in an adjacent structure in the lot across the street (at Spaulding; $5.00) or on the street (but pay attention to posted parking restrictions). A 1986 addition to the museum added the monumental entrance portal and the high, narrow stairway (there's an elevator inside the portal to the right). The complex of buildings, five in all, makes up the largest museum west of Chicago, housing artworks spanning the history of art from ancient time to the present day. LACMA is too big to take in completely in one day, but taking an afternoon to wander through it with someone you're close to, sharing thoughts and feelings about one piece of art or another, can be a deeply bonding experience. Exactly where you go in the museum and what you see is strictly up to the two of you. Here are some of the highlights of the collection to help you formulate a plan of action:

In the **Ahmanson Building,** the collection of American art from the eighteenth and nineteenth centuries includes works by John Singleton Copley (*Portrait of a Lady,* 1771), Rembrandt Peale, Winslow Homer (*The Cotton Pickers,* 1876), and Mary Cassatt. Also in the Ahmanson are collections from ancient Egypt (a gilded wood statue of Osiris dating from 1500 B.C.), Greece, Rome, and Persia; pre-Columbian art; textiles and costumes; decorative arts; and European paintings and sculpture from the early fourteenth through late-nineteenth centuries, including Bellini's *Madonna and Child* (1465), El Greco's *The Apostle Saint Andrew* (1600), and Rembrandt's *Landscape with Dunes* (1649). The Chinese art collection spans 3,000 years; the Indian art collection is the most comprehensive outside India.

In the **Hammer Building,** look for the photography of Stieglitz, Laszlo Moholy-Nagy, and Eileen Cowin, as well as prints and drawings (including works by Van Gogh, Toulouse-Lautrec, Modigliani, Gauguin, Picasso, Matisse, and Stuart Davis), German Expressionist prints and drawings, and late nineteenth-century European art on the second floor. Among the Impressionists and Post-Impressionists, you'll find works by

Degas, Pissarro, Renoir, and Cezanne. The Museum Shop is located off the main plaza in the Hammer Building.

The **Anderson Building,** which fronts Wilshire Boulevard, opened in 1986 to accommodate the museum's burgeoning collection of twentieth-century art. Here you'll find George Braque's *Still Life with Violins* (1914), works by Picasso, Magritte, Rothko (*White Center,* 1957), Frank Stella, and others.

The **Pavilion for Japanese Art** houses an important collection of screen and scroll paintings, and more than 500 netsuke. Lighting is low in this gallery to suggest that illumination is filtered through *shoji* screens. A ramp descends from the top of the pavilion, a la the Guggenheim Museum in New York.

Recently the museum expanded its facility by transforming the former May Company department store building, a 1939 Streamline Moderne-style landmark one block to the west, into additional exhibition space called **LACMA West** (323-933-4510). Here you can expect to find major special exhibitions like "Van Gogh's Van Gogh: Masterpieces from the Van Gogh Museum, Amsterdam," which was the inaugural exhibit at LACMA West. (LACMA West maintains the same hours as the main museum, but there can be an additional ticket cost for special exhibitions.)

DAY ONE: *Afternoon*

When it's time for lunch, skip LACMA's so-called cafe (a cafeteria-style setup, plastic-wrapped food and Styrofoam cups). Instead walk across the adjacent park to Callenders' Wilshire on the corner of Wilshire and Curson Avenue. By exiting LACMA between the Ahmanson and Hammer Buildings into the park, you can walk by the **La Brea Tar Pits** and the **George C. Page Museum of La Brea Discoveries** (5801 Wilshire Boulevard; 323-934-7243). The Tar Pits, as everyone knows, is an Ice Age fossil site that has yielded magnificently preserved fossils of plants and animals, including a giant mammoth. You can backtrack to the Page Museum after lunch, if you wish, to watch bones being cleaned by technicians in a glass-walled paleontology lab.

LUNCH

The flagship restaurant of the Marie Callender chain, **Callender's Wilshire** (5773 Wilshire Boulevard; 323-937-7952; moderate) has an inviting brick-walled patio where you can sit under umbrellas while you have lunch. The menu features an updated and upgraded selection: hand-carved turkey on focaccia bread, grilled vegetable platter, grilled porto-bello burger, Santa Fe chicken pasta, cappuccino and latte, and microbrew beers.

This stretch of Wilshire Boulevard isn't called Museum Row for nothing. And after lunch you have a choice of which of four other museums to visit.

Right across the street from Callender's is the intimate **Craft and Folk Art Museum** (5814 Wilshire Boulevard, Miracle Mile; 323-937-5544). A single gallery serves as the exhibition space for rotating shows from the permanent

Gifts of Love

Be sure to go into the museum shops at LACMA and CAFAM, where you'll find jewelry, glassware, books, scarves, toys, and note cards. When my friend Dave and his wife, Judy, visit a museum, they give each other fifteen minutes to shop for a small gift for each other and a spending limit of $15. On their last visit to LACMA, Judy bought Dave two art magnets for the refrigerator ("because he likes to stand in front of the fridge with the door open and memorize the contents," she says). Dave wisely went a bit over budget and surprised Judy with a necklace of Venetian glass beads.

collection of masks, textiles, tools, basketry, instruments, pottery, toys, and other everyday objects from around the world. The limited exhibition space may seem constricting, but it also promotes informality and interaction among visitors that's hard to come by in other stuffier museum environments. While we were looking at photographs of women in southern India decorating the ground in front of their homes with intricate designs each morning, we met an Indian couple from the same region who explained more about the unique custom than any exhibition signage could have communicated.

On the same side of the street and down the block, at Ogden Drive, is the **Carole & Barry Kay Museum of Minatures** (5900 Wilshire Boulevard; 323-937-6464), a pint-size world of world landmarks, like the Vatican; historical figures, like America's First Ladies; and a turn-of-the-century soda fountain. It's open Tuesday through Saturday, 10:00 A.M. to 5:00 P.M., and Sunday, 11:00 A.M. to 5:00 P.M. Admission is $7.50.

If automobiles, motorcyles, automotive history, and LA car culture pique your interest, then walk one more block west to **Petersen Automotive Museum** (6060 Wilshire Boulevard at Fairfax Avenue; 323-930-2277). This entertaining and informative museum is open Tuesday through Sunday, 10:00 A.M. to 6:00 P.M. Admission is $7.00.

The most recent arrival on Museum Row is the **Southwest Museum at LACMA West** (6067 Wilshire Boulevard at Fairfax Avenue; 323-933-4510), a satellite facility of the Southwest Museum, LA's oldest museum, which is located across town in Mt. Washington. The Southwest Museum is renowned as one of the nation's finest collections of Native American art. But its Mount Washington location, with its vast holdings, had been bursting at the seams for years. The 8,000-square-foot satellite location on Museum Row allows the museum to present exhibitions of nineteenth-century Pueblo and Navajo rugs and textiles and other objects that have never been publically displayed. Designed to suggest the interior of an adobe shelter, the Southwest Museum at LACMA West is well worth a visit, a lovely way to wrap up the day on Museum Row.

For More Romance

On the weekends, LACMA offers ongoing series of free outdoor jazz concerts (Friday evenings), film screenings (Friday and Saturday evenings), and chamber music concerts (Sunday afternoons). Call the museum for schedule and ticket information.

Beside the Garden Wall
HUNTINGTON LIBRARY, ART COLLECTIONS, AND BOTANICAL GARDENS IN SAN MARINO

It's been called "the best place to kiss" in Los Angeles. And that it may be—exquisite gardens, flower-decked bowers, and benches tucked away in shady seclusion offer innumerable spots to steal a kiss. A couple I know, Liza and Gregory, visited the Huntington on their first date and later became engaged here when Gregory proposed to Liza in the Rose Garden Tea Room.

But it's also the combination of treasures found at the Huntington Library, Art Collections, and Botanical Gardens that makes this place such a special destination. Three art galleries and a library compose this magnificent cultural institution, showcasing a collection of rare books and manuscripts, and British, French, and American art. Then there are the 150 acres of botanical gardens and sweeping lawns. An oasis of art and culture —that's about as neat a description of the Huntington as you'll come up with—tucked away in the exclusive residential suburb San Marino.

The Huntington is a calendar of color—something is always in bloom. Whether your idea of a perfect date includes discussing the romance of Shakespeare's plays, admiring the pastoral playfulness of eighteenth-century French tapestries, or just walking hand in hand down a garden path, the Huntington has it all.

PRACTICAL NOTES: A romantic afternoon at the Huntington wouldn't be complete without English tea in the **Rose Garden Tea Room** (626–683–8131; inexpensive). Because the tearoom is very popular, especially on weekends, call a few days in advance to make reservations. Ask to be seated in the Herb Room, the smaller—and much quieter—back room, where you can linger over finger sandwiches and miniature sweets while you sip your tea. Tea is served Tuesday through Friday, noon to 4:30 P.M.; Saturday and Sunday, 10:45 A.M. to 4:30 P.M.

The **Huntington Library, Art Collections, and Botanical Gardens** (1151 Oxford Road, San Marino; 626–405–2100 or 626–405–2141) is open to the public Tuesday through Friday from noon (10:30 A.M. summer) to 4:30 P.M., and Saturday and Sunday from 10:30 A.M. to 4:30 P.M. Admission is $8.50 for adults. (Admission is free to all visitors on the first Thursday of every month.) Docent-guided tours are offered at 1:00 P.M. and as posted, Tuesday through Sunday. Self-guided tour brochures are 50 cents. Because the Huntington is not immediately accessible to any freeway exit, it's best to call for directions.

As perfect as the place is for picnics, visitors are not allowed to bring food onto the grounds. Nor are pets allowed. But do bring a small blanket to spread out under a tree on the lawn, bottled water (not permitted

Romance
AT A GLANCE

✶ Before you begin your visit to the Huntington, stop at **Julienne** (2649 Mission Street; San Marino; 626–441–2299; moderate), an excellent little bistro, for a light, fluffly breakfast omelette. Then while away the rest of the day at the **Huntington Library, Art Collections, and Botanical Gardens** (1151 Oxford Road, San Marino; 626–405–2100, –2141), with its acres of gardens, rare books and manuscripts, fine art, and teahouse restaurants.

✶ Start in the library, where you'll find such treasures as a fifteenth-century copy of Chaucer's Canterbury Tales, an early copy of the Magna Carta, and one of the world's few surviving Gutenberg Bibles printed on vellum. Then after a turn around the **Rose Garden,** where there are more than 1,500 varieties represented, have tea and sandwiches in the **Rose Garden Tea Room** (626–683–8131; moderate).

✶ Later stroll along a hillside pathway above the **Japanese Garden** and explore the jungle and desert gardens. Along the way feel free to pause for a rest under a shady tree or on one of the benches dappled by sunlight. Make your way back to **Main Gallery** for a look at the two most well-known paintings in the art galleries: Thomas Gainsborough's Blue Boy and Thomas Lawrence's Pinkie.

in the library or galleries), sunscreen, a camera, and perhaps a small pair of binoculars for bird-watching. Because you'll want to walk around as much of the estate as possible, wear comfortable walking shoes.

DAY ONE: *Morning*

BREAKFAST

It's worth arriving early—no later than 9:00 A.M. on a Saturday morning —at **Julienne** (2649 Mission Street, San Marino; 626-441-2299; moderate) for a cozy breakfast on the colonnaded small patio. Inside the tiny bistro a huge floral arrangement on the bakery counter competes with an antlered trophy head on the wall for attention. But no one's really paying attention to the interesting but eclectic decor, anyway, because they're too busy reading a book or the newspaper or chatting with their partners. The omelettes, particularly, taste heavenly no matter where you sit. They're light and fluffy and accompanied by roasted rosemary potatoes and the signature toasted raisin bread. You'll also find quiche, crepes, and golden French toast on the menu. Proper linen napkins and sturdy flatware add a classy touch. Open Monday through Friday, 7:00 A.M. to 3:30 P.M.; Saturday and Sunday from 8:00 A.M. to 4:30 P.M.

From whichever direction you approach the Huntington, you'll pass through one of the most exclusive residential suburbs in the Los Angeles area, San Marino. Drive through the neighborhoods surrounding the Huntington if you wish to take in the fine homes and landscaping. Don't worry about getting lost—all roads in the area eventually will lead you to the right place.

The Huntington was the estate of Henry E. Huntington, a railroad and real estate magnate. Also a lifelong book collector, he amassed a collection of British and French art after marrying his second wife, Arabella, in 1913, when they were both in their early sixties. The couple made careful plans for the use of their collections and property after their deaths, and the institution was opened in 1928, following Arabella's death in 1924 and Henry's in 1927.

When finally you do arrive at the Huntington, and after you've parked your car and found your way to the entrance pavilion, be sure to purchase one of the self-guided tour brochures for 50 cents. The tour outlined in the brochure takes only ninety minutes—hardly a romantic or leisurely enough pace to really enjoy all the Huntington has to offer. But the outlined tour serves nicely as a basic overview of a route to follow. There's a lot to see in the library, galleries, and gardens, and although attendants are available to answer some questions, you might want to go into the bookstore and buy the illustrated guide. It's descriptive and full of photographs, yet lightweight and easy to carry. Smaller pamphlets describing the collections are also available in the bookstore, the entrance pavilion, and the galleries (50 cents each).

Take a moment while you're at the entrance portico to get your bearings, or step out onto the terrace lawn to take in the grounds and buildings. Ahead and below are the Palm and Desert Gardens. To the right are the library; the art galleries; the Shakespeare, Rose, and Japanese Gardens; and the teahouse. Make a mental note about the time you've already reserved for tea so you can plan your visit accordingly.

As you take in the expansive vista, consider the effect Henry Huntington had on Southern California. He saw the potential for the area's growth and developed an efficient, inexpensive interurban railway system known as the Red Cars. Much of the subsequent growth of the city and surrounding areas can be attributed to the railway.

The permanent exhibition room in the **Huntington Library** is softly lighted to protect the delicate books and manuscripts on display. Dark paneling covers the walls. Look up and notice the gallery, where the walls are lined with bookshelves with glass doors. The first exhibit you encounter is a beautiful illuminated manuscript (circa 1410) of Chaucer's *The Canterbury Tales*.

Before the development of Gutenberg's printing press in the fifteenth century, all books and documents in Europe were copied by hand. To add beauty to manuscripts, artists in the Middle Ages decorated the pages with miniature illustrations and embellished capital letters with gold leaf and brilliant colors. The gold leaf applied to a manuscript page gave rise to the term *illuminated manuscript*. The Huntington has several fine examples, including this version of *The Canterbury Tales*, known as the Ellesmere Chaucer. It's one of the best-preserved English literary manuscripts in the world. It was made within a decade or two of the poet's death, so it's the earliest complete copy of Chaucer's original text.

Two other important manuscripts on display are an early copy of the Magna Carta, which is the cornerstone of law in English-speaking countries, and a Gutenberg Bible, the first substantial book printed with mov-

Shall I Compare Thee to a Summer's Day?

Strolling through the Shakespeare Garden, which is in colorful bloom year-round, so many famous lines from Shakespeare's plays and sonnets come to mind. But none seems as appropriate as the lines from Sonnet 18:

> Shall I compare thee to a summer's day?
>   Thou art more lovely and more temperate:
> Rough winds do shake the darling buds of May,
>   And summer's lease hath all too short a date.
>
> Sometime too hot the eye of heaven shines,
>   And often is his gold complexion dimmed;
> And every fair from fair sometimes declines,
>   By chance or nature's changing course untrimmed.
>
> But thy eternal summer shall not fade,
>   Nor lose possession of that fair thou ow'st,
> Nor shall Death brag thou wand'rest in his shade,
>   When in eternal lines to time thou grow'st.
>
> So long as men can breathe or eyes can see,
> So long live this, and this gives life to thee.

able type in Europe in the mid-fifteenth century. Johannes Gutenberg, of Mainz, Germany, is credited as the inventor of printing in the West. The Huntington copy is one of the few surviving copies printed on vellum (animal skin), which makes it very rare, considering only between 160 and 180 were printed on vellum or paper to begin with.

Romance has been on the minds of all great writers at one time or another. Shakespeare wrote about the star-crossed lovers Romeo and Juliet, as well as lighter fare such as the romantic romp *Much Ado About Nothing*, in which the obstinate Benedick, a self-proclaimed bachelor, matches wits with the equally stubborn Beatrice. Try as they might—parrying with barbed comments to keep each other at arm's length—they prove no match for the power and mystery of the love that attracts them.

The Huntington's copy of the first edition of this comedy was printed about 1600. A first edition (1824) of Byron's famous poem about the libertine Don Juan is displayed near a handwritten poem (1793) by the Scotsman Robert Burns, who mourns a lost love. In a letter dated 1848, Charlotte Brontë discusses her great romantic novel *Jane Eyre*.

Just outside the library, an expanse of lawn, with its combination of greenery, flowering shrubs, and long lines of sculpture, is reminiscent of a seventeenth-century European garden. On a clear day the San Gabriel Mountains are visible in the distance from this lawn, called the **North Vista**. Bordering the North Vista is a camellia garden. A five- or ten-minute walk along narrow gravel paths that wind through flower-filled bowers under the protective canopy of ancient oaks can be a rewarding side trip. Dappled sunlight filters down onto wooden benches, tucked away in leafy seclusion under the trees. As you enter this garden, look for a small stone temple sheltering the nineteenth-century marble statue of *Cupid Blindfolding Youth*, a reminder that love is blind.

The **Rose Garden** is the floral embodiment of romance. Nearly 4,000 individual rose plants (some 1,500 different varieties) provide an irresistibly stimulating display, from mid-April right up to December. The oldest varieties date back to medieval and Renaissance times. Many of the roses even have romantic names: Secret Love, Careless Love, Sweet Surrender, and First Kiss. You can't pick them, of course, but as you sit under the lacy Montezuma cypress trees, you can revel in the colorful spectacle and take in the heady perfume of thousands of blossoms. Presiding over this garden, fittingly, is *Love, the Captive of Youth*, an eighteenth-century French statue depicting Cupid and his "captor," a beautiful young maiden. Set within a stone temple of love at the top of the garden, this enchanting pair is encircled by a bed of delicate peachy-white French Lace roses.

A stone walkway, trellised with climbing roses, leads from the statue of Cupid and his captor to the entrance of the **Japanese Garden,** which is guarded by two stone lion-dogs (male on the left, female on the right). As you walk down the steps to the terrace overlooking the garden, think how delighted Arabella Huntington must have been with this lovely garden, created for her as a gift from her then-future husband in 1912. A cosmopolitan New Yorker, Arabella was skeptical about the "wild west" of Southern California, and Henry hoped to please her with an exotic garden. With its moon bridge, koi pond, stone lanterns and pagodas, Japanese house, and Zen Garden on the hillside across the pond, it must have enchanted Arabella—just as it has delighted generations of visitors since. Perhaps Henry and Arabella took walks along the path on the hillside near the Japanese house, admiring the magnificent camellias and flowering plum trees. Even on a crowded weekend, it's a fairly quiet and idyllic spot to walk along and hold hands.

DAY ONE: *Afternoon*

LUNCH

The **Rose Garden Tea Room** (626–683–8131; moderate) is an altogether charming little two-room cottage where English tea is served. If you've asked to be seated in the Herb Room, the hostess will escort you through the main room, which is bright and cheerful (and on weekends fairly noisy), to the smaller and much quieter second room that looks out to the herb garden. A small basket of warm scones will be brought to your table, and you'll be given a choice of teas. At the back of the room, a buffet table is laden with an assortment of finger sandwiches—chicken and walnut, cucumber and cream cheese, open-faced salmon, watercress—fresh fruit, and miniature tarts and sweets. Don't be fooled by the diminutive size of the offerings. After scones, several finger sandwiches, sweets, and a pot of tea, you'll be quite satisfied and ready to explore the rest of the Huntington's gardens and galleries. (A cafeteria-style restaurant serving sandwiches and salads is connected to the tearoom if, later on, you require some further nourishment.)

From the tearoom retrace your steps through the Rose Garden and past the Japanese Garden. Follow the path down the hill toward the **Subtropical Garden,** one of the most colorful areas on the estate year-round, but especially during middle to late summer. As you walk along the path of the sloping garden, look off to the left toward the great lawn. You'll probably see couples and families resting in shady spots under the trees or sunning themselves on the lawn. Also visible is an eighteenth-century French marble statue, *Allegory of Louis XV Guided by Love*, set in a small stone temple.

You will come to the **Jungle Garden** next, with a series of lily ponds with water lilies, lotus flowers, koi fish, turtles, and ducks. The whoosh of water that you hear is the waterfall high on the slope above, cascading down over moss-covered stones through a lush growth of orchids, bromeliads, and ferns. A winding path leads up the slope toward the Beaux Arts Huntington mansion, where the main art galleries are located.

The mansion, once home to Henry and Arabella, now houses a distinguished collection of mostly British art from the eighteenth and early ninteenth centuries. Much of it may seem formal and stuffy by contemporary standards, but there are several highlights worth seeking out. In the North Passage, on the way to Main Gallery, look for a delightful collection of miniature portraits. Delicately painted on ivory and encircled with jewels, these were the ultimate tokens of affection from one eighteenth-century lover to another. Some of the miniatures include elaborate woven borders made from locks of hair.

The most famous paintings in the collection are in the **Main Gallery.** *Blue Boy,* painted by Thomas Gainsborough in 1770, is a portrait of the son of a successful hardware merchant who was a close friend of the artist's. Hanging directly opposite is *Pinkie,* the daughter of a wealthy plantation family in Jamaica, painted by Thomas Lawrence in 1794. Although the two paintings have long been popularly linked, there was never an association between the two works until they arrived together at the Huntington in the 1920s.

Perhaps the most charming painting in the collection is from mid-eighteenth-century France, Jean-Baptiste Greuze's *Young Knitter Asleep,* a tender portrait of a young girl who has fallen asleep while knitting in her chair. In another small gallery two scenes of Venice by the Italian painter Canaletto are typical of the small paintings collected as souvenirs by English gentry.

American art is the focus in the **Virginia Steele Scott Gallery of American Art,** where Mary Cassatt's *Breakfast in Bed* (1897) is one of the most eloquent of the painter's many Impressionist treatments of the mother-and-child theme. Lovers of fine wood craftwork will quickly notice the American Arts and Crafts furniture of the Pasadena architects Charles and Henry Greene.

As the afternoon winds down, you might want to make your way back toward the **Desert Garden** for a stroll through a startling and strangely beautiful Eden of cacti and other ribbed, spiny, and spiky desert plants.

There's one last stop to make as the day draws to a close. Beyond the North Vista, next to the orange grove, is the **mausoleum of Henry and Arabella.** The spot was a favorite location for the Huntingtons; the couple used to walk to the hillock during their evening strolls. It's said that on one of those strolls Arabella expressed her wish to be buried at that spot. Henry had John Russell Pope, one of America's foremost architects of the time, design the graceful structure. Pope modeled it on a double-colonnaded Greek temple, because it presents "a perfect front from every angle." Pope would later employ the same style in the construction of the Jefferson Memorial in Washington, D.C.

In many ways the Huntington stands as a testament to love, not just between Henry and Arabella, but also to the romance that has always inspired great art and literature. And the Huntington provides an unrivaled setting for contemplating the vicissitudes of love portrayed in art and literature, and for experiencing the joy of being with someone you love.

FOR MORE ROMANCE

This one-day itinerary could be combined easily with Itinerary 5, "Pasadena Pas de Deux."

Rainbow Gap Romance
TEMECULA VALLEY WINE COUNTRY

SOUTHERN CALIFORNIA HAS ITS OWN WINE COUNTRY, thanks to what's called the Rainbow Gap in the coastal mountains near Temecula, about 80 miles south of Los Angeles, off Interstate 15. The cool ocean breezes that blow through the gap help create a microclimate in the Temecula Valley that's ideal for growing premium wine grapes. It's also ideal for early morning hot air balloon rides, which have become one of the area's principal attractions. Temecula even has an annual balloon and wine festival, usually in April, to celebrate its signature attractions. Vineyards, citrus groves, and avocado trees drape the rolling hillsides of the valley, a dozen or more wineries have sprung up, golf courses have been built, and more people are discovering this spot as a convenient two-day destination.

PRACTICAL NOTES: When booking accommodations at Temecula Creek Inn ask about special packages, such as Wine Country Holiday, which is offered year-round and includes deluxe room; breakfast; a four-course, wine-pairing dinner; and a picnic lunch. There are also bicycle winery tour packages and golf packages, or the inn will help you customize your own package. Many of the wineries in the Temecula Valley offer special winemaker's dinners and Valentine's Day dinners, but these events tend to fill up fast. For more information and a free wine country map brochure listing the wineries, contact the **Temecula Valley Vinters Association** at

(909) 699–3626 or (800) 801–9463. Try to arrange your hot air balloon ride two or three months in advance, especially if you want to coordinate it with a particular date, such as a birthday or anniversary. For more general information about the Temecula Valley, the annual balloon and wine festival, and other events, contact the **Temecula Valley Chamber of Commerce** at (909) 676–5090 or visit the chamber's Web site: www.temecula.org.

Romance

AT A GLANCE

✳ *Book a room at the rustic **Temecula Creek Inn** (44501 Rainbow Canyon Road; 909–694–1000, 800–962–7335; $125–$195) for a weekend of wine tasting and hot air ballooning. Before or after you arrive at the hotel, visit several of the area's wineries for wine tasting.*

✳ *Bring along your own picnic lunch (call Bailey Wine Country Cafe in advance; 27644 Ynez Road at Rancho California; 909–676–9567) or set up a guided trail ride through the vineyards, with stops along the way to taste wine and have a picnic (JT's Winery Trail Rides and Gourmet Picnics; 909–302–0633 or 909–302–0728).*

✳ *In the evening, enjoy the polite informality of **Bailey Wine Country Cafe** (27644 Ynez Road at Rancho California; 909–676–9567; moderate for dinner), where you can match Temecula Valley wines with your food choices.*

✳ *The next morning, it's early to rise for a hot air balloon flight above the vineyards of Temecula (A Grape Escape Balloon Adventure, 909–698–9772). On descent and landing, there will be a champagne toast and a continental breakfast. After freshening up, spend the rest of the day exploring **Old Town Temecula**, with its many antique shops.*

DAY ONE: *Morning*

Nobody can prove the claim, but wine lovers will tell you that a wine tastes better if it's sampled in the region in which it is produced. There are about a dozen wineries dotting the vineyard-covered rolling hills of the Temecula Valley, so there are plenty of opportunities to test the theory (although a few of the wineries produce wines with grapes grown elsewhere in California). Most of the wineries have tasting rooms where for a small fee you can sample the winery's products, and of course you can purchase bottles of the wines. Tasting rooms generally open about 10:00 A.M.; the tasting fee should run no more than a few dollars. Some wineries have set up picnic areas, usually nothing more than a few picnic tables under a gazebo. A few wineries also offer tours of their facilities.

For a very memorable wine-country experience, consider a guided trail ride through the vineyards, with stops along the way to taste wines and have a picnic. Teri Herriott and Jayme Matheny, who own **JT's Winery Trail Rides and Gourmet Picnics** (909–302–0633 or 909–302–0728), will trailer in horses and meet the two of you at a predetermined location (usually at one of the wineries) at around 10:00 A.M. Before hitting the trail, you'll start off with a champagne toast, then ride a short while through the vineyards to the first winery. This is an easy ride, so even if you haven't been on horseback in years, you won't feel intimated. After wine tasting, you'll ride on to the next winery. Altogether you'll probably visit about three or four wineries, stop for a picnic lunch along the way, and return to your starting point three to five hours later. The cost of the trail ride and picnic lunch comes to about $150 per person.

If wine tasting and driving (or horseback riding) don't mix well for you, you can corral the horses and park the car and still have the chance to do some wine tasting. The **Temecula Shuttle** (909–695–9999, 888–464–9947) operates customized private limousine tours of the region. The price—about $52 an hour—includes the driver's gratuity. There's a four-hour minimum on Saturdays; three hours on weekdays and Sundays.

DAY ONE: *Afternoon*

LUNCH

If you saddle up with JT's Winery Trail Rides and Gourmet Picnics, Teri and Jayme will bring you to a spot in the vineyards they've scouted out for a picnic lunch. But don't expect paper plates and saran-wrapped sandwiches. Your picnic will be spread out on a table covered with a lovely picnic tablecloth, and you'll eat off china (if it's just the two of you or a small group) or nice plasticware. The fare might be baked Brie, roasted pork loin with chardonnay-mustard sauce, grilled polenta with sun-dried tomatoes, and a cobbler for dessert, or perhaps sausage-stuffed mushroom caps, salad with champagne vinaigrette, pesto chicken focaccia, and lemon bars and black walnut sorbet.

There are a couple of other lunchtime alternatives. One is the **Vineyard Terrace** cafe at Callaway Vineyard & Winery (32720 Rancho California; 909–676–4001; inexpensive). This outdoor cafe sits on a small hillside terrace overlooking the Callaway vineyards and serves salads and sandwiches. A second option is to call at least twenty-four hours in advance for a picnic lunch from **Bailey Wine Country Cafe** (27644 Ynez Road at Rancho California; 909–676–9567; inexpensive for lunch) to take with you as you drive through the wine country. The boxed lunches are named for wines: for example, the Riesling (chicken Caesar salad), the Sauvignon Blanc (pasta and fresh vegetables), the Chardonnay (chicken ravioli salad), and the Cabernet Sauvignon (sliced sirloin).

Even though the **Temecula Creek Inn** (44501 Rainbow Canyon Road; 909–694–1000 or 800–962–7335; $125–$195) is well known regionally as a golf resort—the inn has three nine-hole courses—nongolfers should find the inn's rustic atmosphere appealing as well. All of the eighty rooms and junior suites have golf course views, but the Shady Knoll building (rooms 110 through 129) seems to offer the most rustic, tree-shaded setting. Rooms are large and comfortably furnished, with a king-size bed or two queen-size beds. Amenities, depending on the room you choose, may include a hair dryer, coffeemaker with fresh beans to grind (grinder included), makeup mirror, and thick terry robes or bath towels. Throughout the inn pottery shards and other relics of the region's native populations have been mounted in shadowboxes and displayed on the walls.

DAY ONE: *Evening*

DINNER

With all those lovely vineyards just a few miles away, it seems a shame that **Bailey Wine Country Cafe** is stuck in a corner of the parking lot of a shopping center (27644 Ynez Road at Rancho California; 909–676–9567; moderate for dinner). Don't be put off by the unromantic setting, however, because the restaurant has been handsomely decorated to create a contemporary and casual ambience. Besides that, somebody is paying attention where it counts—in the kitchen. Ask about the day's fresh fish; it might be grilled ahi, drizzled with a teriyaki-mango glaze and paired with snow peas and a confetti of orzo, tomato, and cilantro. Other choices from the menu might be chicken ravioli tossed with a champagne-tarragon cream sauce or a hearty New York steak sandwich topped with grilled onions, mushrooms, and melted Stilton cheese. Servers of course will help you match Temecula Valley wines with your food choices (by the way, you'll be pleasantly surprised by the very reasonable prices on the wine list).

Take advantage of the fact that there's not much to do in Temecula after dark and return to the inn after dinner. There's entertainment in the lounge at the inn on Friday and Saturday nights. But remember, tomorrow's activity—the hot air balloon ride—lifts off quite early.

DAY TWO: *Morning*

If you've never witnessed a new day dawning as you float in a hot air balloon above vineyards and citrus groves, an amazing experience awaits you. Sure, you've got to get up even before the crack of dawn, because early morning is the best time for hot air balloon flights over the Temecula Valley. The early wake-up call, however, is a minor annoyance compared with the exhilaration of floating 2,500 feet above the awakening world below. You will receive precise instructions about where and when (by 6:00 A.M.) your balloon flight will depart and how to dress when you call **A Grape Escape Balloon Adventure** to arrange the balloon flight (909–698–9772; standard rate of $130 per person; private flights available). But here's an idea of how it all works.

Rusty Manning, an FAA-certified balloon pilot, and his crew will arrive before you do to inflate A Grape Escape's seven-story balloon by using fans to blow heated air into the balloon. You can help, if you wish, probably by holding the "skirt" of the balloon open as the air is blown in. Once the balloon is properly inflated, you and several other passengers will climb into the wicker gondola of the balloon. Lifting off in a hot air balloon is not like flying in a plane or even ascending in an elevator. There's hardly a sensation of motion; the Earth seems to drift away below you, rather than your being lifted off the ground. Once aloft, drifting on the currents of air of the new day, there is virtually no sense of motion, and aside from the periodic whoosh of the burner and the conversation of passengers, the world is silent. A bird may

On Cloud Nine

Rusty and Cherise Manning, owners of A Grape Escape Balloon Adventure, report that one young man proposed to his girlfriend in the hot air balloon. After the balloon lifted off the ground, the Grape Escape crew turned over a sign on the ground that spelled out will you marry me? The answer, happily, was "yes."

fly by, other balloons may be in sight, but for the next hour, you're suspended in a special world of peace and quiet high above the vineyards and citrus groves of the Temecula Valley. Down below a chase truck monitors your flight and will greet you when you descend.

On landing, the pilot leads passengers in a traditional balloonist prayer: *The winds have welcomed you with softness, the sun has blessed you with his warm hands, you have flown so high and so well that God joins you in laughter and sets you gently back into the loving arms of Mother Earth.* A champagne toast follows. While the crew is packing up the balloon, a light breakfast of bagels and cream cheese, fruit, and Danish pastries is served to passengers, after which the chase truck returns you to the starting point.

After having been awakened so early in the morning for the balloon ride, most people like to return to the hotel to shower and change clothes. Checkout time is noon for the Temecula Creek Inn, so you may have to pack and check out before heading to Thornton Winery for brunch or lunch and Old Town Temecula for an afternoon of antiques shopping.

DAY TWO: *Afternoon*

LUNCH

Cafe Champagne at Thornton Winery, with its dusty rose and wine color scheme, is the prettiest little restaurant in Temecula (32575 Rancho California Road; 909–699–0088; moderate). On Sunday from 11:00 A.M. to 3:30 P.M., an elegant brunch is served at the cafe, which is very popular, so it's wise to make reservations. Perched on a small hilltop, the cafe has an adjacent patio dining area, even its own tiny herb garden. Brunch might include chicken almond crepes; an omelette of Black Forest ham, potato, and green onion; or a croissant filled with crab and shrimp. A glass of sparkling wine is included. After brunch you can join one of the hourly tours of the winery (weekends only) or tastings (daily).

If you'd prefer to keep things a bit simpler, you'll come upon several little restaurants as you walk along Front Street in Old Town Temecula. None are fancy, which is part of the appeal. A few are located in historic buildings. The **Bank of Mexican Food,** for instance, occupies what used to be the First Bank of Temecula, built in 1914 (28645 Front Street; 909–676–6160; inexpensive). Inside, the ceiling is wood-beamed. The menu holds no surprises—tostadas, tamales, enchiladas—but the Bank is usually recommended by locals.

One hundred and fifty years ago, stagecoaches made biweekly stops in Temecula, delivering mail and passengers to the outpost. There's still something of an Old West feeling to Front Street, the main drag in historic Old Town Temecula. Many of the old wooden buildings along the street date from the last century. They now house dozens of "antiques" dealers. More than one shop sports *Nana* or *Gramma* or *Grandma* in its name. Predictably, quality varies from shop to shop, and prices can be high, especially for some highly collectible items. But it's possible to spend hours browsing the shops located on Front Street and along side streets as well.

Besides winemakers, balloonists, and golfers, Temecula also attracts artists. **Temecula Art Gallery** (42031 Main Street, upper level; 909–693–1979) represents several local artists. Randy Holland, who owns Temecula Art Gallery, has made arrangements with some of the artists to open up their studios to interested collectors and visitors. The artists who have agreed to show visitors their studios live within a thirty-minute drive of Old Town Temecula. These visits must be prearranged by calling the Temecula Art Gallery and are intended for people who are interested in purchasing an artist's work.

One of the advantages of visiting a spot like Temecula is that besides having created happy memories of a romantic getaway with your partner, you can take a bit of the place back home with you. With at least a bottle or two of Temecula Valley wine packed away as souvenirs, you can uncork the spirit sometime in the future.

FOR MORE ROMANCE

During its spring (April and May) and fall (September and October) jazz series, Thornton Winery presents Sunday evening jazz concerts on its terrace. Depending on the artist, tickets run between $30 and $36 per person. Romantically speaking, Thornton's Gourmet Jazz Supper Package makes the most sense: Typically a three-course meal and a private table for the concert cost about $75–$95 a person. Call Thornton for more information at (909) 699–3021. Extend your stay by a day for spa treatments or massages at **Murrieta Day Spa**, in Murrieta, about a fifteen-minute drive north of Temecula. The spa offers limousine service to and from the Temecula Creek Inn and has several different packages available. Call the spa at (909) 677–8111 for more information.

When You Wish Upon a Star: DISNEYLAND

AUGHTER, GOOD TIMES, EVEN THE CHANCE to act a bit silly— it's all part of love and romance, otherwise, what's the point? Disneyland is one of the fun times, because "the happiest place on Earth" is as entertaining for adults to visit as it is for the kids. From the sophisticated Hook's Pointe & Wine Cellar at the Disneyland Hotel to the reserved seating on the Dessert Balcony at the nighttime *Fantasmic!* spectacular, there are plenty of opportunities for grown-up fun in the Magic Kingdom.

PRACTICAL NOTES: The **Disneyland Hotel** is the logical place to stay for many reasons. Special value-priced packages that include accommodations ($270–$503 for two nights, for example) and park admission (individual adult admission alone to Disneyland is currently $63 for a two-day passport) are a good value. The resort aspects of the hotel offer additional opportunities to share good times. Book a room in the Sierra Tower, preferably on one of the concierge floors (ninth, tenth, or eleventh floors) overlooking the new NeverLand pool complex. The standard rooms are the same as elsewhere in the hotel—spacious and comfortably furnished—but the $65 upgrade for the Concierge Floor buys you access to a concierge lounge on the eleventh floor, with its view of the park. A generous continental breakfast is served in the lounge each morning from 6:30 to 10:00 A.M. (a great way to beat morning crowds in the restaurants); hors d'oeuvres and wine are served in the afternoon between 5:00 and 7:00 P.M. The environment is definitely more grown-up, and the child-crying decibel factor is considerably reduced. Whichever floor or tower you choose (there are three towers: Marina, Sierra, and Bonita), you can always order romantic amenities like champagne, roses, or chocolate-dipped strawberries to make your visit special. Hotel guests can also have purchases made in the park delivered, free of charge, to the hotel instead of having to lug them around all day.

A few things to keep in mind when planning a visit to Disneyland (recorded information, 714–781–4565; Web site: www.disneyland.com): The park is busy year-round—it draws millions of visitors annually. The big crush is summer, of course, and then again during Christmas. But from September to Christmas, things quiet down quite a bit, and this might be the time to plan a weekend visit. The park's entertainment operates only on weekends during the off-months. One resource worth investing in to help you plan a Disneyland visit is Birnbaum's *Disneyland: The Official Guide*. It's comprehensive, updated annually, and, frankly, invaluable when it comes to planning a visit.

Romance

AT A GLANCE

✳ *Check reality at the door of your room overlooking the new Never Land pool at the* **Disneyland Hotel** *(1150 West Cerritos Avenue, Anaheim; 714–956–6425 or 714–778–6600). Arrive at the park in the afternoon and cruise the Rivers of America aboard the* **Mark Twain steamboat.** *Then enjoy a live stage performance, a musical show based on one of the Disney animated feature films.*

✳ *Explore the renovated hotel complex and make plans to have dinner at one of its restaurants—***Hook's Pointe & Wine Cellar** *(moderate) or* **Granville's Steak House** *(expensive). Or return to the park for dinner at the atmospheric* **Blue Bayou** *(moderate) in New Orleans Square. You should return to the park anyway at night to see the spectacular pyrotechnical effects, fiber optics, and lasers of the* **Fantasmic!** *show from your reserved seat on the balcony of the Disney Gallery.*

✳ *The next day, after breakfast, enjoy some of the old-time favorite attractions at Disneyland—the Pirates of the Caribbean, Haunted Mansion, Jungle Cruise. Or check out the new look and entertainment in* **Tomorrowland.** *Before it's time to go home, stop by* **New Orleans Square** *and let one of the artists capture you and your partner in a pastel-chalk caricature sketch.*

DAY ONE: *Afternoon*

Check-in time at the Disneyland Hotel (1150 West Cerritos Avenue, Anaheim; 714-956-6425 or 714-778-6600) isn't until 3:00 P.M. Surely you don't want to wait until then to arrive to begin your Disneyland-for-grownups itinerary. So arrive earlier in the day, park at the hotel, check in, and leave your bags with a bellhop. When you return later in the afternoon to register, your bags should be waiting for you in your room. The hotel is connected to the Magic Kingdom by the Monorail, which arrives and departs every few minutes from the hotel's Travelport. Complimentary trams to Disneyland's main gate also leave from Travelport every fifteen to twenty minutes. Admission Passports to Disneyland may be purchased at the Monorail Station or at the front desk of the hotel in Marina Tower.

Leave the gritty reality of the world behind as you enter Disneyland through the main gate or as you step off the Monorail in the new Tomorrowland. For the next two days, at least, you can forget about adult worries like civil wars in Africa, crime in the streets, and political muckraking and instead plunge headlong into a make-believe world where everybody's dreams come true. And when your eyes light up in wonder at the thrilling fireworks display or you shriek in feigned fright as a ride plunges you into momentary darkness, you share a lot with each other about who you are and what your fantasies may be. (*Note:* The sequence of activities in this chapter, as in all the other chapters, is just a suggestion for a way to organize your time. By no means are all of Disneyland's themed areas or attractions included, so you should feel especially free to modify this itinerary to suit your own preferences.)

Decide on dinner plans as soon as you arrive. If the Blue Bayou restaurant in New Orleans Square in the park is your choice, as it was ours, then walk over to the restaurant and make reservations as soon as you get into the park. The hotel concierge may also be able to make the reservation for you. (The Blue Bayou is very popular, and on busy weekends it may not be possible to obtain a reservation.) For the hotel's fine dining restaurant, Granville's Steak House, reservations are also necessary and should be made right away.

The *Mark Twain* steamboat, one of Disneyland's original attractions and now more than forty-two years old, is still chugging along Frontierland's Rivers of America. The paddle wheeler was built to five-eighths scale; nevertheless, it's a grand presence on the waterway, steaming around Tom Sawyer Island. Take advantage of this fourteen-minute ride to get away from the crowds, enjoy the breeze, and lose yourselves for a few minutes in the re-created Missouri frontier of the past century. Then walk around to the rafts that ferry visitors across the waterway to **Tom Sawyer Island.** If you ran along the island's paths as a kid, the place might seem a bit smaller today, but now you're likely to be strolling and holding hands, so you won't mind. The Suspension Bridge wobbles and heaves and is still fun to cross.

Check the performance schedule for the current live show. (Shows are scheduled five times daily during the summer and Friday through Sunday the rest of the year.) Disney's live stage extravaganzas guarantee a dazzling display of singing, dancing, and special effects. The high caliber of performance should impress you.

By now it should be time to settle into your room at the hotel. Get your hand stamped as you leave the park for reentry later on. If you haven't already surveyed the grounds of the hotel, you may be surprised because the Disneyland Hotel is huge—three towers, more than a thousand rooms, sixty acres, a lap pool for adults, a waterfall you walk under, the new Never Land pool with its water slide and winding "shoreline," restaurants, and shopping arcades. If fact, the hotel complex has been undergoing several changes recently as construction continues on the new California Adventure park and entertainment district (scheduled to open in 2001). Your standard room will be comfortably furnished, most likely with two double beds. If you requested and received a room in the Sierra Tower, you'll have the best view of the Never Land pool below.

DAY ONE: *Evening*

DINNER

Hook's Pointe & Wine Cellar (moderate) is new, part of the renovation of the hotel complex. The decor relies on a rich mix of deep blues, dark wood, and brass, and the addition of a display kitchen lends a contemporary note. The revamped menu features mesquite-grilled entrees, such as cognac-marinated steak with veal glaze and fire-roasted corn, Chilean sea bass with citrus sauce and fried beets, and chicken with sweet pea risotto.

You might want to begin the evening in the wine cellar with a glass of wine or ask to do a "Wine Flight" tasting. For the tasting, you choose among one of five groups of wines—chardonnay, cabernet sauvignon, California white, California red, or California sparkling. Four wines from the one group you choose are brought in two-ounce samples for you to taste. You and your partner may taste the same group of wines, but it's more fun to each taste a different group.

For me, however, it's the fireflies flickering in the dark that makes **Blue Bayou** (Royal Street, New Orleans Square next to Pirates of the Caribbean ride; moderate) my favorite restaurant in the park. Heavy on atmosphere—a terrace on a bayou, Spanish moss hanging from a simulated weeping willow tree, Japanese lanterns (for some reason) strung overhead, make-believe stars twinkling in the sky, and an amusing symphony of frog croaks and background jazz music—Blue Bayou features Cajun and Louisiana-style food. The spice has been turned up a bit in some of the dishes, like the jambalaya, reflecting a more authentic take on the theme. Crab cakes, chicken étouffé, blackened steak, and barbecued shrimp are also featured. Ask for a table on the moonlit lagoon to savor the full effect.

Granville's Steak House (expensive) is the Disneyland Hotel's fine dining restaurant. Tables are set with fine china and silverware, tablecloths, and fan-folded napkins. Lighting is soft, and etched-glass-front cabinets hold fine cognacs and brandies. The menu, completely a la carte, consists mainly of meat—steak, prime rib, veal, lamb—but includes some fish, lobster, and chicken. A waiter will "present" the menu by wheeling over a small wooden sideboard with a marble top. Cuts of meat representing about half the day's entrees are displayed on the marble. After the presentation, the waiter will hand you a small printed menu card to help you remember what's what. Later, a two-tiered cart, laden with desserts like a twenty-layer chocolate castle cake and peanut butter pie, will be rolled over.

Disneyland is never more romantic than after dark, when the lights come on and the stars, real or fiber-optic, come out. One of the most magical of the theme lands at night is **Fantasyland**. A lot of adults skip Fantasyland altogether, thinking it's just for the little ones. But there's a timelessness and, therefore, agelessness to this "land," where village lanes twist around storybook houses with chimneys and weather vanes. **Sleep-**

ing Beauty's Castle, illuminated in a wash of colored lights, dominates the nighttime landscape at this end of the park. It's as enchanting a sight now as it was more than forty years ago when the drawbridge was lowered to welcome the first guests.

Besides Sleeping Beauty's Castle, **King Arthur's Carrousel,** and **Peter Pan's Flight** (for a skyful of tiny fiber-optic stars and a twinkling miniature model of nineteenth-century London), wander into **Snow White's Grotto,** a quiet corner tucked between the moat on the eastern side of the castle and the Matterhorn. Standing beside the waterfall, while a recording of "I'm Wishing" (sung by Adriana Caselotti, the original voice of Snow White), plays in the background, who could resist tossing a coin into the pool at the bottom of the cascade and making a wish?

(Here's a bit of adult trivia: *Forced perspective* is a set designer's technique for making something seem taller than it is. The technique was employed on Sleeping Beauty's castle, Main Street buildings, and the Matterhorn. The first floor of a structure is designed in seven-eighths scale, the second in five-eighths, and the third in half scale.)

Disneyland always gets high marks for the technical wizardry used to achieve the special effects. One of the most impressive displays is *Fantasmic!*, the nighttime sound and light spectacular that's performed on the water at Rivers of America. A dazzling spectacle of pyrotechnics, lasers, fog, fiber optics, live performances, and giant props makes *Fantasmic!* an extravanganza of special effects. First, Mickey Mouse appears at the tip of Tom Sawyer's Island and uses the magical powers of his own imagination to create fabulous wonders, such as giant water fountains, enormous flowers, and fantasy creatures. Then a band of Disney villains, such as Maleficent from Sleeping Beauty, invades Mickey's imaginary world, turning dreams into nightmares. Mickey must overcome these villains with his powers of goodness, which, of course, he does quite handily. Mickey conjures up his visions on three giant mist screens, which measure 30-feet high by 50-feet wide and on which film images are projected.

The best spot for watching *Fantasmic!* is from the balcony of the Disney Gallery, which is right above the entrance to Pirates of the Caribbean. Seating is very limited, expensive ($30 per person for a seat and dessert buffet), and by reservation only (make reservations at the Guest Relations window at the main entrance to the park). If you can't book a seat on the Dessert Balcony, the next best option is the area in front of the French Market restaurant or Pirates of the Caribbean in New Orleans Square. Don't take up positions too close to water's edge, especially on the sides, because you surely will get wet when jets of water are sprayed high into the air. The show is performed twice nightly during the summer and on holidays.

After witnessing the high-tech wonders of *Fantasmic!*, a simple fireworks display may seem a bit pedestrian. But *Fantasy in the Sky,* which starts around 9:45 on summer evenings, is the kind of rousing, old-fashioned extravaganza that's hard to beat. From a site outside the park, fireworks rockets are set off and timed to burst in the sky when they seem to be right over Sleeping Beauty's Castle. The display is as magical as any you've ever seen, and for the moment at least, from where you stand, Disneyland may indeed seem to be the happiest place on Earth.

Fairy Tales Can Come True

Forget the white limousine and an organ. For a Fairy Tale Wedding at the Disneyland Hotel, the bride will arrive like Cinderella in a horse-drawn glass coach to a trumpet fanfare. White doves will be released. And no Disneyland Fairy Tale Wedding would be complete without a visit from Disney characters. The hotel hosts about 400 different kinds of weddings a year. For diehard Disneyphiles, weddings can now be arranged in the gardens near Sleeping Beauty's Castle.

DAY TWO: *Morning*

BREAKFAST

If you're staying on a concierge floor, continental breakfast is served for you in the Concierge Lounge from 6:30 to 10:00 A.M. Otherwise there's room service or one of the restaurants within the hotel complex. Goofy's Kitchen and Hook's Pointe both serve breakfast daily.

A point of logistics: **Pirates of the Caribbean** is one of the most popular rides in the park, and during peak seasons the wait to board the ride can extend to an hour, so you might want to make it your first stop this morning to avoid a long wait. Pirates of the Caribbean was the last ride on which Walt Disney himself worked extensively (he died in 1966), and the master's touch is evident throughout, from the uncannily realistic details to the expert pacing and momentum of the thirteen-minute voyage.

If it's too early in the day for a thrill ride like Indiana Jones or Star Tours, then head over to the **Haunted Mansion** in New Orleans Square or the **Jungle Cruise** in Adventureland. Both are amusing, not jolting, and are venerable Disneyland attractions, a bit corny perhaps by today's thrill-ride standards, but at least you know the ghouls in the Haunted Mansion are harmless and the alligators on the Jungle Cruise don't really bite. With no harrowing twists and turns on these rides, you can stick close to each other and hold hands.

The new Tomorrowland—with its bronze-and-gold industrial look—debuted in 1998. At the entrance to Tomorrowland is the spaceship ride, **Astro Orbitor.** Just beyond is **Rocket Rods,** which speeds along a track originally designed for the slow-moving PeopleMover, is now the longest and fastest ride at Disneyland. Nearby is the interactive fountain, **Cosmic Waves,** which occasionally drenches guests with unexpected bursts of water.

Checkout time at the hotel is 11:00 A.M. You can ask for a late checkout, but if that's not possible, leave your bags with the bellhop for retrieval later on.

DAY TWO: *Afternoon*

LUNCH

Grab a bite to eat at one of the restaurants on Disneyland's Main Street. The full-service **Carnation Cafe** (moderate) offers a menu of hamburgers, deli-style sandwiches, and salads. Treat yourselves to an ice-cream sundae or a milk shake.

New Orleans Square, with its wrought iron balconies, tiny specialty shops, and live and recorded jazz and Dixieland music, has always been one of the more enchanting and evocative areas of Disneyland. Recent changes—the addition of zydeco, funk, and blues music, more authentic food items, such as poor boys and mufelattas;; and different kinds of daily celebrations—have created an even more authentic New Orleans atmosphere. The shops are a far cry from the souvenir emporiums you'll find on Main Street and in Adventureland. Le Gourmet sells red-beans-and-rice mixes and other Cajun and Creole foods, along with pralines and Cafe du Monde products. The Mardi Gras cart sells Mardi Gras–themed merchandise and candies. La Mascarade D'Orleans carries a lineup of Italian-made aromatherapy bath products and an original line of leather Mardi Gras masks.

As souvenirs go, nothing could be more delightful as a memento of a romantic holiday here than a pastel chalk cartoon sketch rendered by one of the **artists in New Orleans Square**. For about $25 and thirty minutes' sitting time, you can go home with a profile sketch of the two of you; $50 and an hour rewards you with a full-view sketch. An additional $11 buys a very nice wooden frame.

When it comes time to leave Disneyland, I hope you'll take a joyful sense of your own powers of imagination with you. It takes everything from sophisticated computer technology to age-old techniques like forced perspective to create the magical world of Disneyland. It also takes one thing that no computer has yet been able to duplicate—the human imagination. After all, nothing much in Disneyland is real, aside from some ducks that have made the place home and some of the plants and trees. It all looks real, of course, and we adults never cease marveling at that. But the magic only takes place if we can go with the flow, let our imagination take hold, and, just for a moment, believe it *is* real.

FOR MORE ROMANCE

Bring your dancing shoes if you're in the park on a summer Friday or Saturday evening. On Friday, dance to live swing music at Carnation Plaza Gardens; Saturday is big band night. Combine this itinerary with a visit to Laguna Beach (see Itinerary 12) or Newport Beach (see Itinerary 30).

Hideaway Havens

The Lap of Luxury
BEL-AIR

EFORE YOU'VE WALKED COMPLETELY ACROSS the stone-arched bridge that leads to the magnificently landscaped grounds of the Hotel Bel-Air, you'll know you've found the most seductively romantic spot in all of Los Angeles. The high-rise towers of downtown Los Angeles are 12 miles away, but the Hotel Bel-Air, tucked into a heavily wooded canyon off Sunset Boulevard in one of the most elegant residential neighborhoods in the world, may as well be on another planet. The privacy and tranquillity have made the Hotel Bel-Air a long-time favorite of movie stars, presidents, and dignitaries who want some peace and quiet. If you truly want to get away from it all, sleep late, lounge by the pool, dine sumptuously, and be treated like an honored guest at a magnificent private estate, then look no farther than the Hotel Bel-Air. Just bring a good book, a smart swimsuit to wear at the pool, and lots of money.

PRACTICAL NOTES: The Hotel Bel-Air is smallish: only ninety-two rooms and suites. It's a very popular wedding location, especially from April to June. As for which or what kind of room to book: Much of that will depend on your budget and the room availability. Suffice it to say that all accommodations are elegant and luxurious, appointed with fine French-country furnishings, and many with fireplaces. The rooms are so comfortable and the grounds so sylvan that you may well abandon any plans you have to visit Westwood, Beverly Hills, Century City, or Santa Monica during your stay.

DAY ONE: *Afternoon*

Turning off Sunset Boulevard onto Stone Canyon Road to reach **Hotel Bel-Air** (701 Stone Canyon Road, Los Angeles; 310–472–1211, 800–648–4097; $350–$2,500) is to detour into an exclusive world of luxury and privilege and a chapter of Los Angeles history that goes back to the 1920s and is linked to real-estate development. Oil-rich developer Alphonzo E. Bell bought a chunk of land in 1922, christened the area Bel-Air (a play on his own name and the former Spanish name for the area, Buenos Aires), and built an arcaded mission-style planning and sales office from which he directed his plans to develop the region north of Sunset Boulevard into the most desirable neighborhood in Los Angeles. He subdivided the land into estate-size properties and laid out winding roads to complement the existing terrain. For residents who did not want to keep horses at their estates, Bell erected the Bel-Air Stables and a riding ring just north of his sales office. More than 60 miles of riding trails were also constructed throughout Bel-Air, allowing homeowners to ride their horses into the chaparral-covered hillsides. Most homes built at the time in the Bel-Air subdivision cost $100,000.

In the 1940s Bell sold off his holdings to a Texas-born investor, Joseph Drown, who converted the Bel-Air land offices and stable into a hotel. Carefully preserving the original 1920s style and charm of the original structures, Drown created a rambling complex of patios and porticos and converted the oval horse paddock into a pool. It was the age of

Romance
AT A GLANCE

* You'll enter a rarified, privileged world when you book a room at **Hotel Bel-Air** (701 Stone Canyon Road, Los Angeles; 310–472–1211, 800–648–4097). Come for lunch (or weekend brunch), then find a shady bench in the sylvan garden, filled with flowers, scented by jasmine and herbs, and shaded by magnificent trees.

* In the evening, dine in one of the most romantic settings in Los Angeles, alfresco on the **Terrace**, overlooking the hotel's famous Swan Lake and wedding gazebo. Later, retire to your luxurious room and sip champagne in front of the fireplace.

* The next day, linger in your room or on its patio with breakfast, then follow the lead of Marilyn Monroe and other Hollywood stars and just lounge by the pool.

leisurely travel before jet planes and corporate rates, when hotel guests valued privacy and unobtrusive service, not frequent flyer points. The elegantly rustic tranquillity appealed to powerful people like Howard Hughes and the Fords, Kennedys, and Rockefellers, and to privacy-seeking movie stars like Gary Cooper, Marion Davies, Greta Garbo, Audrey Hepburn, Grace Kelly, Sophia Loren, Marilyn Monroe, and Gregory Peck.

Privacy, tranquillity, and personal service are still the hallmarks of the hotel; little has changed in that regard over the past fifty years. By the time you've pulled into the car park, walked across the stone bridge that leads into the grounds, and checked into your room, you should feel the calming effects of this rarefied world.

The hotel comprises several two-story pink-stucco buildings, all connected by porticoed walkways and brick paths. Guest rooms and suites are laid out in a variety of sizes and floor plans and are individually decorated. Some of them have private garden entrances or patios, wood-burning fireplaces, and terra-cotta tile floors. Floral motifs, reflecting the lush floral world just outside the French doors, predominate in draperies, bed canopies and coverings, and exquisite needlepoint carpets. (If you're starstruck and would get a kick out of staying in one of the rooms frequented by Hollywood movie stars, see "Starstruck.")

Starstruck

The Hotel Bel-Air has welcomed many celebrity guests during its fifty-year history. Marilyn Monroe was still a starlet the first time she stayed in one of the poolside rooms. She returned many times over the years, to rooms 133 or 135, alone and with husbands Joe DiMaggio and Arthur Miller. Room 160 was a favorite of Grace Kelly and heiress Barbara Hutton. Judy Garland preferred Room 118, Tyrone Power liked 136, Bette Davis requested 140, and David Niven favored 99. The hotel has a policy of not revealing celebrities' favorite room choices until after they've departed for good. We'll just have to wait a while longer to find out the favorite rooms of guests like Prince Charles, Luciano Pavarotti, Kathleen Turner, Paul Simon, and Robin Williams.

LUNCH

The **Restaurant** (expensive), an elegantly appointed room of warm, nutty colors and richly upholstered chairs, is located in the mission-style main building of the hotel. The seasonal French-California menu features fresh, natural ingredients, many of them locally grown. (The chef maintains a working herb garden at the south end of the grounds.) If it's a nice day, dine alfresco on the bougainvillea-draped **Terrace,** where the stone floor is heated during the winter. The Terrace overlooks the hotel's famous Swan Lake (the resident swans, by the way, also enjoy the culinary skills of the chef, who feeds them salad). Take your time, order something like a roast salmon salad with fresh-shaved fennel, artichokes, pine nuts, and an herb vinaigrette, and a bottle of wine from the extensive (and expensive) list. The food, the storybook setting, and the afternoon are yours to enjoy.

After lunch a stroll of the grounds will reveal the seemingly organic, spontaneous environment of the hotel. Nothing is contrived or out of place, from the wrought iron balconies to the bell tower to the picturesque chimneys. Each turn reveals something new: an intimate courtyard, perhaps, where water springs from the top of a small pineapple-shaped fountain.

Your walk around the property is a tour of an enchanted garden where meandering footpaths follow a shrub-and-fern-lined stream, and a waterfall and the Swan Lake form a storybook setting for outdoor weddings. Many of the Bel-Air's trees and shrubs are rarely seen in Southern California, among them the grove of coast redwood trees growing along the stream; the 12-foot high, white-flowering bird of paradise trees; and above Chalon Road, the tipu tree that turns into a cloud of yellow blossoms. A sixty-year-old lonchocarpus tree, indigenous to the East Indies, is the only one in California. It blossoms in the spring with pale mauve flowers. Canopying the terrace restaurant is a Monterey pine; elsewhere, ancient sycamores and California live oaks stand guard. The 50-foot-tall silk floss tree, native to South America, is the largest of its kind in California.

Color is everywhere—from the pink primose to the red azalea, from the white and pink hyacinths to the flowering peach and apricot trees— and the air is redolent with jasmine and orange blossom, ginger and gardenia. If you explore the grounds as they slope up the back hill, you'll pick up the aromatic bounty of the herb garden.

If the serene setting of the hotel isn't enough to keep you occupied for the afternoon, the shopping mecca of **Beverly Hills** is less than 3 miles away (see Itinerary 3, "Faraway in Beverly Hills"). To the west is the new **Getty Center** arts and cultural campus, set on a hilltop above the Sepulveda Pass in the Santa Monica Mountains (see Itinerary 4, "West Side Story"). Admission is free, but advance parking reservations are required (call 310–440–7300, or TDD line at 310–440–7305). Farther still, you can experience the trendy exclusiveness of Montana Avenue shops in **Santa Monica.** The front desk can provide directions.

DAY ONE: *Evening*

DINNER

For the most romantic effect, try to arrange to dine outside on the terrace at table 50, 51, 52, or 53. These tables are set in little canopied alcoves right on the edge of the lawn, so they feel quite private, and they look out to the Swan Lake and the lighted grounds around it. Chef Gary Clauson's seasonal menu tonight might include an appetizer of terrine of smoked salmon and trout with cucumber-horseradish relish and caviar crème fraîche, or lobster-fennel ravioli in tomatoes and herbs. Entrees could include curried pork medallions with mango-lemongrass sauce, veal tournedos with vegetable ragout and caramelized figs, or whitefish with an onion crust and garlic mashed potatoes.

The **Bar,** which is next to the restaurant, is a clubby little spot, with a fireplace, lots of rich wood paneling, and leather-upholstered chairs. It's the sort of place early Bel-Air's horsey set would have frequented. In the evening there's piano entertainment and the Bar becomes a meeting place of sorts for residents and hotel guests.

Have a bottle of champagne chilled and waiting in the room, build a fire in the fireplace (the service is provided complimentary), and let romance orchestrate the evening. If you get hungry later on, room service is available around the clock.

DAY TWO: *Morning*

BREAKFAST

Why not simply call room service this morning and have coffee, juice, and bakery items sent up? That would be an especially pleasant scenario if your room has a private little patio or terrace on which to linger in your robes over coffee and breakfast pastries. Later you can make your way down to the Restaurant or Terrace for breakfast (or weekend brunch). Lemon pancakes with raspberry syrup and fresh raspberries are worth getting up for. So are huevos rancheros.

If you haven't yet discovered the hotel's pool, now may be the time. Bring the paper, let the pool attendant help you select a comfortable location, and lounge the morning away. Lounging around the pool is a well-honored tradition at the Bel-Air. Years ago it was not uncommon to see the famous actors Hume Cronyn and Jessica Tandy sunning by the oval pool. Marilyn Monroe posed for glamour shots beside the pool back in the 1950s. Monroe also posed for photographs in a bungalow that was formerly called the Marilyn Monroe Cottage. It has since been converted into the twenty-four-hour fitness center.

DAY TWO: *Afternoon*

Here's a way to extend your Hotel Bel-Air getaway a bit longer. Before checking out order boxed picnic lunches to take with you ($20–$38). There are five choices: lobster, shrimp, and crab salad; lobster salad sandwich; poached salmon with cucumbers; smoked chicken salad; and herb-crusted ham and cheese. Everything's packed in a pink-and-gray box, including utensils, plates, napkins, roll and butter, and condiments. When it's time to check out, pick up your picnic lunches and head off to the beach or some other location (the sculpture garden on the UCLA campus is a delightful spot) for a picnic.

FOR MORE ROMANCE

Combine a stay at the Hotel Bel-Air with an evening at the theater (the **Shubert Theater** in Century City is only minutes away), shopping in Beverly Hills (see Itinerary 3), or a visit to the Getty Center (see Itinerary 4), or an afternoon at the beach.

California Dreamin'

PLAYA DEL REY

I F IT'S TIME FOR THE TWO OF YOU TO GET AWAY FROM IT ALL for a couple of days but there's no time to drive up the coast or fly off to another destination, then slip away to a beachside bed and breakfast without really leaving the city. From the deck of your room in a spacious Cape Cod–style summerhouse, you can still see the bright lights of the big city at night. In the morning, though, you may spot a snowy egret or blue heron highstepping through the marsh grass of protected Ballona Wetlands right outside your window. Then you'll wonder why it took you so long to finally travel the short distance to Playa del Rey, a hidden corner of Los Angeles, sandwiched between Marina del Rey and a seaside hill near the airport.

PRACTICAL NOTES: The **Inn at Playa del Rey** has twenty-one rooms and suites, with king- and queen-size beds. It's about a 5-block walk from the beach, located on a protected wetland habitat called Ballona Wetlands. Culver Boulevard is an important local thoroughfare, so some of the inn's twenty-one rooms and suites get a little traffic noise. The best bet is to ask about the availability of the "Romance Suites" 204 and 304 ($275)—king-bed suites with decks overlooking the wetlands, fireplaces in the bathroom, and Jacuzzi tubs for two. Because it's on the top floor, 304 has a peaked cathedral ceiling. Another option is the corner suite 307 ($245), with a queen bed, a living room with a small dining table and chairs under the window, wetlands view, fireplace, and two bathrooms, one with a Jacuzzi tub. All the rooms at the inn are wheelchair accessible. The inn does not require a minimum nights' stay on weekends. Breakfast and afternoon wine and cheese are included in the price. Don't forget beach chairs, a beach umbrella, sunscreen, and swimwear. You may want to pack a pair of binoculars for a good look at the herons, egrets, and other birds that populate the wetlands.

DAY ONE: *Afternoon*

Plan to arrive earlier than the post-3:00 P.M. check-in time at the inn. Wear swimwear under your clothes, because if your room isn't ready, you can leave your car in the private lot at the inn and walk down to the beach.

LUNCH

Take an impromptu picnic with you to the beach. Walking west on Culver Boulevard, you'll come to the mom-and-pop grocery **Gordon's Market** (303 Culver Boulevard; 310–822–7227), where you can pick up sandwiches at the deli counter, fruit, soft drinks, and anything else you may want for your beach picnic. From Gordon's it's about 2 more blocks to the beach, Dockweiler State Beach.

Playa del Rey is tucked into a little area between the entrance channel to Marina del Rey and the Ballona Wetlands, an ecological preserve. The fluttering colorful sails of the boats entering and leaving the marina are always in sight. A hill buffers

Romance
AT A GLANCE

✴ Get away from it all in Playa del Rey, a hidden corner of Los Angeles, where you can stay at the romantic New England-style **Inn at Playa del Rey** (435 Culver Boulevard; 310–574–1920; E-mail: playainn@aol.com; Web site: www.inatplayadelrey.com; $145–$275), which sits right on the edge of a fragile environment, the Ballona Wetlands.

✴ Buy a picnic lunch at **Gordon's Market** (303 Culver Boulevard; 310–822–7227) and a kite from Epic Kite (423 Culver Boulevard; 310–822–9550 or 310–219–1410), then idle away the afternoon on the beach.

✴ Back at the inn, have a catered dinner for two in your room at the inn or on the deck. Or walk down the block to a popular local restaurant, **La Marina** (119 Culver Boulevard; 310–823–9535; moderate). Or make the drive into Marina del Rey for dinner at **Shanghai Reds** (13813 Fiji Way, Marina del Rey; 310–823–4523; moderate) or over to Main Street in Santa Monica for Wolfgang Puck's specialties at **Chinois on Main** (2709 Main Street, Santa Monica; 310–392–9025; expensive.

✴ Borrow bikes from the inn the next morning and follow the bike path around the picturesque waterways of Marina del Rey, then over to the ever-lively **boardwalk** in Venice.

Playa del Rey from the sight and most of the sound of Los Angeles International Airport, which is to the south. Planes take off over the ocean and are visible, though engine noise is not especially noticeable or intrusive.

Your hotel, the **Inn at Playa del Rey** (435 Culver Boulevard; 310–574–1920; E-mail: playainn@aol.com; Web site: www.innatplayadelrey.com; $145–$275) sits right on the edge of the Ballona Wetlands, a 350-acre remnant of a much larger salt marsh lost to development over the years. The marsh and lagoon attract migrating birds from Canada on their way to winter homes in Mexico. Bring a pair of binoculars with you to watch the show from the deck of your room. Beyond the wetlands is Marina del Rey, the masts of boats harbored there are clearly visible. Farther still the high-rise corridor along Wilshire Boulevard and Century City is silhouetted against the backdrop of the Santa Monica Mountains.

Owner Susan Zolla was already a successful innkeeper (she owns Channel Road Inn in Santa Monica) when she decided to open the Inn at Playa del Rey, her second. She asked architect Gerald Li to design the weathered-looking Cape Cod–style structure of gray-and-white clapboard. It took four years to obtain the necessary permits to build on the environmentally sensitive site, and after a year of construction, the Inn at Playa del Rey opened in 1995 with twenty-one rooms. No two rooms are exactly alike, although the overall effect is consistent—the casual good life at the seaside: polished natural oak floors and sisal carpeting; fireplaces and whirlpool tubs; whitewashed, hand-painted headboards; wrought-iron deck furniture; sunny porches and decks; bay windows; down comforters and chenille bedcovers; blue plaid table linens; iron and brass canopy beds; and handmade seashell tiles in a bathroom. A handwritten note and a plate of home-baked chocolate chip cookies welcome guests to their rooms.

After the sunshine and salt air have left you both feeling tingly and maybe a bit worn out, treat yourself to in-room massages (arrange these through the inn's staff) and an afternoon nap.

DAY ONE: *Evening*

DINNER

Deciding on where to go for dinner may depend on what wardrobe you packed and whether you want to get in the car and drive. The Ocean Park section of Santa Monica is a quick drive for a fancy evening at Wolfgang Puck's **Chinois on Main** (2709 Main Street, Santa Monica; 310-392-9025; expensive), for example. Marina del Rey is within walking distance (at least a twenty-minute walk); the fresh fish, pasta, and steaks at **Shanghai Reds** (13813 Fiji Way, Marina del Rey; 310-823-4522; moderate) come with views of the marina and the dinner cruise boats as they come and go.

If one of your reasons for "escaping" to Playa del Rey was to get away from the high-profile goings-on of places like Santa Monica, then walk down the street to **La Marina** (119 Culver Boulevard; 310-823-9535; moderate). It's beachy and unpretentious, a bit dated in decor, certainly nothing fancy: green velourlike wallpaper, lots of exposed brick, and heavy doors with etched-glass panes. But there's a cozy booth in the back room to the right of the fireplace, and the staff is very friendly. The menu is straightforward—no fusion here—chateaubriand for two, lightly battered sand dabs with a shrimp and white wine sauce, and New Zealand rack of lamb, for example. After 9:00 P.M. on Friday and Saturday nights, the bar area gets pretty lively with a DJ and dancing; other nights a piano player entertains. With some advance planning, you could follow the lead of one customer who arranged a private, romantic dinner for two in the Wine Cellar room, a small brick-walled room used for private parties. A violinist was on hand to serenade, and flower petals were strewn on the table and across the floor.

Another option is to ask the inn's staff to help you arrange a catered dinner to be set up on the main-floor deck at the inn. It's one of the common areas of the inn, so it's not totally private, but certainly a charming alternative. If you booked the living-room suite 307, which has a small dining table and chairs set under the window looking out to the wetlands, you've got yet another possibility: a private, catered dinner for two in your suite.

Arrange beforehand to have a chilled bottle of wine or champagne waiting for you when you return to the inn. Then it only takes the flip of a switch or two to create a romantic ambience—the warm glow of a gas fireplace, the therapeutic, bubbling whirl of the Jacuzzi. Outside, beyond the dark expanse of wetlands, the lights of civilization twinkle, so near, yet, happily, so far away.

Ready for Commitment?

More than sixty years ago, a young football player and his girlfriend sat on a bench on a bluff at Loyola Marymount University and made plans for their future life as husband and wife. Since then, nobody knows how many couples have sat on that bench behind the chapel, looking out over the west side of Los Angeles toward the mountains and the sea, and kissed and dreamed of their future together. Today an ordinary-looking park bench known as the Proposal Bench commemorates the spot where the football player and his sweetheart (they were married for forty-eight years, until her death in 1990) first talked about getting married. The bench, the westernmost one on the bluff between the chapel and Xavier Hall, is designated by a small bronze plaque that reads: "Intended for couples of marriage-able age with reasonable expecta-tions that their present relationship may lead to marriage." The University is a five-minute drive from the inn.

DAY TWO: *Morning*

BREAKFAST

The sunny breakfast room, with its polished hardwood floor, pale yellow walls, small round tables covered with yellow and blue striped table-cloths, and wetlands view, is cheerful and inviting. Breakfast is a generous extended continental affair, and includes, besides fresh juice and fruit platters, plenty of homemade baked goods like a vanilla streusel and scones. If you just can't be convinced to leave your room this morning, ask to have breakfast for two sent up.

Make it funky this morning: Ride bikes over to **Venice Beach,** Los An-geles's nonstop outdoor sideshow of the weird and wonderful. Borrow bikes from the inn and pick up the paved beach path at the foot of Cul-ver Boulevard. The path quickly veers away from the beach, to navigate by the inlet channel to Marina del Rey and around the marina itself. When it returns you to the beach, you'll be in Venice along Ocean Front Walk. Here you can rent Rollerblades, get your fortune told by a palmist or tarot-card reader, watch street entertainers, buy T-shirts and sunglasses, and watch bodybuilders pump up at Muscle Beach.

If the exercise of bicycling and the eccentricities of Venice hold no sway for the two of you, then maybe you should go fly a kite. Stop in at the tiny **Epic Kite** shop (423 Culver Boulevard; 310–822–9550 or 310–219–1410), two doors west of the inn, and pick up a rainbow nylon delta kite ($15–$25) and a 500-foot spool of monofilament ($5.95) for a morning of kite flying on the beach. According to owner Russell, there's nothing to flying this model; with the two-handed spools now being used, even small children can do it.

All good things must come to an end, so unfortunately, you'll have to keep an eye on the time, for noon is the checkout hour at the inn. (If you want to extend your stay a bit, ask about leaving your car at the inn for a while so you can spend more time at the beach.)

FOR MORE ROMANCE

Call before you arrive at the inn and have flowers delivered to your room or suite from **Playa del Rey Florist** (307 Culver Boulevard; 310–821–0984 or 800–327–0772). During warm-weather months, Malibu Ocean Sports (310–456–6302) leads **moonlight kayak tours** around Marina del Rey, between 7:00 and 11:00 P.M.

Hills of Enchantment
EL ENCANTO HOTEL AND GARDEN VILLAS, SANTA BARBARA

QUAINT COTTAGES PERCHED ON A HILLSIDE above Mission Santa Barbara and secluded behind tropical plantings and swaying palms. Sweeping views of the Pacific Ocean from a sunny patio restaurant. Nothing to do except sink into a lawn glider, hold hands, and dream that it will never end. El Encanto Hotel and Garden Villas could be too good to be true. But Hollywood celebrities have been coming here for decades to escape the rigors of stardom. Even if you don't have agents, producers, and *Vanity Fair* editors hounding you, but you want to escape for a day or two to an enchanting place, El Encanto will welcome you and your partner.

PRACTICAL NOTES: **El Encanto Hotel and Garden Villas** (1900 Lasuen Road; 805–687–5000, 800–346–7039; $229–$1,000) sits on ten acres set on a hillside, which gives slope to most walkways on the property. Plan to book one of the deluxe cottages ($429–$469) that has a view of the ocean and channel. The newly refurbished one-bedroom cottage 303, for example, is a lovely choice, with a sunny sitting room and ocean view, a fireplace, and a king-size bed in a large bedroom. Cottage 311 is another good choice for a view of the ocean, this time directly from the bed. It's also where John Travolta once stayed for several months. The Honeymoon Cottage is large and airy, with a fireplace, king-size bed, and a big front porch. El Encanto is a historical property, and some rooms (312, for instance) retain a more "quaint" historic charm (read: smaller, not very luxe). Rooms 401–420, which are in 1970s-style stucco buildings near the tennis courts, lack charm of any kind, although they are spacious, and the second-level rooms command great views. These buildings are scheduled for refurbishment, however, which should make them more desirable. Only two rooms on the property, number 415 and cottage 353, are wheelchair accessible, but neither is handicapped equipped.

When making plans to visit El Encanto, remember that weekend stays may require a two-night minimum; holidays, three-night. The hotel has an excellent award-winning restaurant, but aside from a movie theater showing foreign films, which is located just outside the grounds, there are no other restaurants, shops, or services in the immediate area. El Encanto is in a residential neighborhood, and you must drive down into Santa Barbara for more entertainment.

DAY ONE:
Afternoon

LUNCH

Romance
AT A GLANCE

* Decamp to a luxury cottage in a hilltop garden setting with an ocean view at **El Encanto Hotel and Garden Villas** in Santa Barbara (1900 Lasuen Road; 805–687–5000 or 800–346–7039; $229–$1,000). Arrive in time for a casual lunch on the patio of the dining room, which commands sweeping views of Santa Barbara and the Pacific Ocean and is the perfect place to linger over bowls of cioppino.

* In the afternoon stroll the lushly-planted grounds of El Encanto. Settle into one of the canopied lawn gliders and lose yourself in reverie, hold hands, or read your favorite book. Return to your room later for a scheduled theraputic massage.

* After dinner in El Encanto's dining room, you can catch a foreign or independent film playing at the **Riviera Theater** (805–963–9503) across the street from the hotel's main entrance.

* The next day, there's time to visit **Mission Santa Barbara** (2201 Laguna Street at Los Olivos; 805–682– 4713) just down the hill from El Encanto, or stop at the **Santa Barbara Museum of Natural History** (2559 Puesta del Sol; 805–682–4711) for an introduction to the life and culture of the Chumash, the region's original inhabitants.

Don't wait until the official check-in time (3:00 P.M.) to arrive at El Encanto. One of the joys of this place is sitting out on the terrace of the dining room (expensive), under a peach-and-green awning, surrounded by potted pink geraniums with flowers as big as hydrangeas. The sun is warm and invigorating, and the breeze is cooling and sensual. The sweeping panoramic view takes in the mountains and ocean, the red-tile roofs of the city below, and the silhouette of the offshore Santa Cruz Island. Then there's the food, a winning combination of classic themes with new-world tastes: local field greens with blue cheese, pear, and aged balsamic vinaigrette; *cioppino*, a hearty, flavorful seafood stew of halibut, sea bass, scallops, mussels, and clams in a broth redolent of tarragon and fennel; angel-hair pasta with roasted garlic, basil, yellow peppers, tomatoes, and pine nuts. Once you've seen the view and tasted the food, you'll see why lunchtime can be busy. You may have to wait a few minutes for a table. If that's the case, retire to the adjacent lounge and settle back in one of the cushy love seats. And make reservations for dinner tonight.

As you go to your cottage, don't fail to notice the giant birds of paradise planted along the walkway above the pool, which is flanked by a thick stand of banana trees. In fact, the entire hillside compound is a garden-like setting of lush plantings and verdant lawns. One of the most tranquil spots on the grounds is the lily pond, which is surrounded by an arbor densely covered in wisteria. Elsewhere you'll see a wonderfully gnarly dragon tree and regal Canary Island palms.

Also notice how the villas and cottages of El Encanto are a mixture of Craftsman-style cottages, Spanish Colonial Revival-style white-washed adobe villas from the 1930s, and, near the tennis courts, apartment-style buildings dating from the 1970s. The oldest cottages date back some eighty years, when El Encanto was an artists' retreat. Today the hotel is a charter member of the Historic Hotels of America and was featured in 1996 on a PBS television show about historic hotels and country inns.

People come to El Encanto to retreat into a private world of serenity and beautiful surroundings. Aside from a stroll around the grounds, a game of tennis, or a swim in the pool, you may decide to do nothing more than settle into one of the lawn gliders and get lost in the watercolor scene of sailboats in the distance, skimming across the silvery ocean.

If the tranquil beauty of the place isn't enough to cure what ails you, then maybe a massage in your room might do the trick. El Encanto has arranged with certified, licensed massage therapists to provide its guests with a range of massages, including Swedish, deep tissue, shiatsu, and reflexology. (Here's a quick review: classic Swedish massage involves kneading and stroking aimed at increasing circulation; deep tissue massage is a technique used to release built-up muscle tension; shiatsu is a 5,000-year-old Japanese technique that was focused pressure to balance the body's energy flow; and reflexology is massage therapy of the hands and feet.) Cost for the different massages varies from about $45 for a half-hour reflexology treatment to about $90 for a one-hour massage. Appointments must be arranged in advance.

DAY ONE: *Evening*

DINNER

Tonight dine inside at El Encanto's dining room (expensive), where the setting is a bit more formal than outside on the terrace. (Although it doesn't seem to be a policy strictly adhered to, men are requested to wear jackets at dinner.) The menu changes nightly, but the variations are conducted within a classic framework, with preparations of fresh fish from local waters, vegetables and fruits grown by area farmers, and fresh-baked breads and pastries. Here are some of the dishes on the menu the week we visited: risotto of black truffle with morel and enoki mushrooms, roasted free-range pheasant, rack of lamb with Provençal herbs, and sauteed sea bass with a tarragon mustard crust. One of the signature dishes is El Encanto paella, with green lip mussels, Manila clams, rock shrimp, sea scallops, chicken, and cilantro; it's an excellent dish for two. Another specialty is striped bass baked in parchment paper with chardonnay and garnished with julienne vegetables, parsley, and thyme. Whatever you order, do save room for the classic Floating Island dessert, a luscious "island" of meringue floating in a satiny crème anglaise.

Aficionados of foreign and independent films might want to check out the film schedule at the **Riviera Theater** (805–963–9503). The cinema is right across the street from the hotel. The small complex of historical buildings in which the theater is located was the original site of the University of California, Santa Barbara.

DAY TWO: *Morning*

BREAKFAST

Order room service this morning, and if your room or cottage has a porch or patio, sit outside and linger over coffee and croissants. Have champagne and orange juice sent up to make mimosas. Read the paper, do the crossword puzzle, or . . . there's no rush.

Checkout time isn't until noon, which still leaves time for a swim in the pool, another game of tennis, or a last stroll around the grounds.

DAY TWO: *Afternoon*

If you've never visited **Mission Santa Barbara** (2201 Laguna Street at Los Olivos; 805–682–4713), stop by on your way down the hill from El Encanto. The mission's twin towers will be recognizable from postcard images you've no doubt seen. Built in 1786, the tenth of twenty-one Franciscan missions in California, it's known as the Queen of the Missions for its graceful beauty. Tours are self-guided (a modest fee is charged), taking visitors through rooms displaying historical items, including religious manuscripts and embroidered vestments. Outside is a lovely landscaped garden and a serene old cemetery. Across Los Olivos Street are the remains of tanning vats, a pottery kiln, and parts of an early water system.

Two blocks north of the mission and just past Rocky Nook Park is the **Santa Barbara Museum of Natural History** (2559 Puesta del Sol; 805–682–4711). The 50-foot skeleton of a young blue whale is the first thing you'll see in the entrance courtyard. Inside the complex of buildings, several exhibits about birds, marine life, fossils, and plants focus on the natural history of the West Coast. Among the most interesting is Chumash Hall, which depicts and explains the life and culture of the area's original inhabitants. Serendipity may brighten your visit with a seasonal exhibit about, for example, the monarch butterfly's wintering grounds in nearby Goleta. The museum is open Monday through Saturday; 9:00 A.M.

to 5:00 P.M.; Sunday, 10:00 A.M. to 5:00 P.M. Adult admission is $5.00 per person (last Sunday of the month is free).

Missions and natural history museums don't hold interest for everybody. If that's the case, perhaps a chance to take a look at the spot where the newlyweds John and Jacqueline Kennedy spent part of their honeymoon will spark your interest. Among the most exclusive retreats in the country is **San Ysidro Ranch** (900 San Ysidro Lane, Santa Barbara; 805–969–5046, 800–368–6788). Drive down to take a look around the elegantly rustic retreat set in the foothills off San Ysidro Road near Montecito.

At Long Last

It took fifty years, but a honeymoon couple in their seventies finally made it to El Encanto, according to the hotel's sales director. The couple had originally planned to honeymoon at El Encanto but World War II spoiled their plans. Half a century later, they finally got the honeymoon they never had.

You can park, take a walk around, and have a drink in the Plow & Angel. Laurence Olivier and Vivien Leigh were married at the ranch, and other famous couples who've retreated here at one time or another are Mick Jagger and Jerry Hall, and Meg Ryan and Dennis Quaid.

FOR MORE ROMANCE

Extend your stay another day and take a **wine country tour** through Santa Ynez Valley, about 35 miles north of Santa Barbara. Call the Santa Barbara County Vintner's Association at 800–218–0881. For other romantic itineraries in Santa Barbara, see Itinerary 10, "Jewel of the Coast," and Itinerary 28, "Set Sail."

Mountain Magic

LAKE ARROWHEAD

THERE MAY BE PLENTY TO DO IN LAKE ARROWHEAD—hiking, ice skating, shopping, bird-watching—but part of the reason for going up to the resort high in the San Bernardino Mountains is to escape from a life of scheduled activities and do nothing more than swing in a hammock, build a snowman, or count stars. The world is a different place up here. The air is cleaner, the stars are brighter, and the moon is about 1 mile closer, just enough to inspire most of us to wax poetic.

PRACTICAL NOTES: Lake Arrowhead is a year-round resort, although the warm months are busiest, especially weekends. During the summer try planning to arrive on Sunday afternoon; the crowds will be decamping for home in the basin, and you'll pretty much have the place to yourself. In winter it's wise to carry chains to ensure your ability to travel on mountain roads in case of snow. If you plan to hike in the forest, bring along appropriate footwear, as well as a small backpack or daypack to carry water, sunscreen, and a pair of binoculars for bird- and animal-watching (and stargazing at night). Lake Arrowhead's elevation is about 5,000 feet, which is enough to cause some shortness of breath. Contact the **Lake Arrowhead Communities Chamber of Commerce** for more information at (909) 336–1547 or visit the Web site at www.lakearrowhead.net.

DAY ONE: *Afternoon*

As you ascend the San Bernardino Mountains, the basin below may be shrouded in a gauzy haze of coastal fog or smog, and you'll know you made the right decision to take off for a place where the air is clear and fresh and the night sky is filled with a galaxy of stars. The route up from San Bernardino, State Highway 18, delivers you to State Highway 173, which leads you right into Lake Arrowhead Village, a natural starting-off point for your visit. *Village* may be something of a misnomer. A multilevel parking structure and acres of parking lot surround several mountain-chalet-style buildings that house various retail tenants, including several factory outlet stores. The effect, unfortunately, is less mountain village than shopping mall. The saving grace is the beautiful lake. During warm months sailboats scud across the sparkling deep-blue waters, and small power boats skim by, sometimes pulling skiers behind. Surrounding the lake stands a ring of conifer-covered mountain peaks, a forest of green in summer, a snow-covered wonderland in winter.

LUNCH

Woody's Boathouse (Building B-100, Lake Arrowhead Village; 909–337–2628; inexpensive) is strategically situated dockside for a good view of the lake and all the recreational activity on the water. The food—specialty one-third-pound hamburgers, salads, and thick sandwiches—is reasonably good, and the casual atmosphere draws

Romance
AT A GLANCE

✻ Arrive in the San Bernardino Mountain resort of Lake Arrowhead in time for lunch and a stroll around the village. Then check into the country bed-and-breakfast inn **Château du Lac** in Lake Arrowhead (911 Hospital Road; 909–337–6488 or 800–601–8722), where the views of the lake are spectacular. Pass the afternoon swinging in the hammock on the deck overlooking the lake.

✻ Dine intimately in an antique-filled cottage that evening at **Casual Elegance** (26848 Highway 189, Agua Fria; 909–337–8932; moderate). Later enjoy the stargazing possibilites afforded by the clean mountain air. Call the **Mountain Skies Astronomical Society Science Center** for program information (909–336–1299 or 909–336–1699).

✻ After breakfast the next morning, take a nature walk at **Heap's Peak Arboretum** (909–336–2282) or join a guided tour conducted by the Forest Service). You could also head off on your own along the miles of hiking trails. Call the Arrowhead Ranger Station for information (28104 Highway 18 at Arrowhead Villas Road; 909–337–2444).

✻ Before you descend from the mountains for the drive home, stop off in Blue Jay for a turn at ice-skating at the **Iceoplex** (27307 Highway 189, Blue Jay; 909–337–5283).

a diverse crowd, from families in shorts and T-shirts to a young couple gently arm wrestling in one of the back booths to a thirty-something well-dressed pair sipping bloody Marys and gazing into each other's eyes.

After lunch take a stroll through the **festival area,** where there may be a Renaissance fair replete with entertainers and magicians or some other special event taking place. There's a shady little grassy slope on the lake side of the festival stage that's an inviting spot to relax for a few minutes.

Because Lake Arrowhead is private, about the only way to actually get out onto the lake is to take one of the cruises aboard *Arrowhead Queen* or *Lake Arrowhead Princess* (909–336–6992). The *Queen* is a small, sixty-five-passenger paddle wheeler. Some improvements have been made to the vessel, so it's not as noisy as it used to be, although the horn that's honked to announce the boat's arrival and departure is shrill. Nevertheless, the forty-five-minute narrated tour reveals something of the lake's history, and the cruise gives you a chance to see some stunning lakeside homes. More than that, however, as it cruises across the sparkling water, the *Arrowhead Queen* provides a splendid opportunity for the two of you to marvel at the incredible setting. The *Princess* is a twenty-passenger wooden speedboat. It departs twice hourly for twenty-minute turns around the lake. Adult tickets are about $10 per person.

Meanwhile on a bluff overlooking the north side of the lake, innkeepers Oscar and Jody Wilson have taken pains to create a completely relaxing and tranquil environment at their country bed-and-breakfast inn, **Château du Lac** (911 Hospital Road; 909–337–6488, 800–601–8722; Web site: www.ramonamall.com/chateau.html; E-mail: chateau@js-net.com; $125–$225). The soaring interior space, with

Starlight, Star Bright

On a clear night in the mountains, the absence of big city lights guarantees a heaven full of stars. The planet Venus, the brightest object in the sky apart from the sun and the moon, has beguiled earthbound stargazers since ancient times. Venus is called the evening star when it appears in the west at sunset, though it is never visible for more than three hours after sunset. As the morning star, when it appears in the east, Venus is visible for three hours before sunrise.

its fireplaces, wood beams, library landing, cozy tower sitting room, window seats, and five spacious guest suites with queen-size feather beds, would be enough to recommend the place. But when you step onto the west-facing deck outside the dining room and get a load of the million-dollar unobstructed view of the lake, you may not want to move from the spot. The afternoon breeze and sunlight paint the lake sparkling silver, and speedboats cut foamy white arcs across the surface. If you've been able to book the Lakeview Suite (about $225), you'll have the same glorious view from your own private deck and from the window over the spa tub in the suite's bathroom. The more masculine Loft Suite ($195) doesn't have a view, but it's got a private entrance, a big brick fireplace, as well as a spa tub. If you're as entranced by the setting as most people who come here, you'll probably want to stray no farther than the hammock stretched between two posts on the main deck's gazebo.

If it's winter and there's snow on the ground, you could always build a snowman and then go inside to warm up before a fire and sip tea or wine. Later unwind from the trip with a soak in the spa tub (a preview of what might come in the evening as the glow of the fireplace lights up your darkened room?).

DAY ONE: *Evening*

DINNER

The menu may change weekly at **Casual Elegance** (26848 Highway 189, Agua Fria; 909–337–8932; moderate), but the intimate setting—a storybook, antique-filled cottage aglow in candlelight—remains one of the most romantic in Lake Arrowhead. Dress casually but expect to linger over an elegant dinner presentation of beef, fresh fish, poultry, lamb, or pasta. Call for reservations on weekends.

At night crystal-clear skies set the stage for, literally, a star-studded evening—Orion in the winter, Scorpio in summer. Lake Arrowhead is a year-round stargazing wonderland. Best of all the only thing you have to do is look up. For more formal stargazing activities, call **Mountain Skies Astronomical Society Science Center** (909–336–1699), which offers scheduled starwatches during the summer, or call the center's twenty-four-hour recorded Sky Report (909-336-1299) for daily updates on sky happenings. (You can also pick up star maps at the center.)

On chilly autumn or winter evenings, don't forget to make good use of the fireplace in your room or in the château's living room.

DAY TWO: *Morning*

BREAKFAST

The Wilsons serve a hearty cooked breakfast—eggs, quiche, or a specialty from Jody's B&B cookbook, along with croissants, muffins, scones, and fruit—at 9:00 A.M. on the terrace or in the dining room each morning.

As the snows melt and spring approaches, wildflowers start to bloom all over the place, in the pine forests, along rocky hillsides, and in lush meadows. Monkey flowers, geraniums, violets, buttercups, poppies, lupine, lilies, sunflowers, orchids, and penstemons burst forth in a riot of color. An interpretive nature walk at **Heap's Peak Arboretum** (on Highway 18 between Lake Arrowhead Village and Running Springs; 909-336-2282) highlights some of these plants, as well as other species, including the giant sequoia and the delicate western bracken fern. The arboretum is open year-round, except after heavy snowstorms.

If you've timed your visit to coincide with the **bald eagle migration** to the San Bernardino Mountains between December and March, you may be able to glimpse these magnificent creatures on a morning tour conducted by the Forest Service. Call (909) 337-2444 for more information.

The miles of **hiking trails** through the forest around Lake Arrowhead range from rugged to easy. Trail maps for hiking in the forest are available (for a $1.00 fee) at the Arrowhead Ranger Station in Skyforest (28104 Highway 18 at Arrowhead Villas Road; 909-337-2444), where you must buy a parking permit for $5.00. A couple of easy hikes include the 1/2-mile Indian Rock Trail, which begins at the Rock Camp Fire Station on Highway 173 near Deer Lodge Park; and a 1-mile Tunnel Two Trail near Grass Valley Lake. Not too far from Château du Lac is the North Shore

Recreation Trail, a moderately difficult 1.7-mile trail with elevation gain that begins at the North Shore campground on Hospital Road. Just remember that checkout time at Château du Lac is 11:00 A.M.

DAY TWO: *Afternoon*

If there's a bit of Kristi Yamaguchi or Scott Hamilton in you, then stop off at **Iceoplex Ice Castle** (27307 Highway 189, Blue Jay; 909-337-5283) before leaving Lake Arrowhead to descend the mountain to the basin. The rink is open on three sides, so not only do you have the mountain scenery to set the stage, you've got plenty of pine-scented air to breathe in while you perform those toe loops and axels.

FOR MORE ROMANCE

Call Jim Manson of **Romantic Fancy** (909-337-0620) to find out about the annual Starlight Picnic he organizes. It's usually held in August on a lakeside lawn and includes dancing, poetry readings, strolling musicians, and lake cruises. Guests are greeted with flowers, a complimentary photo, and unlimited champagne. Tickets for the Starlight Picnic are about $55–$65 per couple.

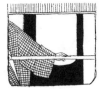

Desert Chic
PALM SPRINGS

I N THE DAYS BEFORE CELLULAR PHONES, Hollywood movie stars like Clark Gable and Carole Lombard would retreat to the rural Palm Springs desert in the 1930s and 1940s for secluded, romantic weekends. Even though Gable and Lombard wouldn't recognize the place now—development has turned the Palm Springs area into a sprawling conglomeration of desert cities totaling a quarter million people—they'd probably be happy to know that they still could hide away here for a day or two in surroundings that might seem familiar. A bit of Old Palm Springs—updated, of course, to contemporary standards—can still be found amid the chain hotels, motels, restaurants, and multiplex cinemas. You can hide away at the Willows Historic Palm Springs Inn, a seventy-two-year-old Italianate villa (where Gable and Lombard slept), pamper yourselves with spa treatments for two at Two Bunch Palms (another longtime celebrity haunt), and hike out to a remote box canyon to watch the moon come up over the desert. Bring your significant other, but leave the phone or the pager at home.

PRACTICAL NOTES: Weekends during the winter high season (mid-January through mid-April) and holidays bring a crush of visitors to Palm Springs. If you want to avoid the crowds, plan your getaway for midweek or arrive in town on a Sunday afternoon as everybody else is preparing to head home. During July and August, when temperatures often top one hundred degrees, many restaurants and other businesses are closed. The Willows requires a two-night minimum stay on weekends and is closed in July and August. For more information about Palm Springs and the other desert resort cities of Cathedral City, Desert Hot Springs, Indian Wells, Indio, La Quinta, Palm Desert, and Rancho Mirage, contact the **Palm Springs Desert Resorts Convention and Visitors Bureau** (760–770–9000 or 800–967–3767; Web site: www.desertresorts.com; E-mail: psdrcvb@earthlink.net).

DAY ONE: *Afternoon*

From whichever direction the two of you approach Palm Springs, follow Highway 111 as it turns into Palm Canyon Drive and comes into downtown Palm Springs. To reach the Willows, follow the signs for the Desert Museum. At Tahquitz Canyon Way, turn toward the mountain and drive the 2 blocks to the end of the road and the Willows, the grand Mediterranean-style villa on the right, practically at the foot of the mountain.

Arriving at the **Willows Historic Palm Springs Inn** (412 West Tahquitz Canyon; 760–320–0771 or 800–966–9597; $175–$500) is a bit like arriving at the home of rich, gracious friends half a century ago. Instead of registering at a desk, guests are met at the gate by an innkeeper and escorted to their rooms, where they then sign the registration form. During the check-in hours between 4:00 and 7:00 P.M., a pianist may be at the keyboard in the Great Hall, or living room, where wine and hors d'oeuvres are also served.

Built in 1927 by Samuel Untermyer, a former United States Secretary of the Treasury, the villa welcomed many famous guests decades ago. Marion Davies lived here.

Romance
AT A GLANCE

* Retreat to **Willows Historic Palm Springs Inn** (412 West Tahquitz Canyon; 760–320–0771 or 800–966–9597; $175–$550), a Mediterranean-style villa in the old section of Palm Springs and once the haunt of Hollywood movie stars. Spend the afternoon just lounging by the pool at the Willow or strolling around downtown Palm Springs.

* Hike by the light of the stars and moon to a special spot in the desert on a guided moonlight desert expedition with **Desert Safari** (760–770–9191; Web site: www.desertsafari.com). If you miss the moonlight expedition because you've decided to stay in town for dinner, get up early the next day and go along on one of the company's hikes into Palm Canyon.

* In the afternoon, drive over to **Two Bunch Palms Resort & Spa** (67–425 Two Bunch Palms Trail; 760–329–8791; Web site: www.twobunchpalms.com) for a romantic and theraputic candlelight soak in a Roman tub or for a side-by-side Swedish massage. Don't rush away—linger at the spa for dinner.

* Before you leave Palm Springs the next day, take a cable car ride up a mountain on the **Palm Springs Aerial Tramway** (Tramway Road off State Highway 111; 760–325–1391; fare about $18 per person). The ride up lasts about fourteen minutes and ascends some 6,100 feet; along the way, you'll pass through several climate changes before reaching the tram station on Mt. San Jacinto.

Clark Gable and Carole Lombard honeymooned here. New York mayor Jimmy Walker hid out here. And Albert Einstein slept here. But as happens to so many aging beauties, the ravages of time took their toll on the villa. In 1996 physicians Tracy Conrad and Paul Marut bought the Willows and set out to rescue it from years of neglect. The couple restored the mahogany beams of the Great Hall, removed a Budweiser sign hanging from a frescoed ceiling in the dining room, and otherwise resuscitated their sick patient with an infusion of expert care and love, not to mention money. The result: eight sumptuous guest rooms, furnished with fine antiques, claw-foot tubs, pedestal sinks, and handmade draperies.

In the Einstein Garden Room ($300–$425), French doors open to a private patio beside the garden waterfall, which cascades down the mountain. Befitting the legend of its namesake, the Marion Davies Room ($375–$500) is romantically elegant, with a balcony, a grand fireplace, and a chaise longue in the pillowed stone floor bathroom. Gable and Lombard honeymooned in the Library ($375–$475), a handsome, masculine room encased in mahogany, with a coffered ceiling and a private entrance. The Loft ($225–$350) and the Waterfall Room ($250–$375) both have private staircases and views of the waterfall and mountains. Once the two of you have settled in, explore the villa, the garden, and the stone path that leads to a secluded lookout on the hillside. If the Willows' tariffs seem a little high, keep in mind that a full breakfast is included and that you won't be nickel-and-dimed for phone calls (local calls are free) or any extras that may be offered or that you may request, such as bottled water or soft drinks at the pool.

Note: If you're interested in spa treatments at Two Bunch Palms tomorrow, call now (760–329–8791) to schedule appointments, if you haven't already done so.

DAY ONE: *Evening*

DINNER

If you don't want to travel any farther than across the street, and you don't object to spending a lot of money, then reserve a table at Le Vallauris (385 West Tahquitz Canyon Way; 760–325–5059; Web site: www.levallauris.com; very expensive), the "grande dame" of elegant desert dining: Mediterranean-

Californian cuisine that includes sea scallops provençal, escargot, goat cheese, ravioli with grilled peppers and parmesan, and Grand Marnier soufflé.

If Le Vallauris sounds too high profile, ask Tracy, Paul, or one of the innkeepers on duty to suggest something. They might propose a small Greek taverna just a few blocks away that's family run and a favorite with locals or a Japanese restaurant on the north end of town that Paul says is "expensive, but wonderful" and also off the beaten path. Or you can strike out on your own. Palm Canyon Drive is lined with restaurants within walking distance.

If your visit to Palm Springs coincides with that month's full moon cycle, the two of you might want to join a guided four-hour "moonlight expedition." That means you'd have to skip dinner altogether, opting instead for a light meal in the late afternoon. **Desert Safari** (760–770-9191; Web site: www.desertsafari.com) leads the monthly expeditions across the silent desert, miles away from the lights of civilization. The cost is about $90 per person, which includes round-trip transportation, gate fees, a hip pack of two bottles of water, and a flashlight. The expedition reveals a desert landscape that is otherworldly, stark and with little vegetation. The group gathers on a ridge to watch stars appear in the eastern sky as the sun begins to sink in the west. Then, as the moon rises, you hike down into a still, silent world of moonlit canyons, arroyos, and washes. You soon come to a "secret" location, hidden in the shadows, where you'll have a chance to explore if you wish, or you can gather around a single lighted candle to contemplate in silence, gaze at the moon and the stars, or listen to the occasional serenade of an owl. Even though you're with a group of other people, tension melts away, and the experience can be quite spiritual and bonding. When you leave, you'll see that the moon, having risen higher, drapes shadows across different canyon walls, in effect creating an entirely different route for you.

DAY TWO: *Morning*

Early risers who missed Desert Safari's moonlight hike can explore the Indian canyon called Palm Canyon (two hours) with a guide or test their stamina with a more strenuous hike to Fern Grotto (four hours). Call for details and reservations.

BREAKFAST

A morning hike, however, would mean pulling yourselves away early in the morning from the understated luxury of the Willows and missing the three-course breakfast (puff pancakes, baked eggs with white truffle sauce, bread pudding, homemade granola, praline-pecan bacon, and more), served on Wedgwood in the dining room, which opens to the waterfall. But you'll get another chance tomorrow if you miss it today.

Remember to call Two Bunch Palms to schedule spa treatments for later in the day. Then the two of you can idle away the rest of the morning relaxing by the pool at the Willows or visit the **Palm Springs Desert Museum** (101 Museum Drive, just west of Desert Fashion Plaza; 760–325–7186).

DAY TWO: *Afternoon*

LUNCH

You only have to walk 2 blocks over from the Willows to Palm Canyon Drive where, within a block in either direction, you'll find a dozen restaurants ranging from the Italian **Trilussa** (123 North Palm Canyon Drive; 760–323–4255; moderate) to the desert editions of chain restaurants like **California Pizza Kitchen** (123 North Palm Canyon Drive; 760–322–6075; moderate) and **Hamburger Hamlet** (123 North Palm Canyon Drive; 760–325–2321; moderate).

Allow about thirty minutes to drive from the Willows to **Two Bunch Palms Resort & Spa,** about 12 miles away in Desert Hot Springs (67–425 Two Bunch Palms Trail; 760–329–8791; Web site: www.twobunchpalms. com). There's no sign announcing the spa, which is one of the most famous in the world. But you shouldn't have any trouble finding the place if you look not for two bunches of palm trees, but rather for the gray-green tamarisk trees that surround the property. A guard at the gate will admit you and give you parking instructions. The little sign in the driveway that warns of a roadrunner crossing isn't a joke. The creatures are evident, as are rabbits, who seem to be hopping around all over the place. Nor are the posted requests to keep noise down a joke. The restorative effects of Two Bunch Palms, aside from the mineral hot springs, mud baths, and special massage therapies, begin with the absence of "big city" noises—no horns honking, no cellular phones, no kids or pets, no loud music. Special "Romance Treatments" at Two Bunch include a side-by-side Swedish massage for the two of you in a wooden tropical pagoda, set on the lawn overlooking the lake (about $180 per couple); Watsu a Deux, a warm mineral water Yoga relaxation therapy for you and your partner conducted in a private pool (about $180 per couple); and Roman Tub Rejuvenator, side-by-side massages for the two of you, followed by a twenty-minute private lavender Epsom salt bath, by candlelight, and polarity energy balancing (about $250 per couple). Other therapies, such as side-by-side mud baths and body wraps, are also available for couples. Two popular "day at the spa" packages are the Day Break (about $225 per person), which includes two spa treatments, lunch at the restaurant, access to the pool and grotto, taxes, and gratuities and The Sunset (about $235 per person), which includes one treatment, grotto soaking, dinner, a spa robe to keep, taxes, and gratuities. As day visitors, you and your partner are also permitted to use the natural hot springs and saunas. The spa will provide towels, but you'll have to provide your own robes and slippers.

DAY TWO: *Evening*

DINNER

No need to break the spell of relaxation that descended on you during the spa treatments. In the evening Two Bunch Palms' **Casino Dining Room** (moderate) is quite a pretty place, with fine old dark-wood sideboards and hutches and lots of candles illuminating the room. The menu, which changes seasonally, is happily not a severe spa regimen but includes an eclectic array of such mainstays as melon and prosciutto as appetizers, paper-wrapped salmon, pork loin, free-range chicken, and pasta. The house specialty entree is a succulent rosemary lamb. Cocktails, beer, and wine are available. Make a reservation for dinner when you schedule your spa treatments.

DAY THREE: *Morning*

BREAKFAST

If you missed breakfast at the Willows yesterday because you went on a hike, stick around this morning to sample the wonderful specialties and to admire the dining room's frescoed ceiling and the cascading waterfall right outside.

End what has largely been a low-key visit to Palm Springs with a unique, spectacular cable car ride up a mountain. One of the wonders of living in Southern California is the region's proximity to so many climatic conditions and environments. Nowhere is the point driven home more dramatically than by riding the **Palm Springs Aerial Tramway** (Tramway Road off State Highway 111; 760–325–1391; fare about $18 per person) up Mount San Jacinto, a fourteen-minute ride that ascends from an elevation of 2,400 feet to 8,500 feet (the summit of the mountain at more than 10,000 feet). From Highway 111 on the north side of town, the steep Tramway Road winds up

Yeah, but Can She

Keep the Moon from Setting?

The Westin Mission Hills Resort (Dinah Shore and Bob Hope Drives, Rancho Mirage; 760–328–5955) takes romance seriously. The Rancho Mirage hotel has a "director of romance" on its staff. Charged with making sure that the hotel property, from its cascading waterfalls and meandering garden paths to its reception rooms, evokes a romantic mood, the director helps couples plan their engagement parties, weddings, anniversaries, and other special romantic events. A new trend in weddings at the resort is for the bride to arrive at the ceremony in a horse-drawn carriage.

a hill to the tramway station. Two enclosed cable-operated trams transport passengers back and forth every half hour, ascending and descending 6,100 feet through the rugged Chino Canyon, starting at 10:00 A.M. weekdays and 8:00 A.M. weekends and holidays. In moments that are reminiscent of a Hitchcock movie, the trams pass within what seems to be only inches of sheer cliff walls. Within minutes, you've risen from a desert environment to alpine; at the top, the temperature can be forty degrees cooler, and even into warm-weather months, snow may cling to these rocky crevices. (If you take your ride in winter, be sure to bring a warm jacket to wear.) This is a little side trip that could really help put things in perspective, because from the mountain the view to the Coachella Valley below is awesome. The mountain station has a cocktail bar and rather dreary cafeteria, but with plenty of hiking trails fanning out from the station, don't waste your time inside if the weather's nice. Take a walk and let the cool mountain air, the winter snowscape, or the springtime wildflowers cast a spell.

FOR MORE ROMANCE

Drive about 50 miles north of Palm Springs to **Joshua Tree National Park** for a look at the spectacular desert landscape of massive granite boulders and gnarly Joshua trees. Call the visitor center (760–367–5500) for more information.

Fit for Love

ITINERARY 25
One day

Two on the Trail
HIKING IN THE SAN GABRIEL MOUNTAINS

THE SAN GABRIEL MOUNTAINS, those snow-capped peaks that tower thousands of feet above the Los Angeles basin, and on clear days providing a postcard-perfect backdrop for the vast city, are *the* mountains for hiking in Los Angeles. Countless trails crisscross the mountains in the Angeles National Forest, but there's one hike in particular that offers an excellent introduction to these peaks. It's not a difficult hike, so even inexperienced hikers can enjoy part or all of it. A portion of the Gabrielino Trail meanders through the upper reaches of the Arroyo Seco ("dry gully") and leads to a perennial waterfall. You can hike to a point above the waterfall and picnic there. Best of all, you don't have to drive far to reach the trailhead, a serious consideration for Los Angeles hikers. After all, who wants the pleasant effects of the day's hike erased by an endless commute home?

PRACTICAL NOTES: This hike can be enjoyed year-round, but the hiking experience will be different from season to season. Autumn brings some fall color to the oak and sycamore trees in the canyons, while winter and spring can bring wet weather and lots of water in the streambed. Summer temperatures in the mountains can be hot, although they're generally cooler than those in the basin and valleys. Any adventure in the great outdoors, even a short, easy hike like this one, requires some preparation, such as dressing appropriately. The weather and temperature can change in the mountains, especially at higher elevations, which in this area are between 3,500 and 5,000 feet. So don't go off in a tank top, shorts, and flip-flops just because it's sunny and warm when you leave home. If you don't have hiking shoes, wear good, sturdy sneakers. Bring along a hat, sunscreen, and insect repellent. You can pack your picnic lunch in two knapsacks to share the load (pack a plastic bag for the refuse and carry it out with you). Think about taking along a book of poetry to read aloud or a small cassette recorder and a favorite tape to play while you picnic. And don't forget to let a relative or a friend know where you're going and when you expect to return. For more information on the Gabrielino and other trails in the Angeles National Forest, phone (818) 574-5200.

Before parking your car at the trailhead, you must stop at the Clear Creek Station (State Highway 2 and Angeles Forest Highway N3) and purchase a National Forest Adventure Pass, which is really a parking permit. The pass is $5.00 for the day or $30 for the year. The Clear Creek Station is open only on weekends, so if you plan to hike in the forest during the week, you'll have to stop in the town of La Cañada Flintridge to buy a pass at Jay's Shell Station (4530 Angeles Crest Highway; 818-790-3836) or Sports Chalet (920 Foothill Boulevard; 818-790-9800).

Romance
AT A GLANCE

* Follow State Highway 2 into the Angeles National Forest above Los Angeles to hike a portion of the **Gabrielino Trail.** Your first stop (if you're hiking on the weekend) should be the Clear Creek Station (State Highway 2 and Angeles Forest Highway N3) to buy a parking permit. During the week stop in La Cañada Flintridge at Jay's Shell Station (4530 Angeles Crest Highway; 818-790-3836) or Sports Chalet (920 Foothill Boulevard; 818-790-9800) to buy a parking pass.

* From the trailhead in the Switzer picnic area, hike along the shaded portion of the Gabrielino Trail that parallels a mountain stream and eventually leads to a waterfall. Bring along your own picnic and pause along the trail—under an ancient oak tree or above the waterfall—to picnic and observe nature.

DAY ONE: *Morning*

To get to the trailhead, take the **Angeles Crest Highway** (State Highway 2) north from I-210 in La Cañada Flintridge for about 10 miles. The highway itself, which is wide for a mountain road, is something of a wonder. Spanning deep chasms and chiseled out of solid rock walls in some

Poet's Corner

Sure, it's a little corny to suggest taking along a book of poetry from which to read aloud. But, so what? It's just the two of you, and if you've never done something like that, it could be fun to profess your love through the words of Shakespeare, Burns, the Rossettis, Emerson, or another voice. In today's world of hard rock and rap music, lyrics like "Come live with me and be my Love," by the sixteenth-century English dramatist Christopher Marlowe, can sound refreshingly sweet.

places, it extends for 55 miles to Brightwood. Construction, which started in 1929, took almost thirty years.

Stop at the **Clear Creek Station,** just past the junction of State Highway 2 and County Highway N3 (Angeles Forest Highway), for maps and updated information about trail or road closures, fire danger, and other information about the forest. Then drive on another ½ mile until you see the sign for **Switzer Picnic Area** on the right. Follow the steep paved road for ½ mile to the picnic area parking lot. If the gate is locked, go back up to the highway and park in one of the small dirt lots along the highway and walk down the road.

On a nice day, the picnic area may be overflowing with people, but most of them don't venture past the picnic tables. The name of the picnic area, Switzer, comes from the name of the man, Perry Switzer, who established a mountain wilderness camp in the area in the 1880s. Before the highway was built, people would travel up to the camp via stagecoach and burro to fish and hike. A 1938 flood destroyed most of the camp.

From the Switzer Picnic Area, pick up the **Gabrielino Trail** by walking over the small wooden footbridge. A sign points the way to Switzer Falls. The trail at this point is paved in spots and parallels the stream on its meandering course through the rugged Arroyo Seco. After hiking for about 1 mile, you'll come to the remains of the Switzer wilderness camp. At this point, you have two choices. One is to continue hiking along the creek trail, which will lead you to a picnic spot on the rocks just above the waterfall. If you follow this trail, it's not very far to the top of the waterfall. (Please heed the warning signs posted to discourage people from climbing down the slippery rocks of the falls; recently, a man ignored the warnings and fell, severely injuring himself on the rocks.)

The other option is to ford the stream across from the camp and continue up the Gabrielino Trail. Depending on the time of year, the stream may be only a trickle. In the winter, however, rains can swell the creek up to 10 or more feet wide. The Forest Service has been known to place a log here to aid people in crossing. Up to this point, the hike has been more of a shady walk than an outdoor adventure. But on the other side of the stream, the trail makes a fairly steep ascent before leveling out and narrowing along the side of the ridge for the next several hundred yards. You can look down to the stream and waterfall, although there's little shade and no beckoning picnic spot along this part of the trail. So keep on hiking as the trail descends once again into the canyon. Keep to the left and follow the creek upstream for $1/4$ mile into the canyon to an area known as the Cascades. From Switzer Falls, which you've viewed from the trail, the water travels down the rocky streambed to cascade into two small pools in the rocks. You can climb the 30 feet to the upper pool, but be careful on the narrow, steep ledge from which you must scramble down, using your backside to reach the cool, sandy-bottomed upper pool. Later, climb back down and spread yourselves out on a couple of the large, smooth boulders that rim the lower pool and enjoy your picnic. Generally, you can expect to enjoy yourselves in privacy, but do remember that other hikers and picnickers may come by (some couples apparently forget they are in public and get a bit carried away). The hike in from the parking lot to the picnic spot at the Cascades should take about an hour as should the return to the trailhead.

FOR MORE ROMANCE

After a day hiking in the mountains, you'll both be dusty and tired and ready for a long, hot bath. Plan ahead and have plenty of your favorite bath oils, scented candles, and a chilled bottle of champagne waiting at home or your hotel, and order in food from your favorite restaurant or from hotel room service.

☆jai Idyll

HATEVER KIND OF LOVERS you and your partner are, Ojai has something to offer the two of you. Ojai (pronounced *O-hi*) is a small town tucked away in a verdant coastal valley 75 miles northwest of Los Angeles. Its sunny hillsides are draped in avocado trees and citrus orchards. Movie lovers will remind you that the Ojai Valley and the Topa Topa mountains that ring it stood in for Shangri-La in Frank Capra's 1937 film *Lost Horizon*. Music lovers throng into town for the annual Ojai Music Festival. Art lovers praise local artists, none more famous than potter Beatrice Wood. People escaping the big city like to spend a few days in Ojai to get away from it all, slow down a bit, read a book, and spend time with their partners. For outdoor and nature lovers, Ojai means great golf, horseback riding into the hills, bicycling through town, and hiking in the mountains.

PRACTICAL NOTES: Long known as a fine golf resort, **Ojai Valley Inn & Spa** (Country Club Road; 805–646–5511, 800–422–6524; Web site: www.ojairesort.com; $235–$2,000) is just as popular with nongolfers who instead take advantage of the new Spa Ojai and the inn's other activities—horseback riding, bicycling, hiking, swimming, tennis, water aerobics, power walking. It's like a summer camp for grown-ups— a very classy summer camp, to be sure, with a full service spa and great food, where nobody has to sleep on a lumpy cot or in a sleeping bag. Accommodations here are all first class, with the most romantic quarters being the twenty-two rooms in the historic original Hacienda building. Each room in this wing has been redecorated in the California Spanish Revival style popular in the 1920s, with four-poster beds; handmade furniture, such as Morris chairs and Mission armoires; pedestal sinks; hardwood floors; and decorative hand-painted tiles. Altogether the inn, one of the Historic Hotels of America, has 206 guest rooms and suites, many with fireplaces. Ask about one of several Escape Packages that combine accommodations with breakfast or activities like golf, tennis, horseback riding, or a Jeep tour. A two-night minimum stay is required for these packages, which range in price from about $210 to $300 per night. The Spa Ojai Discovery Package (about $518 double, two-night minimum) includes accommodations, unlimited use of spa facilities, and two spa treatments per person, per night. And during the holidays, the inn offers a special Shopping and Pampering Package that comes in at just about $100 per person. Besides casual resort clothes to wear to restaurants in the evening, plan to bring appropriate wardrobe for the outdoor activities: golf shoes, a hat, hard-sole shoes for horseback riding, shorts for bicycling, and hiking shoes. Depending on the season, a warm jacket might come in handy on a cool evening.

DAY ONE: *Afternoon*

Just because check-in time at Ojai Valley Inn isn't until 4:00 P.M. doesn't mean you two can't enjoy an afternoon of bicycling around the

Romance
AT A GLANCE

✶ Pack a good pair of hiking boots, shorts, and casual resort clothes for an activity-filled escape to the **Ojai Valley Inn & Spa** (Country Club Road; 805-646-5511 or 800-422-6524; Web site: www.ojairesort.com; $235-2,000). Arrive at the inn early in the afternoon, borrow bicycles and peddle into town to explore Ojai's shops and have an alfresco lunch at **La Veranda** (109 North Montgomery Street; 805-646-3733; inexpensive). After lunch, visit **Bart's Books,** a treasure-trove of used books, magazines, and sheet music (Matilija Street at Canada Street; 805-646-3755).

✶ That evening, plan to dine at the inn, either at the signature dining room, **Maravilla** (expensive), or at the more casual Oaks Cafe (moderate). Both offer inventive, freshly-prepared dishes and special ambience.

✶ After breakfast the next morning, get the next day off to a hearty start with a guided trail ride through the surrounding hills. In the afternoon, choose among a variety of spa treatments and massages at the inn's new Spa Ojai, or take off on a guided sunset Jeep tour into the Los Padres National Forest. Call **Pink Moment Jeep Tours,** 805-653-1321 or 805-646-3227, or make arrangements with the concierge.

✶ Before you leave Ojai the next day, have the concierge arrange a guided walk around Lake Casitas to bird-watch or a hike into the hills above the avocado and orange groves, following a trail to a mountain stream.

small town. You can also stop to have lunch in one of the little restaurants along the main street and browse in some of its galleries and shops. If you check in early at the inn and your room isn't ready, park the car, leave your luggage with the bellhop, and borrow complimentary hotel bicycles to pedal the mile into town. A bike path begins at Country Club Road and parallels Ojai Avenue, the main street through town. It's a short, easy ride that delivers you quickly to Libbey Park, right in the center of town. The park is the site of the world-famous annual Ojai Music Festival.

Downtown Ojai, with its one main street and its Spanish-style shopping arcade, resembles a village (except for the steady stream of traffic). Lock the bikes in one of the bike stands located intermittently along the arcaded side of the street and spend some time strolling through the downtown area. Of the shops along the arcade, **Tottenham Court** (242 East Ojai Avenue; 805–646–2339), the English gift shop and tearoom, is well known as the place to buy china, crystal, and silver gifts or to have tea and sandwiches. Ojai, however, is considered an artists' community rather than an outpost of British imperialism, so you simply must visit any of the galleries. **Primavera Gallery** (214 East Ojai Avenue; 805–646–7133) specializes in glass (such as the Inhabited Planet spheres of glassmaker Josh Simpson), wood, and jewelry. Look for little 1-inch glass hearts here; at between $22 and $38 apiece, they're perfect little gifts.

Rings, of course, can symbolize the bond of love. At **HumanArts** (310 East Ojai Avenue; 805–646–1525), jewelry maker and proprietor Hallie Katz showcases a collection of contemporary rings, jewelry, and crafts. Simple, half-round sterling bands designed by Mikal Deese have eye-catching corner bindings of 18K gold; Santa Barbara jewelry maker Thomas Rhodes has placed moonstone in a ring setting of sterling silver and 14K rose and yellow gold for a hip, elegant look. Katz herself has a dramatic flair to her own ring designs that makes each one unique, and she works with clients to custom design pieces that are quite affordable.

LUNCH

Our favorite lunchtime option is **La Veranda** (109 North Montgomery Street; 805–646–3733; inexpensive), which is half a block off Ojai Avenue. Under the shade of a big wisteria tree, the two of you can sit outside on the wooden porch, where jasmine climbs up the posts and classical music plays in the background, and order from a menu that has a European-Mediterranean bent: tabbouleh and grape leaves, baked eggplant, salad niçoise, and artichoke or spinach and feta quiche.

After lunch, ride your bikes over to **Bart's Books** (Matilija Street at Canada Street; 805-646-3755), as much for the opportunity to browse through more used books, magazines, and sheet music than you could imagine (something like 100,000 items) as for the unique setup. Most of Bart's books are organized and stacked on shelves built outdoors on a patio and shaded by an old oak tree. A small cottage holds collector's editions. Several shelves of used paperback and hardcover books line the sidewalks. After hours, customers are on the honor system to pay the marked price for these books by slipping the money through the slot in the door.

DAY ONE: *Evening*

DINNER

Dine at either of the inn's restaurants: Chef Brent Wuest's signature room, **Maravilla** (expensive), or the more casual **Oak Cafe** (moderate), which also has alfresco dining on the patio. Both have a rustic, but classy, atmosphere and feature Wuest's lauded Pacific Provincial cooking. Wuest stocks his kitchen with foods from local farmers and growers, and he has planted an herb garden at the inn. The menu at Maravilla changes daily, but you can expect to find dishes like French turbot in sesame-orange brown butter, natural chicken breast and local Channel Islands lobster with pink peppercorn lobster sauce, seared yellowtail snapper with plum tomato concasse, grilled elk with pumpkin rosemary spaetzle, or roasted rack of lamb with goat cheese polenta. Chef Wuest also prepares a prix fixe spa menu (about $60 per person) and a five-course *menu gastronomique* (about $65 per person). Each course of the menu gastronomique can be paired with a specially selected California wine, which adds about $40 per person to the cost. Exposed wood beams, fine Italian leather chairs, art work, and roaring fireplaces create a stately atmosphere at Maravilla, which serves dinner Wednesday through Sunday.

The Oak Cafe offers a more casual atmosphere and menu: red chili tortilla soup with ranchero cheese and avocado salsa, smoked salmon with warm potato pancake, oak-smoked rib eye with caramelized onions, spit-roasted chicken, pizza, and pastas. You can dine inside, where a wintry evening is warmed by the fireplace, or outside on the terrace, where summer nights are balmy and romantic under the stars.

Here are your after-dinner options: Stroll hand in hand around the grounds of the hotel to gaze at stars, have a chilled bottle of champagne waiting for you in your room, enjoy the piano music in Maravilla on Friday and Saturday evenings, or check out the poetry reading, musical performance, or book signing that may be taking place at **Local Hero Bookstore** downtown on a Friday evening (254 East Ojai Avenue; 805–646–3165).

DAY TWO: *Morning*

BREAKFAST

Take breakfast this morning in the **Vista Dining Room** (moderate), which has grand views of the tenth hole of the golf course and the surrounding ridges. There's nothing Spartan about the continental breakfast buffet that begins at 6:30 A.M.: Sideboards are loaded with baskets of muffins and breads, juice, fresh fruit, cereal, yogurt, and other goodies. You can also order a full cooked breakfast.

If you're not playing golf, take a guided horseback ride into the surrounding hills (make arrangements for this activity when you book your room or as soon as you check in). You'll meet your guide and other riders at the inn's stables at **Rancho Dos Rios**. The guide will help the two of you mount your horses and give you basic instruction in holding the reins and using them to direct the horses. Then you're off on a pleasant ride through surrounding hills, fields of spring wildflowers, and waist-high purple sage. The ride is more interpretive than adventure, with the guide pointing out different plants and trees, such as the California live oak (interior oak), the bright yellow and fragrant flowers of the Scotch broom, the shiny three-leaf cluster of the poison oak, hummingbird sage, owl's clover, and mistletoe, which grows in this region as a parasite hanging from the branches of the sycamore tree.

DAY TWO: *Afternoon*

LUNCH

Sit on the inn's **Oak Cafe** terrace under an arbor of wisteria and the dappled shade of ancient oak trees. Try a salad (for example, warm grilled chicken salad with lettuce, apples, roasted walnuts, blue cheese, and port wine vinaigrette), a sandwich (grilled local vegetable sandwich with herbed goat cheese on sourdough), burger, or entree (pasta or fish). The setting is idyllic: the rolling green expanse of the golf course backed by the Topa Topa Mountains in the distance.

Don't eat too much at lunch if you've scheduled afternoon massages at Spa Ojai. In fact, you may want to head down to the spa early and pick up a sandwich or salad and eat at the poolside cafe, Acorn. The spa compound looks like a little Mediterranean village, with a bell tower rising 50 feet over the central courtyard and fountain. The little courtyard, which is surrounded by an artist-in-residence studio, the Yamaguchi hair and nail salon, the boutique, and the cafe, can be a busy place, but with all the comings and goings, there is no sense of urgency, but rather of serenity. Inside, sculpted and plastered ceilings, tile floors, hand-stenciled walls, and fireplaces, evoke a sense of balance and well-being, which are the guiding principles at **Spa Ojai.** You've got a choice of a number of different therapeutic treatments, massages, skin and hair care treatments, and exercise programs. But the signature treatment at Spa Ojai is something called "Kuyam" (*Koo-yam*), a Chumash word meaning "a place to rest together." This fifty-minute treatment combines cleansing mud, dry heat, and steam, along with inhalation therapy.

Perhaps you prefer a more active, exciting afternoon. How about a sunset Jeep tour to Chief's Peak, the highest and most prominent peak in the Topa Topa Mountains around Ojai. (Make your arrangements for

Jeep tours with the concierge on arrival.) **Pink Moment Jeep Tours** (805–653–1321 or 805–646–3227) operates several different tours, using off-road four-wheel-drive Jeeps to access the rugged terrain of the mountains, which are part of Los Padres National Forest. Watching the sun set behind a mountain ridge from a vantage point of 5,500 feet is dramatic and romantic, especially if the moment includes a picnic basket of fruit and cheese and champagne. You'll take off from the inn in the late afternoon (departure will vary depending on the time of year) in an open Jeep for a three-and-one-half-hour tour high into the forest. Your guide is trained to entertain and inform guests about the history and folklore, the geology, and the flora and fauna of the forest. Once into the forest, it's a rugged, bumpy ride on unpaved fire trails to a spot below Chief's Peak. Along the way you may spot a red-tailed hawk and other wildlife—and possibly the offshore Channel Islands, many miles to the west. The tour is timed to arrive at Chief's Peak, which is about 5,500 feet above sea level, in time for a view of the sun setting into the ocean, beyond the ridges to the west. It can be a magical moment together (just remember to bring warm jackets, in case even the summer evening turns chilly). The company has several options if this tour seems too rugged.

The Pink Moment

How could there not be magic in a place where the mountains that ring the valley are blushed with pink in the glow of the setting sun? Ojai's Pink Moment is a seasonal event, from late October through January, when the sun is low in the sky. The magenta rays of the setting sun fire the Topa Topa Mountains with a rosy blush. The best places at the Ojai Valley Inn to view the phenomenon are outside in front of the lobby and from the terrace by the Hacienda building.

DAY TWO: *Evening*

DINNER

By the time you return to the inn, you'll still be revved up by the Jeep tour, although you'll likely be feeling a bit windblown and dusty from the trip. So head right for the nineteenth hole, the very casual **Club Bar,** to warm up by the fire, have a drink, and order hamburgers from the bar menu. You'll still have time for a romantic bubble bath before slipping into bed.

DAY THREE: *Morning*

After breakfast (room service begins at 7:00 A.M. if you opt to skip the breakfast buffet in the Vista Dining Room), start the day with an 8:30 A.M. hike into the mountains to Gridley Creek. (You must arrange this in advance; check with the concierge upon arrival. The Gridley Creek hike does not go out every day; some mornings a bird-watching walk around Lake Casitas is scheduled instead. There's an extra charge for guided hikes and walks.) Judy, an avid hiker who's also on the inn's staff, will probably lead the hike. After a short drive to the trailhead, you'll start an easy-to-moderate climb, past groves of avocado and orange trees, along the Gridley Creek Trail for the 3-mile hike to the stream. Along the way, you'll pass groves of avocado trees (which are sometimes visited at night by hungry bears). Judy, who has a sharp eye for clues of animals' recent presence on the trail, will point out a bear print or other evidence, like coyote or raccoon scat. When she sees the black sage plants growing trailside, she'll stop, break off a leaf, and urge you to smell it. Farther along, she'll stop again and reach down to stroke the petals of the velvety woolly blue curls. Depending on the pace of your hike, you may not make it all the way to the creek (we didn't), but you'll be able to hear it as you draw closer. In any event you should be back at the hotel by about 11:30 A.M., in time for checkout.

As the two of you leave the Ojai Valley to drive home, don't be surprised if you feel rejuvenated. We all know, of course, that Shangri-La is a mythical place. Or is it? After a few days in Ojai, it's hard to say with any certainty.

FOR MORE ROMANCE

Want a more rigorous Ojai idyll? Sign up for a guided mountain bike tour into the mountains, or rent the bikes, grab a map, and head off on your own. Consult the concierge at the inn for more information.

Sweethearts in the Saddle:

HORSEBACK RIDING IN THE SANTA MONICA MOUNTAINS

IMAGINE A SETTING IN WHICH A FLAT ROCKY LEDGE next to a cascading miniature waterfall becomes the spot where a young man proposes to the woman he loves. When she accepts, they kiss and then toast the moment with a glass of sparkling cider. A scene from a movie? Could be, but the scene I'm thinking of did indeed occur at a lovely dell, shaded by ancient oak trees in the Santa Monica Mountains above Malibu. And to get to the idyllic spot, the young couple rode horses, guided by an experienced trail guide.

PRACTICAL NOTES: If the smell of horses, the buzz of flies, and the threat of poison oak somehow daunt you or your partner, then this is not the activity for you. Even if you're game for this adventure, be prepared to be saddle sore the next day, because although you'll receive instructions about how to "sit" a horse, it takes years of practice to do it properly. **Adventures on Horseback** (31811 Mulholland Highway; 818–706–0888; reservations necessary) has several options for horseback riding, including moonlight rides and the two-and-one-half-hour Sweethearts at Sunset ride. Appropriate dress would be jeans or other long pants and hard-heeled boots, sturdy hiking shoes, or sneakers (no sandals). Depending on the time of day you're riding, you should bring hats and sunblock; jackets or sweatshirts are a good thing to have for a sunset ride. Don't forget water. If you're not familiar with the area, a good map could be useful as well.

DAY ONE: Afternoon

Saddle up, so to speak, a bit earlier in the day by driving into the Santa Monica Mountains through the rugged chaparral and elfin-forest beauty of Topanga Canyon along Topanga Canyon Boulevard. In the heart of the canyon is the community of Topanga, beloved by leftover hippies, New Agers, yuppies, and rednecks, all of whom, somehow, seem to coexist in this erstwhile outpost.

LUNCH

People claim they can feel cosmic and angelic vibrations when they sit out on the terraced patio beside Topanga Creek for lunch at the **Inn of the Seventh Ray** (128 Old Topanga Canyon Road off Topanga Canyon Boulevard; 310–455–1311; moderate). That may have something to do with all those statues of various deities scattered about the place. More likely, they're blown away by the idyllic setting beside Topanga Creek, shaded by a canopy of trees and viny flowering plants. A few tables for two have been discreetly set apart in a shady alcove and under a small gazebo, perfect for a lingering lunch—grilled ahi, a free-range chicken salad sandwich, heavenly salads—and a glass of wine. You won't find a more bucolic spot in Los Angeles. And if the cosmic vibrations really are better here, who could complain?

Romance
AT A GLANCE

* Call **Adventures on Horseback** (31811 Mulholland Highway; 818–706–0888; reservations necessary) in advance to make reservations for a Sweethearts at Sunset horseback ride through the Santa Monica Mountains above Malibu.

* Start the adventure earlier in the day with lunch on the terrace at the **Inn of the Seventh Ray** (128 Old Topanga Canyon Road off Topanga Canyon Boulevard; 310–455–1311; moderate) in the rugged Topanga Canyon. Then drive west along Mulholland Highway or take the freeway to Adventures on Horseback's Malibu location. Your guide will lead to a waterfall and along ridges covered in wild sage and ancient oak trees. From a mountain meadow, you can, on a clear day, see the Pacific Ocean and watch the sun sink behind the next ridge.

* Then, retreat to the **Westlake Village Inn** (31943 Agoura Road, Westlake Village; 818–889–0230) for a relaxing evening with whirlpool bath and fireplace.

It's a long, winding drive on Old Topanga Canyon Road to Mulholland Highway, which will eventually bring you to Kanan Road, about 10 miles west as the crow flies (bring along a map). An easier route is to take Topanga Canyon Boulevard north to the San Fernando Valley and the 101 (Ventura) Freeway west. Exit at Kanan Road, travel south about 7 miles into the mountains to Mulholland Highway and turn right (west). In about a mile, you should see a sign on the right, ADVENTURES ON HORSE-BACK. Turn down the dirt drive and find a place to park under the trees next to the corral.

Adventures on Horse-back is located on Saddle-rock Ranch, a private estate often used as a movie location and wedding site. When the two of you arrive, proprietor Angela Locascio and her staff will greet you and ask you to sign a liability waiver form. Then you'll be asked about your riding experience, and appropriate horses will be selected for you. Once you've mounted the horses, the stirrups will be adjusted, and you'll be given instructions about how to sit in the saddle, use the reins, and ride a horse. Then you'll be off on your ride.

Angela created the two-hour Sweethearts at Sunset ride as a private experience for couples only ($175–$200 per couple). It's a popular choice for couples celebrating a birthday or anniversary, and it's gentle enough for inexperienced or novice riders. Angela adds a romantic touch by including a little picnic of cheese and crackers, fruit, and sparkling cider (for an extra charge, you could customize the picnic, by having chicken or something else added). She's found a delightful spot next to a small waterfall, where you'll stop for half an hour. As the guide tends to the horses, you two climb down to a ledge next to the waterfall, pop the cork on the cider, and nibble on cheese and fruit. At least one wedding proposal has been proffered on this spot and accepted, says Angela.

It's OK to Kiss the Horse, Too

The laconic actor Gary Cooper, who starred in High Noon, one of the all-time great Westerns, was once quoted as saying, "In Westerns, you were permitted to kiss your horse but never your girl." ("Well, It Was This Way," Saturday Evening Post, March 17, 1958)

The ride continues up into the hills, along ridges covered in wild sage, wildflowers, ancient oak and sycamore trees, even poison oak (your guide will remind you how to identify it and alert you as you come upon it). After riding for twenty minutes or so, you'll arrive at a mountain meadow. From your 2,000-foot vantage point, the Pacific Ocean may be visible miles away. A cool breeze rustles the grass that the horses are quietly nibbling. The timing should be right to watch the sun sink behind the next ridge, the sky turning to flame. For the next ten minutes, the world seems a peaceful place. (Don't get so lost in the moment that you forget to take pictures. The guide will probably offer to snap one of the two of you, too.)

Returning to the ranch, part of the ride may be in the dark, an interesting, if somewhat unnerving, experience. But horses are supposed to see well in the dark, so I've been told. And when you've finally dismounted, don't forget to hug your horses and tip the guide.

DAY ONE: *Evening*

Retreat to **Westlake Village Inn** (31943 Agoura Road, Westlake Village; 818–889–0230) and pamper yourself by booking a suite ($155–$250) with a fireplace and whirlpool tub. To reach the hotel, leave Saddlerock Ranch and retrace your route to the 101 (Ventura) Freeway. Travel west about 3½ miles to the Lindero Canyon Road exit. Turn left on Lindero Canyon, cross over the freeway, and turn right at Agoura Road. In less than 1 mile, you'll see the hotel on your right.

FOR MORE ROMANCE

This itinerary could be incorporated into the Malibu itinerary (see Itinerary 8, "Beach Blanket Romance").

Set Sail

WEEKEND SAILING COURSE IN SANTA BARBARA

*L*EARNING TO SAIL TAKES A LOT MORE TIME than a weekend. But then the point of this weekend isn't to become accredited sailors; rather, it's to learn a few fundamentals, get some fresh air and exercise, and have fun doing something different. And instead of spending the night in a nondescript motel, you can stay on board a 30-foot sailboat. That means roughing it a bit (you'll receive a key card to use the marina shower-restroom), but that's part of the fun.

PRACTICAL NOTES: **Santa Barbara Sailing Center** is accredited by the American Sailing Association as a sailing school. The center is located in the harbor off Cabrillo Boulevard at Harbor Way, next to the public boat launch, in Santa Barbara (805–962–2826 or 800–350–9090; Web site: www.sbsailctr.com; E-mail: charter@sbsailctr.com). The weekend Resort Course is designed for novices who would like to learn the basics of sailing (no ASA certification is awarded for this course). The cost— $350 per couple—includes eight hours of sailing instruction and the overnight sailboat accommodations, plus a 10 percent port tax. Besides packing shorts, T-shirts, boating or tennis shoes, sunscreen, and a hat, bring along a windbreaker and some sort of rain jacket (just in case). You can bring your own sleeping bags and towels or pay an additional $20 cleaning fee per person to have sheets and towels provided for you. You can also bring food aboard the boat (but cooking is not allowed), although most people take advantage of the nearby restaurants.

DAY ONE: Morning

Instruction at the Santa Barbara Sailing Center begins promptly at 10:00 A.M. and lasts until 2:00 P.M. (Eat a light breakfast before you arrive and bring along a few snacks, because you won't have a chance to eat again until after instruction is over.)

After meeting your instructor, you'll get right to work aboard your "classroom": a 21-foot stable keelboat. When you scheduled your weekend, some instructional materials and a loaner video that introduced some of the fundamentals were mailed to you to study. Now you'll find out how well you studied your lessons. Pretty soon you'll know your bow from your stern, starboard from port, and you'll be using terms like *lines* and *sheets* instead of the landlubber word *ropes*. You'll practice how to *rig* the boat (set the sails) and learn about wind direction, setting a course, and using the wind to sail from point A to point B. You'll get in some real sailing time that first morning, too, by casting off and practicing what you've learned by sailing around the harbor. You'll feel what it's like to have a breeze fill your *jib* (front sail), and you'll find out how to *come about* (turn into the wind). If the wind is light, you'll sail past the breakwater and head out into the Pacific Ocean.

Romance
AT A GLANCE

✳ Learn and practice some of the fundamentals of sailing by signing up for a two-day sailing course at the **Santa Barbara Sailing Center** (Cabrillo Boulevard at Harbor Way, next to the public boat launch; 805–962–2826 or 800–350–9090; Web site: www.sbsailctr.com; E-mail: charter@sbsailctr.com).

✳ Spend the day aboard your "classroom"— a 21-foot stable keelboat practicing techniques and applying them while sailing around the harbor. Learn "bow" from "stem" and "starboard" from "port." Practice rigging the boat and using the wind to turn it.

✳ When class is over in the afternoon, have lunch at **Shoreline Beach Cafe** (801 Shoreline Drive; 805–568–0064; inexpensive). Then explore **Stearns Wharf** and lower State Street or rent bicycles at **Cycles for Rent** (101 State Street; 805–966–3804). That night, as harbor lights twinkle in the background, dine at one of nearby waterfront restaurants. When it's time to turn in, you'll sleep aboard a sailing yacht at the Sailing Center.

✳ Class resumes the next morning at 10:00 A.M. Before you complete your abbreviated sailing course, you'll get a chance to apply what you've learned in a practice sail around the harbor or past the breakwater into the ocean.

DAY ONE: *Afternoon*

By 2:00 P.M. your sailing lessons will be over for the day. Back at the dock you'll be escorted to the boat that you'll be staying on overnight. The size of the boat will vary between 30 and 42 feet, but the idea is the same: a "cozy" but comfortable berth, wood paneling, a galley, and refrigerator. Sort of a floating Winnebago. Small quarters can quickly get stuffy, so open the windows, er, portholes, to clear the air. You have to go off the boat to use the facilities, and you'll be given a key card for that purpose.

LUNCH

There's no indoor seating at **Shoreline Beach Cafe** (801 Shoreline Drive; 805-568-0064; inexpensive) on Leadbetter Beach, which is a short distance from the marina. Umbrellas protect tables on the glass-enclosed deck, or you can sit at a table right on the beach and dig your toes into the sand. Then dig into steamed clams, shrimp, grilled ahi salad with roasted peppers and tangy vinaigrette, or the very popular Hawaiian plate: two or three selections of fresh fish or steak, two servings of sticky rice, and salad. It's an ideal choice for two.

The rest of the afternoon is yours to explore Santa Barbara. By walking south along the beach path, it's about ½ mile from the marina to **Stearns Wharf** and lower **State Street**. To keep the nautical theme of your day going, walk out onto the wharf, where you'll find souvenir stands and restaurants, as well as the **Sea Center** (805-962-0885). This interpretive "window" on the Santa Barbara Channel looks at the impact of oil exploration on the channel and presents life-size models of whales, dolphins, and seabirds; an indoor aquarium and tide pool; and Chumash Indian artifacts.

State Street is Santa Barbara's main drag. The upper end of State is the important shopping district; lower State is looking better these days, with new shops and cafes moving into the renovated buildings along this stretch of avenue. To see more of State Street, hop on the MTD Downtown-Waterfront shuttle. It runs every ten to twelve minutes, until about 6:00 P.M., and costs twenty-five cents each way. If you haven't had enough exercise for the day, you can rent bicycles at **Cycles for Rent** (101 State Street at Mason; 805-966-3804) to pedal along the beach path.

DAY ONE: *Evening*

DINNER

There's something immediately familiar about long wooden piers like Stearns Wharf. The smell of old, damp splintered wood and tar sends me back thirty-five years to childhood vacations at the Jersey shore and summer nights at the amusement pier on the boardwalk. There's also something comforting about wharf restaurants: the aged timber, the lobster tank, the constant motion of waiters and kids. **Harbor Restaurant** is no exception (210 Stearns Wharf; 805–963–3311; moderate). It's been there forever and is immensely popular. For the most part, the food—grilled fresh fish entrees, shrimp scampi, lobster salad, coquille of scallops and crab—is turned out well, although salads can come out a bit overdressed and vegetables might be frozen, not fresh. Desserts are big and gooey, and the service is pleasantly efficient. Then there are those harbor lights twinkling on the water—they should make up for any lapses in the kitchen.

At night a shroud of fog can envelop the coast, eerily diffusing light and sound. In the distance the moan of a foghorn can suggest mystery and romance. And after a day of fresh salt air, sunshine, and exercise, the two of you should drift off to sleep, safe and snug in your berth.

DAY TWO: *Morning*

BREAKFAST

Fuel up for the day's sailing lesson with a good breakfast at a delightful little cafe on State Street, **Pierre Lafond** (516 State Street; 805–962–1455; inexpensive). A breakfast bagel topped with scrambled eggs mixed with feta cheese and spinach is nice and filling, as are huevos rancheros, French toast, pancakes, or eggs with country potatoes. Steaming cups of café au lait are just right to take the chill off a misty morning.

Class starts again at 10:00 A.M. Only today, you'll spend all four hours on the water. Again, depending on the wind, your instructor will confine you to the harbor or let you out past the breakwater into the ocean. The big lessons today are learning to *tack* (change direction by using the wind to turn the boat) and the rules of etiquette at sea (who's got the right of way, that sort of thing).

By the end of the day's lesson, you should have discovered some of the pleasures of sailing (if, as a nonsailor, you didn't already appreciate them), if nothing more than having learned to *jibe* (turn while going downwind) without getting clonked in the head by the boom as it swings across the boat.

FOR MORE ROMANCE

For more ideas about what to do and see in Santa Barbara, see Itinerary 10, "Jewel of the Coast," and Itinerary 22, "Hills of Enchantment."

Ocean Kayaking
ADVENTURE IN MALIBU

S URFING'S NOT THE ONLY GAME IN MALIBU. Ocean kayaking is the hot new sport that everyone wants to try. From a beach next door to Malibu's famous surfing strand, the two of you can set out on a weekend morning's easy kayaking adventure along the coastline. Or you can take kayaking lessons and then set off on a short scenic exploratory paddle. Either way you get to see Malibu from a different perspective while enjoying plenty of fresh air and exercise together.

PRACTICAL NOTES: Make arrangements with **Malibu Ocean Sports** (22935 Pacific Coast Highway; 310–456–6302) for the kayak tours, kayaking lessons, or kayak rentals. The tours last about two and a half hours, include some basic instruction, and cost about $50 per person. Tours are offered only on weekends and, due to weather, only between April and October. Kayaking lessons are offered in groups ($49 per person, plus tax) or privately at your convenience ($74 per person for two hours). The kayaks used for the tours and lessons are sit-on-top kayaks; they're safe and easy to use, so previous experience is not necessary, but you should each be able to swim at least 50 yards. Plan to wear swimwear and appropriate footwear, such as Tevas or Aqua Socks. You probably won't tip over, but if you're wearing glasses, you may lose them, so it's a good idea to secure them with some sort of headband. Don't forget to bring along a hat, sunscreen, and a towel.

DAY ONE: *Morning*

The coastline kayak tour takes off at 9:00 or 10:00 A.M., so the two of you will have to get up a bit early to arrive in Malibu a few minutes before. The early start is because the wind and ocean conditions are generally calmer in the morning. It's also the time when the dolphins make their transition from traveling south to north, and chances are good you'll spot several of them within several yards of your kayak.

When you arrive at Malibu Ocean Sports, across the street from Malibu Pier, you'll be asked to sign a waiver of liability. If you've forgotten anything like sunscreen or a headband for your glasses, you can buy it there. When everybody in your group is present and accounted for, you'll start the most dangerous part of your adventure—crossing Pacific Coast Highway to the beach where the kayaks await.

On the beach for the next fifteen or twenty minutes, you'll receive basic instructions about paddling techniques and safety. The type of kayak used is the Cobra, a wide, stable sit-on-top kayak that's easy to get in and out of and that has scupper holes that automatically drain water out of the cockpit. An adjustable backrest helps you sit upright in the kayak. The paddle is more than just a long pole with flippers on both ends. It's aerodynamically designed to help reduce wind drag as you lift one end out of the water to dip the other end in. It's brightly colored and can also be used in an emergency to signal for help or alert an approaching boat of your presence. Paddling itself, as you'll soon find out, is a self-correcting technique; once in the water, you'll get the hang of it rather quickly. Don't forget your disposable camera (one you won't mind getting wet), or you will miss photo opportunities before and after the trip.

The instructor-guide explains about wave sets and counting waves, a trick surfers also use to calculate when to launch into the surf without being swamped by a crashing wave. The same technique is applied when it's time to come in, so you use the waves to help propel you toward the

Romance AT A GLANCE

✷ Explore the beautiful Malibu coast on a morning kayak tour with **Malibu Ocean Sports** (22935 Pacific Coast Highway; 310–456–6302). After receiving some basic instructions in safety and paddling, you'll launch your kayaks and begin your tour.

✷ Paddling about 200 yards offshore, you'll share the world with seabirds, seals, dolphins, pelicans, and other creatures. Your guide will explain other kayaking techniques and inform you about the Malibu ecology.

beach. Novice kayakers want to know, of course, what to do if the kayak tips over and they're dunked in the water. The kayak is lightweight and easy to right. You'll be shown the correct way to pull yourself out of the water to get into the kayak. You'll also learn the international hand symbols to signal for help (one arm waved over the head) or an emergency (both arms cross-waved overhead).

When you're finally launched, it may take a minute or two to get your bearings and feel coordinated in your kayak. By the time you've paddled out about 200 yards, just beyond the surf line, you'll be noticing the long-necked shorebird, a cormorant perhaps, that skims by just a feather's breadth above the shimmering water. As you and your partner turn up current to paddle along the coast, seagulls soar overhead and a formation of brown pelicans glides by, a majestic flying escort. Sailboats scud silently along the horizon, and waves that "crashed" onto the beach a few minutes ago now seem to slip almost silently into the sandy shore. Seals, curious about your presence, pop up to take a look, and if you're lucky, in a moment that feels like Flipper meets Jacques Cousteau, dolphins may make an appearance.

Moonlight Over the Marina

If you want a little moonlight with your kayaking, ask Malibu Ocean Sports about the Marina Moonlight Paddle, a four-hour group excursion around the placid moonlit waters of Marina del Rey, followed by optional drinks and dinner.

The paddling tour covers about 2 miles of the coast, past Malibu Lagoon and the exclusive Malibu colony residences. Along the way, the instructor-guide explains how wave action affects a kayak, the best way to cross the wake of a boat, and other kayaking techniques. He'll also do his best to answer questions about the topography and ecology of the Malibu coastline.

Paddling will give you exercise, but it shouldn't seem extreme or difficult. The return trip will be easier, because you'll be traveling down current. When the two of you come ashore, someone will be there to help you pull your kayaks onto the beach. If you've enjoyed the excursion or the lesson, show your appreciation by tipping your instructor-guide (the amount is up to you, but the customary 15 to 20 percent would be appropriate).

LUNCH

Slip on clean T-shirts and shorts over your swimsuits, and drive north along Pacific Coast Highway to Zuma beach, about a 10-minute drive. At Westward Beach Road (look for the Malibu Country Inn), turn left and drive up the hill to the **Hideaway Restaurant** (6506 Westward Beach Road at Pacific Coast Highway; 310-457-9622; inexpensive). Once you're there, you can sit out on the deck, order a salad or sandwich, and enjoy views of the ocean and the surrounding mountains.

FOR MORE ROMANCE

Combine this itinerary with a longer stay in Malibu (see Itinerary 8, "Beach Blanket Romance").

Biking Around the Bay
NEWPORT BEACH

OU'D NEVER KNOW IT FROM ALL THOSE steel-and-glass office towers that dominate the landscape along the freeway, but Newport Beach is something of a recreational paradise. Boating, of course, goes without saying—Newport Bay is one of the world's largest small-boat harbors. You don't have to be a millionaire yacht owner, however, to rent a couple of kayaks for an hour or two to paddle around the bay. Most surprising to discover, perhaps, is the Upper Newport Bay Ecological Reserve, a 752-acre coastal wetland that's been maintained in one of the most highly urbanized corridors in Orange County. Skirting the reserve are miles of paved bikeway, offering an easy, scenic route for cyclists of all skills. From Los Angeles, Newport Beach is an easy drive 60 miles south on the 405 Freeway.

PRACTICAL NOTES: The bikeway around Upper Newport Bay Ecological Reserve does include some hills, though nothing too strenuous. Call the **Newport Beach Department of Public Works** (City Hall, 3300 Newport Boulevard; 949–644–3311) and ask to have a copy of the "Bikeways" map sent to you. It shows all the bike trails in Newport Beach. To rent bicycles, expect to pay a per bike day rate of between $12 and $18 for a beach cruiser ($5.00 to $8.00 hourly) and about $18.00 for a mountain bike (about $6.00 hourly). On Balboa Peninsula, **Bob's Bikes and Skates** (118 23rd Street at Newport Pier; 949–673–8480) rents beach cruisers and mountain bikes. On Upper Newport Bay rent beach cruisers at **ResortWatersports** at Newport Dunes Resort (Coast Highway at Jamboree Road; 800-585-0747) or **Hyatt New-porter** (1107 Jamboree Road; 949-729-1234). For paddling around Newport Harbor, rent kayaks at **Boat Rentals of America** (949-673-7200) next to the auto ferry and the Balboa Fun Pavilion on Balboa Peninsula. Kayak rentals run between $10.00 and $15.00 an hour, plus a deposit (about $50, cash or credit card), and a California license or other photo ID. One of the biggest challenges facing visitors to Newport Beach is parking. On Balboa Peninsula metered spaces in lots around Newport Pier fill up fast on summer weekends especially; meters accept only quarters (a quarter buys fifteen minutes; maximum time is three hours). There's an attendant lot at Balboa Pier (about $7.00 for the day). Hotels have guest parking, which may or may not cost extra. On Balboa Island there's only very limited street parking. For more information on Newport Beach, contact the **Newport Beach Conference & Visitors Bureau** at 949-722-1611 or 800-942-6278.

Romance

AT A GLANCE

* Reserve a room in the romantic Victorian **Doryman's Inn** (2102 West Ocean Front at Newport Pier; 949-675-7300 or 800-541-8749; Web site: www.DorymansInn.com; $129–$259) or at the beachfront European-style **Portofino Beach Hotel** (2306 West Ocean Front; 949-673-7030; Web site: www.portofinobeachhotel.com). Arrive in Newport Beach in time for a ferry ride to **Balboa Island** and lunch. Then rent kayaks (Boat Rentals of America; 949-673-7200) and paddle around Newport Bay.

* For a romantic dinner that evening, take an oceanfront walk to **Renato** (2304 West Ocean Front; 949-673-8058; moderate to expensive), or return to Balboa Island and dine in the cozy little family-owned trattoria, **Amelia's** (311 Marine; 949-673-6580; moderate).

* After a walk along the beach the next morning, discover the beauty of **Upper Newport Bay Ecological Reserve**. Bike around this ancient geological formation, one of California's last remaining coastal wetlands. From the deck of **Back Bay Cafe** on the edge of the reserve (Newport Dunes Resort, 1131 Back Bay Drive; 949-729-3863; inexpensive), you can reflect on the day's events.

DAY ONE: *Afternoon*

Be as patient as possible as you exit the 405 Freeway at Highway 55–Newport Avenue and join the heavy traffic heading toward Balboa Peninsula. You'll soon pass all the commercial centers that line the highway and cross over the bridge at Lido Village onto the peninsula for your first look at Newport Bay. More than 9,000 private yachts and boats call this bay home, making Newport Bay the largest small-boat harbor in the world, so local boosters claim. Small beach cottages and luxurious residences share close-knit quarters on the peninsula and the bay's two islands, Lido and Balboa. Keep left as Newport Avenue becomes Balboa Boulevard, and head south to Balboa Pier (Balboa Boulevard at Main Street), about midway down the peninsula. Park in the lot there and walk 3 blocks toward the bay to the auto ferry. The ferry, a low-slung, narrow barge, is a throwback to the old days when the ferry was the only way to get back and forth from Balboa Island and the peninsula. Quaint, but practical and fun, it transports cars, bicyclists, and pedestrians from one point to the other in about three minutes. The fare is fifty cents for pedestrians (more for cars and bikes). Once on Balboa Island, it should take about fifteen minutes to walk along Bay Front to Balboa Island's main drag, Marine Avenue.

Balboa Island, with its small-seaside-town atmosphere and narrow, alleylike streets, seems to exist in a universe light years away from the anonymous subdivided residential sprawl and office-park blight that's come to symbolize so much of Orange County over the years. Clearly the owners of the cottages on the island have taken great pains to personalize their homes, as evidenced by the different styles and decoration—ultramodern glass-and-steel boxes, fanciful New Orleansesque cottages, Cape Cods, Spanish bungalows. Take the stroll at a leisurely pace, and don't feel shy about holding hands or stopping for a few minutes to sit on one of the many benches and look out to the bay.

LUNCH

On Marine Avenue, Balboa Island's eucalyptus tree–lined main street, you'll find gift boutiques and small shops, as well as a few cafes like **Wilma's Patio** (225 Marine; 949–675–5542; inexpensive), a casual, cheerful, family-dining spot that's perfect for a quick burger, a club sandwich, soup and salad, or an all-day breakfast. Lunch of pasta or fresh fish becomes more of a lingering affair at **Amelia's** (311 Marine; 949–673–6580; moderate), the most romantic little restaurant on the island. Each of three rooms in this charming, family-owned trattoria is cozy and inviting. Amelia's is an excellent choice for dinner, too.

As you step off the ferry, look for the **Boat Rentals of America** (949–673–7200) concession stand to the right. That's where you can rent single or double kayaks for the afternoon to paddle around the bay and Balboa Island. Life preservers are stored on the kayaks; wearing them is recommended but not mandatory. The waters of Balboa Bay are quite calm, although heavily trafficked with boats of all shapes and sizes—from 17-foot runabouts and 20-foot canopied electric boats to million-dollar yachts. It's about 1,200 feet across the bay to Balboa Island, the circumference of which is about 3 miles. The lower part of the bay itself is about 4 miles from end to end. Make sure you've brought along hats and plenty of sunscreen.

Midafternoon (3:00 P.M.) brings check-in time at your hotel. There's a preponderance of large, corporate chain hotels and motels in Orange County. But on Balboa Peninsula two bed-and-breakfast inns come recommended for their beachside locations, romantically influenced decor and design, private guest parking, and the fact that no minimum stay is required, even on weekends.

Doryman's Inn (2102 West Ocean Front at Newport Pier; 949–675–7300; Web site: www.DorymansInn.com; $175–$325) dates back to the nineteenth century, when the building was a boardinghouse for the fishermen who sailed each morning in their narrow, flat-bottomed, high-bowed boats, called dories, and returned to sell their catch in an open-air market next to the pier (dory fishermen still carry on this tradition a century later). Today, the inn has ten guest rooms, carefully designed in classic Victorian style: floral swag draperies, bedcovers, and carpets; gilt-edged beveled mirrors; antique furniture; and ornate moldings and wallpapers. Each room has a fireplace. Although the bathrooms are small, they all have skylights and sunken marble tubs; one has a whirlpool tub. Number 8 ($325) is a corner master suite with an ocean view, canopied king-size bed, and whirlpool tub. It also has a table placed in front of the window, a perfect setup for a catered dinner for two. An elevator makes this inn wheelchair accessible, although the bathrooms are not handicapped equipped. Breakfast is served in the parlor, out on the deck, or in your room.

Portofino Beach Hotel (2306 West Ocean Front; 949–673–7030 or 800–541–8749; Web site: www.portofinobeachhotel.com; $129–$259), as the name suggests, goes for an old-world European ambience, with a peach-and-pink interior scheme, marble baths, Austrian draperies, and hand-painted murals. Only two of its fifteen rooms—Portofino Suites 1 and 2 ($219–$259)—have full ocean views. In fact these suites were cleverly designed to provide an ocean view from the double-size spa bathtub. In the afternoon, in the hotel's **Bar La Gritta** next to the parlor, wine, beer, and cappuccino are available.

If you prefer full-service accommodations, Newport Beach has several possibilities. One is the **Hyatt Newporter** (1107 Jamboree Road; 949–729–1234 or 800–233–1234; $129–$950). The 410 rooms have about as much charm as any chain hotel can offer, but the grounds are lovely:

well-tended lawns and thick stands of shrubs, groupings of tall palms, hanging baskets of flowers, even a small rose garden. Ask about the Romance Package ($129 per night), which includes an upgrade to a bay-view room, if available, and an amenity of champagne and strawberries. One-bedroom bayview suites start at $250, and the hotel's four three-bedroom villas, each with private swimming pool, start at $750. The other thing the Hyatt has going for it is its location adjacent to the Upper Newport Bay Ecological Reserve, particularly convenient if you plan to bike through the reserve. The Hyatt is two minutes from Balboa Island.

DAY ONE: *Evening*

DINNER

From Doryman's Inn, it's only a few steps around the corner to **21 Ocean-front** (2100 West Ocean Front; 949-673-2100; expensive), which is known for fresh fish, such as sautéed ono served with a garlic cream sauce, or poached salmon with raspberry butter. Ask to sit in one of the banquettes, which look out to the ocean. Lots of wood, etched glass, brass-and-glass chandeliers, and exposed brick give a rich, tradi-tional ambience to this split-level restaurant. **Renato** (2304 West Ocean Front; 949-673-8058; moderate to expensive) is an ele-gant Italian restaurant next door to Portofino Beach Hotel. Seafood is featured here too, like fresh Norwegian salmon poached with a light champagne sauce, along with classic Italian pastas (linguine *alle vongole*), risotto (*ai porcini*), and veal, which is pre-sented in several versions, includ-ing a daily chop special. If you're staying at the Portofino Beach Hotel and would rather have a ro-

Whale Watching

Bring binoculars and a camera and hop aboard a whale-watching cruise leaving from Newport Bay for an up-close look at the annual migra-tion of the California gray whale—southward in December and Janu-ary to the warm breeding and calv-ing waters off Baja California, and northward in February and March to the feeding grounds in the Bering Sea. Contact Davy's Locker at (949) 673-1434 for information.

mantic dinner in your room, arrange with Renato to deliver to your room. On Balboa Island, there's **Amelia's** (311 Marine; 949–673–6580; moderate), which is known for its bouillabaisse, lasagna verde—made from the same recipe for the past thirty years, and homemade tiramisu.

After dinner, you may wish to investigate the **Balboa Fun Zone** (at the auto ferry) on Balboa Peninsula, with its roller coaster, merry-go-round, and arcades. The Fun Zone, which has been around since the 1930s, is one of the last seaside amusement areas in Southern California. The typically lively and colorful scene has a strong appeal for youngsters and teenagers especially, but adults too are drawn to the Fun Zone.

DAY TWO: *Morning*

An early morning walk together on the beach near Newport Pier will give you a glimpse of a local tradition that's been going on for generations: the return of the dory fishing fleet each morning. The fleet at Newport Beach numbers about ten fishermen who depart around 2:00 each morning. They usually return around 8:00 A.M. and sell their catch at an open-air market next to Newport Pier.

BREAKFAST

Fresh fruit, cereal, yogurt, croissants, muffins, and juice are part of the expanded continental breakfast served at both Doryman Inn and Portofino Beach Hotel. You should eat well this morning to fortify yourselves for the bicycling tour around Upper Newport Bay Ecological Reserve. If the offering at the inns isn't sufficient, try the casual little cafe on the peninsula, **Britta's** (205 Main Street; 949–675–8146; inexpensive).

There are a couple of ways to get started with the day's activity—biking through the **Upper Newport Bay Ecological Reserve.** If you rent bikes and want to ride over from Balboa Peninsula, the easiest route is via the auto ferry and Balboa Island. At Coast Highway, Marine Avenue turns into Jamboree Road (which presents you with a nice hill to climb almost immediately). From Jamboree turn off at Back Bay Drive, which leads you to the entrance to Newport Dunes RV Resort and the reserve. Stay to the right, following Back Bay Drive past the resort and into the reserve. If you have your own bikes or want to drive over from the peninsula with rented ones, you can park at Newport Dunes (there's a parking fee of about $6.00) or try for one of the spots in the small Big Canyon lot, which is a few hundred yards into the reserve.

Back Bay Drive is a multiuse trail; that is, it's a paved road with a double-wide bike route. A painted line separates the one-way auto lane from the bike route, which is actually shared by cyclists, joggers, skaters, and walkers. Back Bay Drive extends for about 3³/₄ miles along the eastern portion of the reserve. It joins a sidewalk bikeway in a blufftop residential area before linking up with the northern section of bike route within the reserve. On the western flank of the reserve, the bike route (no cars here) finally gives way to a street bike lane for the rest of the loop. The entire loop is about 10 miles, more than half of which is along dedicated bike routes. Consult the "Bikeways" map for detailed route information (see Practical Notes).

Even though the footprint of humankind is never out of sight or earshot—luxury homes are visible high up on the bluffs surrounding the reserve and the distant roar of jets taking off from John Wayne Airport intrudes occasionally—entering Upper Newport Bay Ecological Reserve is like entering another, ancient world. Marsh grasses and cat-o'-nine-tails edge the bikeway; overhead, red-tailed hawks soar above the bluffs on the lookout for the next meal. Shorebirds wade along the mudflats, and ducks dabble in the shallow water. Sage and scrub cling to the drier slopes of the bluffs.

Upper Newport Bay is believed to be an ancient geological formation, created by erosion during the glacial period of the Middle Pleistocene epoch some 300,000 years ago. Eventually rising seas inundated the bay, and when it reemerged between 10,000 and 25,000 years ago, winter floodwaters deepened its channel. The marshes that flourished there once extended many more miles inland. Natural events as well as human intervention changed the features of the bay, and today Upper Newport Bay supports one of the last remaining coastal wetlands in California. The ecological reserve, which covers only 752 acres, was established in 1975 by the California Fish and Game Commission. It protects a delicate saltwater marsh ecosystem and various forms of rare and endangered fish, birds, and other wildlife that are dependent on the wetland habitat.

DAY TWO: *Afternoon*

LUNCH

Cycle right over to the **Back Bay Cafe** (Newport Dunes Resort, 1131 Back Bay Drive; 949-729-3863; inexpensive) for a hearty bowl of Back Bay seafood chowder and a sandwich. From the patio look out over the portion of the bay that's been developed into the resort's aquatic park. This is also a good spot from which to enjoy the sunset and twilight evening.

FOR MORE ROMANCE

Leave the paddling to **Adventures at Sea** (3101 West Coast Highway, or Route 1 at Riverside; 949-650-2412 or 888-446-6365) on a one-hour ($125 per couple) or two-hour ($175 per couple) gondola cruise on Newport Bay. Sip complimentary champagne or sparkling cider and nibble Godiva chocolates as you glide through the bay. Go all the way and add $100 for a three-course catered dinner, served on crystal, silver, and china.

Recommended Annual Events

JANUARY

Tournament of Roses Parade. Pasadena; (626) 449–4100.
Palm Springs International Film Festival. (760) 778–8979.
Chinese New Year. Chinatown, Los Angeles; (213) 617–0396.

FEBRUARY

Valentine's Day Sweetheart Dance. Avalon, Catalina; (310) 510–1520.
Whale-watching. Santa Barbara, Newport Beach, Long Beach, Ventura, and
    Oxnard.
National Date Festival. Indio; (760) 863–8247.

MARCH

Santa Barbara International Film Festival. (800) 927–4688.
La Quinta Art Show. La Quinta (Palm Springs); (760) 564–1244.

APRIL

Temecula Valley Balloon and Wine Festival. Temecula; (909) 676–6713.
Taste of Ventura County Food and Wine Festival. Oxnard; (800) 269–6273.

MAY

California Strawberry Festival. Oxnard; (805) 385–7578.
Back Bay Run and Walk. Newport Beach; (949) 776–7490.
Cinco de Mayo. Olvera Street, Los Angeles; (213) 625–5045.
Venice Art Walk. (310) 392–8630.

JUNE

Ojai Festival. (805) 646-2094.
Summer Solstice Celebration. Santa Barbara; (800) 927-4688.
Gay & Lesbian Pride Celebration. West Hollywood; (323) 969-8384.

JULY

4th of July fireworks. At the Rose Bowl (626-577-3100); the *Queen Mary* (562-435-3511); Avalon Bay, Catalina (310-510-1520); Hollywood Bowl (323-850-2000); Channel Islands Harbor, Oxnard (800-269-6273).
Lotus Festival. Echo Park, Los Angeles; (213) 485-1310.
Sawdust Festival (949-494-3030), **Festival of Arts** (949-494-1145), and **Pageant of the Masters** (949-497-6582), Laguna Beach.

AUGUST

Ojai Shakespeare Festival. (805) 646-WILL.
Nisei Week. Little Tokyo, Los Angeles; (213) 687-7193.
African Marketplace and Cultural Faire. Los Angeles (213) 237-1540.
Old Spanish Days Fiesta. Santa Barbara; (800) 927-4688.

SEPTEMBER

Chinese Moon Festival. Chinatown, Los Angeles; (213) 617-0396.
Mexican Independence Day. Citywide celebrations.
Catalina Wine Festival (310-510-1520) and **Festival of Art** (310-510-0808).

OCTOBER

Ojai Studio Artists Tour. (805) 646-8126.
Catalina Jazz Trax Festival. (888) 330-5252, (310) 510-2848.
Halloween on Santa Monica Boulevard. West Hollywood; (310) 289-2525, (800) 368-6020.

NOVEMBER

Dia de Los Muertos. Olvera Street, Los Angeles; (213) 625–5045, (213) 485–9777.
Plein Air Painters of America Festival. Catalina; (310) 510–1552.
Doo Dah Parade. Pasadena; (626) 440–7379.

DECEMBER

Holiday caroling and music, Christmas readings, and seasonal floral displays at Huntington Library, Art Collections, and Botanical Gardens. San Marino; (626) 405–2100.
Las Posadas. Olvera Street; (213) 625–5045, (213) 485–9777.
Christmas boat parades. In Santa Barbara (800–927–4688), Newport Beach (949–729–4400); Oxnard (800–269–6273); Ventura (800–333–2989).

General Index

A

B

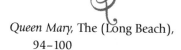

Special Indexes

ROMANTIC RESTAURANTS

Afternoon Tea

Rose Garden Tea Room
(Huntington Library), 127

American

Bernard's (Downtown Los
Angeles), 5

Casino Dining Room
(Two Bunch Palms, Palm
Springs), 177

Casual Elegance (Lake
Arrowhead), 169

Granita (Malibu), 63

Granville's Steak House
(Disneyland), 142

Ivy at the Shore (Santa
Monica), 55

Musso & Frank Grill (Hollywood), 103–4

Raymond Restaurant
(Pasadena), 36

Breakfast and Brunch

Busy Bee (Catalina), 47

Cafe Champagne
(Temecula), 136

Coogie's Beach Cafe
(Malibu), 62

Cottage Restaurant
(Laguna Beach), 89

House of Blues (West
Hollywood), 16

Julienne (San Marino), 124

Le Petit Cafe Bakery
(Oxnard), 70

Old Town Bakery (Pasadena), 37

Original Pantry (Downtown
Los Angeles), 6

Pierre Lafond (Santa
Barbara), 201

Village Coffee Shop
(Hollywood), 102

Cajun

Blue Bayou (Disneyland), 142

ROMANTIC LODGINGS

DAYTIME DIVERSIONS

Special Indexes

EVENING DIVERSIONS

About the
Author

STEPHEN DOLAINSKI IS A FREELANCE TRAVEL WRITER who has lived in Los Angeles for twenty-five years. He's contributed to several guidebooks about Southern California, including Ulysses Press's *Hidden Southern California* and a guide to performing arts in the region. He's also written about Los Angeles and Southern California for regional and national magazines, including *Westways* and *Avenues* (published by the Automobile Club of Southern California), *Los Angeles* magazine, and *Travel Holiday*.